Tahoe Tales
of Bygone Days
and Memorable Pioneers

Tahoe Tales
of Bygone Days
and Memorable Pioneers

Don Lane

Don Lane

To order additional copies of this book, contact:
Xlibris Corporation
1-888-795-4274
www.Xlibris.com
Orders@Xlibris.com
21046

Contents

DEDICATION

This book is dedicated to my family for their support,
and to the staff of Douglas County and Eldorado County Library,
and the Forest Service Heritage Resources Staff,
for all their assistance. The book is also dedicated to the forgotten
men and women that built this country so long ago.

AUTHOR
BIOGRAPHY

Since 1971 Don Lane has been a member of the US Forest Service recreation management team at Lake Tahoe. For many of those years, as the Supervisory Recreation Forester, he has been responsible for the management of all of the National Forest campgrounds, beaches, picnic areas, wilderness, trails and backcountry programs within the Tahoe Basin. A life member of the Lake Tahoe Historical Society, Lane is a graduate of the University of Nevada with degrees in liberal arts, forestry and land use planning. He has taught a number of courses at the Lake Tahoe Community College on Tahoe natural history, forestry and recreational land use planning, and currently lectures at the college's wilderness institute. He has authored a score of magazine and newspaper articles on Tahoe history, and frequently gives lectures on Tahoe history to organizations around the Basin. For several years beginning in the early 1980's, Lane began a radio program for station KTHO focusing on Tahoe and regional history, and the Basin environment, and has since 1995, as a public service, recorded over 2000 segments of a popular program called "Don Lane's Tales of Tahoe," on Lake Tahoe radio station KOWL AM-1490.

LAKE TAHOE
HISTORY
OVERVIEW

Long ago before there were subdivisions, high-rise buildings, asphalt highways and millions of visitors, Lake Tahoe was a quiet place, a secluded mountain lake where only a few scattered bands of migrating Native-Americans and an occasional wandering mountain man came to its shores. The ancient forest around the lake was lush and green with massive Yellow and Jeffrey Pines carpeting the basins slopes. The clear blue lake was teeming with native fish and the skies above were alive with the shrill cry of the osprey and hungry bald eagles as they circled high above the lake's streams searching for a meal. Nineteenth Century poets that did take the long journey to see Tahoe marveled at its size and brilliant colors. One, John Vance Cheney, would describe the lake as a "child of nature . . . with moods that change as freely as the way of the wind." Thomas Starr King came to the lake and fell in love with it, calling it "a gem of blue surrounded by a ring of flaming emerald." Mark Twain was to visit the lake in 1861, and he too was to marvel at the lakes brilliance and beauty, calling it "the fairest picture the whole earth affords." He also marveled at the purity of the mountain air, and declared that he must be in heaven, since it was the same air the angels breathed!

The Lake Tahoe Basin in geological time was formed fairly recently, only several million years ago. The continental crust had been actively breaking along its fault zones into massive blocks. The lake was to evolve through powerful geologic forces that would push massive blocks of the Sierra Nevada and the Carson Range upwards to become mountains. Those same forces would also create a trough or "graben," when a block of granite dropped to form a valley. Molten rock welled up through gaps in the faults, and andesite flows from these vents bisected and dammed the valley, forming a barrier across the lakes natural outlet and reshaping the landscape. As time passed, rain and melting snow combined to fill in the valley, forming a lake. During the last ice age, extensive glaciation was to sculpture the mountains and valleys overlooking the lake, and for a time, was to dam the Truckee River, temporarily raising the level of the lake by nearly 800 feet higher than its present level. Twenty-two miles long and twelve miles wide with seventy-two miles of shoreline, the surface area of the lake covers 191-square miles. With a depth of 1645 feet, Lake Tahoe is the third deepest lake in North America and the tenth deepest in the world!

The first people to settle on the lakeshore during the summer months were the "Washoe." Native Americans who came to the lake each spring and summer to hunt, to fish, trap and gather the bounty of food that could be found in and around the meadows and waters of the basin. To the Washoe, the lake was a sacred place, a place to gather food, and a place to socialize. But they spent little time here during the winter months, for there was too much snow, so they migrated to the lower valleys, to wait until the next spring. The first European-American to report seeing the lake was Lt. John Charles Fremont. He "discovered" the lake on February 14, 1844 and put Tahoe on a map for the first time. But the Tahoe area was quiet for a few more years, with few outside visitors and no permanent settlers. And it may well have stayed that way for many more years, although a nearby discovery was to change the nation.

On January 24, 1848, a few miles west of Lake Tahoe, at Coloma, California, James Marshall discovered gold. And soon the cry rang out across the country, and they came west to California! The trappers, traders, teamsters, the whiskey peddlers, the doctors, lawyers, farmers, ranchers and gamblers. Many traveled near or through the Tahoe Basin, and nothing was the same anymore in the "Golden State." But surprisingly at first, little changed around the basin, as there was no gold strike here to attract the Argonauts, and it seemed that Tahoe would be spared the environmental devastation from the rush to find gold. But another, similar event, another discovery was to occur, and this time the Tahoe Basin would never be the same. In 1859, the Comstock Lode near Virginia City, Nevada was discovered and the rush was on again. They called it the "The Rush to Washoe." This time the fortune seekers, the schemers and the dreamers went east, stampeding past the lake to the Great Basin. To get to the waiting gold and silver ore, mines were dug deep into the earth, thousands of feet down. And timbers were needed to shore up those mines. Timber was also needed to build the cities and the railroads and fuel the steam engines, and the Tahoe Basin was where they went to find the needed trees. And so the basin became a logging camp, and the forests were cut down to send to the Comstock. Over a forty-year period nearly two-thirds of all of the basin's forests were removed, and only stumps and unwanted fir trees remained.

By the end of the 19th century, the Comstock Lode had played out, and a new era began to dawn with the next century. The forests were beginning to re-grow and renew themselves. Resorts began to spring up around the lakeshore and an expanding and improving transportation system began to evolve that allowed people from all over the country to visit this once remote mountain lake. However in the years following World War II, the Tahoe Basin was to experience extensive urbanization and development. That was to have a substantial impact on the basins ecosystem and has created environmental consequences and challenges that has a score of federal, state and local agencies and organizations today working diligently to protect and preserve the famous beauty and clarity of this mountain lake, so that it will always remain as the fairest picture the whole earth affords.

This book is a collection of historic tales about the people and the events that are a treasured part of Tahoe's history, including stories about the gold rush and the Comstock Lode discovery, of pioneer days and people that worked and lived around the lake. Stories about Tahoe's colorful times and famous people, and about those people that history has largely forgotten.

NAMING THE LAKE

What's in a name? Not much if you take Shakespeare literally. For in his classic work "Romeo and Juliet," his Juliet was to first ask: "What's in a name?" Then was to proclaim "That which we call a rose, by any other name would smell as sweet." Or, that the name of an object was less important than its essence. But in the case of our mountain lake, the lake we call "Tahoe," there has been a great deal of debate over what name it should have. A debate that wasn't legally resolved until July 18th of 1945. For on that day, the California legislature passed a statute that once and for all, pronounced the name of the lake to officially be "Lake Tahoe." For before that date, the state had a different "official" name for the lake, calling it "Lake Bigler," in honor of the 3rd governor of the state. Governor John Bigler received this honor after he'd valiantly led a rescue party into the basin during the winter of 1853, and helped free a stranded party of immigrants who'd been trapped in the deep snow. But "Tahoe" has had more names over the years.

The first European explorer to see our lake, John Fremont admired its beauty and was impressed with its size, and decided to give it the name of a man that he had long admired. A French doctor, turned botanist that had spent years accompanying legendary explorer Alexander von Humboldt. The botanist, Aime Bonpland was a man of adventure, and along with Humboldt was to explore South and Central America, conducting scientific experiments in everything from geology, astronomy, botany to ocean currents. So it was that the very first Euro-American name for the lake was "Lake Bonpland." Unfortunately poor Doctor Bonpland was to run afoul of a South American dictator and was sentenced to 10-years in prison, but was able to spend most of that time providing medical care to poor villagers. Perhaps that was why he was so admired by Fremont. But American cartographers didn't like the idea of a French name on an American lake, so they ignored Fremont's name and used names like "Fremont's" or "Mountain Lake." It was just more appropriate. But those names didn't stick either! People wanted a different name. But no one could quite agree on what to call the place. Even the Native American name wasn't all that popular: "Da-ow-a-ga." Some linguists thought that meant "lake," in English! So a shortened "Lake Tah-o" would actually mean "Lake Lake," which of course didn't make any sense! Even the more popular translation for the word Da-ow-a-ga ("Big Water") was derided in an 1870 Truckee newspaper that claimed "Big Water," was actually a Native American slang word for "whiskey." Mark Twain was to claim the name "Tahoe" really meant "Grasshopper Soup," and should never be used. Despite the widespread popular use of the name "Lake Tahoe," no matter what had been said about that Native American name, the official name remained as "Lake Bigler," when finally in July 1945, the popular will could no longer be ignored, as a new statute was passed that once and for all, changed the name of the lake to today's "Lake Tahoe." As for Doctor Bonpland, at least he today has a crater on the moon named after him.

EARLY DAY HOSTESSES

They were Tahoe's earliest hostesses, hotelkeepers, chief cook and bottle washers. But they often were a whole lot more. There was Amanda Jane, a caring, hard-working icon of Glenbrook's "Jellerson Hotel." Along with her brother Frank, she operated this 1880's inn. Welcoming guests, then cooking for them and cleaning up after them, mending their clothes, constantly swapping jokes and tales with them. And always tending after them if they happened to get sick, and counseling them or consoling them if they had family problems. Amanda Jane was to become a Glenbrook legend.

There was also the incomparable Sierra Nevada Phillips Clark. But she was commonly known as "Vade" Phillips. A female dynamo who operated both the "Phillips" way station off Highway 50, and the Rubicon Springs Resort, located west of the lake. Vade worked tirelessly for years to tend to her patrons needs, for along with the usual cooking and cleaning and providing for their welfare, she also ran a dairy, general store, campground and she even made time to be postmistress. And too, there was the beloved "Lydia Clement." Compared to her gregarious husband Yank Clement, she was exceptionally quiet and reserved, but she had a heart of gold, as "Aunt Liddy," as she was known, was a mixture of hotelkeeper and saint-to-be. Back in the 1860's through the 1890's, Aunt Liddy was also the south shores resident midwife, delivering babies, nursing sick residents and patiently dispensing sound advice to everyone who needed her counsel. She was THE person in the community whom anyone could go to for help. The one you could always depend on, rain or shine to be there.

Finally, there was Alice Riggins Scott, a lady who had learned to be tough. For her first husband, an area cattle rancher had died, leaving her to run their Squaw Valley ranch in the 1880's along with raising their three sons. She struggled, but managed to prosper. Later marrying a man who, along with Alice, opened up a small hotel at Deer Park Springs, near today's River Ranch. Here too, she worked hard, doing all the cooking and cleaning, and together they packed their hotel with guests, and Deer Park Springs became known as a popular turn of the century Tahoe resort even though Alice did have one peculiar idiosyncrasy! She insisted that all her guests be in bed by 10:00 pm and even walked around and checked to make sure they were tucked in! And such were Tahoe's early-day hostesses.

EMMA AND ANTOINETTE

From a modest beginning, one lady was destined to become known for her delightful voice. She was to have an exciting singing career, meeting European royalty, traveling the world and performing on the finest and most glamorous stages in the country. But another lady, who also was to perform in the Comstock Country, was to become locally famous and a legend for having an unforgettably bad singing voice. The first lady was Emma Wixom. Born in 1859 in a California gold camp, her family soon moved to Nevada. Her father was a doctor her mother was a dealer in a gambling hall. Young Emma loved the open rangelands, the desert wildflowers, the tough but kind people, and wiled away her early days singing songs she'd made up. Polishing her rhymes, practicing, improving her skills, teaching herself and immersing herself in the beauty of music. Soon others began to notice and young Emma was asked to perform at town gatherings, and her admirers grew. She may have remained a Nevada songbird but fate stepped-in. Her mother passed away, and her father decided to send Emma away, to an eastern school. It was there her talents were to change her life, as she was asked to join a school musical group. And during a tour of Europe, she was "discovered" by a well-connected opera matron who was enthralled with Emma's voice, and so it was that Emma was able to receive the formal training she needed to reach her obvious potential. Emma went on to become a sensation, going on tours throughout Europe and in this country, even singing at the coronation of King George. She was to be dubbed as "Emma Nevada," and became a beloved diva who never forgot her Nevada roots. The other lady was Antoinette Adams. It was the early 1860's, and she'd polished her vocal skills, if that's what you could call them, back in Boston before coming out west. To the Comstock Country, to Virginia City, where she was to make her debut at Max Walters Music Hall. The audience was packed with miners anxious to hear the lyrical notes of a real-life Boston songbird. But when Antoinette started singing they couldn't believe their ears. Her voice was described as being a cross between a braying mule and a squeaky wheelbarrow. She was bad. But she was "so bad," that the audience (for a short while anyway) actually enjoyed hearing her sing. Perhaps it was just desperation for entertainment, and perhaps they felt sorry for Antoinette, they listened to a few songs, but finally had enough; ears could only take so much! But before walking out of the music hall (in a characteristic display of Comstock era generosity), the miners dug into their pockets and tossed gold and silver coins onto the stage. A gift to Antoinette. They also left her a request, to "please" never sing again.

WITH A LITTLE IMAGINATION

With just a little bit of imagination, if you look across the lake towards Mt. Tallac, you'll see a cross of white across its face. It's actually only a crevice filled with snow and ice, but its also a natural landmark that helps to make Tahoe a special place. And if you're willing to use just a little more imagination, you can also enjoy some of the other natural landmarks around the Basin. For example, for a time following a good snow year, if you're up at Rubicon Point looking south towards Freel Peak, you should see the numerals "87" on the west slope of the mountain. And if you prefer to view the lake by boat, just below Cave Rock, you can make out the profile of a fifty-foot high rock outcrop known as the "Lady of the Lake." And just above her, on the upper curve, is a weathered rock outcrop that looks a lot like a profile of a gorilla! There are even rocks on the west shore that look like "Old King Cole" or the head of a whale or even a gremlin.

One of the most interesting natural landmarks overlooks

Glenbrook and that's known as Shakespeare Rock. Though it seems in recent years to be quietly fading against the granite. High up on the right side of the granite wall, is an uncanny profile of the Great Bard himself. Created by a combination of lichens, oxidation and weathering it looked so real to one former resident that he thought it was divine and for years visited the rock on a regular basis. For him, this was also a source of inspiration. During the 19th century, one of the more amusing examples of a unique Tahoe area natural feature, was what appeared to be the head of a grizzled old man sticking out of the notch of a forked tamarack pine. Nothing more than an outgrowth of bark and weathered wood, nevertheless, when viewed with the right lighting, it looked so real that it became an early day South Shore tourist attraction! It received even more attention after a local hotel operator and master of the tall tale, Yank Clement decided to give it a name; calling it "Nick of the Woods," for as Yank said, it did look a lot like old Saint Nick himself. Sadly over the years, the tree grew old and one day was gone and with it, a simple act of nature that with a little imagination created a local landmark.

A DAY ON THE LAKE

Long before the days highways wound their way around the basin, the only way to get around the lake was to take a steamer; a boat trip. Typically around the year 1900, for most people, this journey would begin at Tahoe City. For here was the home berth of a grand steamship. Often called the "Queen of the Lake," the "SS Tahoe," was a luxurious 169-foot long greyhound of the water. Lovingly outfitted with Moroccan leather, lush carpeting, teakwood and mahogany trim. Each morning it sat waiting at the pier, the powerful steam engines quietly idling as the embarkation time drew near. Soon there was a clattering of footsteps on the pier-deck as the passengers began to arrive. As many as 200 of them, often elegantly dressed, the ladies resplendent in their long flowing dresses and wide sun bonnets. The gents dignified in their traveling suits and dapper bowlers or natty straw-hats. With a little assistance from the boat crew, they were all aboard in time for the scheduled 9:05 A.M. departure. With a quick glance to make sure all lines were cast off, the captain yanked on a cord, letting loose a loud blast from the ships airhorn, and signaled the engineer to open the throttles; they were under way. The passengers could feel the vibrations under their feet, the ship beginning to head out into the deep blue lake. The bow of the ship began to cut its way into the waves, while the ship began to gently rock from side-to-side as they picked up speed, perhaps 18 knots worth. When the winds and waves on the lake were stronger, passengers would often need to grab onto a rail for support, but few complained, for this was an excursion. A fun ride across one of the most beautiful lakes in the world. The ship headed south, towards Homewood and a quick stop at the lakes newest resort. From there it steamed to McKinney's Resort and on towards and into Emerald Bay, always a highlight for the passengers and the captain. The steamer took a slow turn around the island, everyone's eyes on the mountains towering high above. From here the Tahoe throttled up and turned towards the resorts on the south shore; the Tallac Hotel, its pier always alive it seemed with seagulls and mud-hens, then to Camp Richardson and Lakeside Park and then on into Nevada, with stops at Glenbrook, Brockway and eventually, after a trip of eight hours, back to the pier at Tahoe City. After a final blast of the airhorn, the captain signaled the engineer to stop the engines. The boat trip around the lake was over. But the next morning, beginning promptly at 9:05 A.M., there would be another.

WASHOE

The first summer inhabitants of the Lake were the people of the Washoe. While they were able to obtain most of their food and clothing needs from the lake, the forest and meadowlands of the region, like most early cultures, they weren't entirely self-sufficient, and relied on trading with neighboring tribes, such as the Maidu and Paiutes for the items they couldn't find locally. Commonly they'd exchange things like deerskins, dried fish, & pinion pine seeds for items like salt, ironware and obsidian for making arrow points. And from time-to-time, the Washoe would undertake a long journey to the interior of California. Traveling even as far as the coast, to bring back articles of trade. Items like seashells. The mollusks on the beaches were eaten on the spot, and their shells would be brought back to the mountains to be made into jewelry, and to be traded to the tribes to the east. One of the staples of their food supply, pinion pine nuts required the Washoe to weave large baskets to carry and store the nuts. During the summers, they would collect willow branches around the basin meadows, and when the winter snows drove the Washoe back into the lower valley areas, they would weave the willows into baskets. Some baskets were later used for trading, especially the finely woven ones that were used to cook in. While all of the women of the Washoe were to learn the practice of basket weaving, there was one lady that was to bring basket-weaving to an art form. But she was also to become an exploited supplier. Her baskets were rarely traded, but sold, and made a great deal of money, though little for her. Her name was Louisa Keyser, but her Washoe name was "Dat-so-la-lee." Louisa was a washerwoman for Amy Cohn, who was the wife of Carson businessman Abe Cohn. Amy soon recognized the unique and impressive quality of the baskets that Louisa was weaving during her free time, and brought them to the attention of her promoter husband, who saw an opportunity to profit from Louisa's innovative and skilled handicraft. And so Abe decided to sell her baskets in his Emporium. The baskets sold well enough, even at Abe's inflated prices (fifty dollars a basket) that he expanded his sales operation to the lake, to Tahoe City, where in 1900 he established a summer sales outlet, to capture the trade of the summer tourists. Abe further stimulated his sales by creating a mystic around Louisa, romanticizing her early life, and by falsely interpreting the patterns on her baskets, claiming they variously represented Washoe stories about hunters or past battles, and by issuing so-called "authentic certificates" to go along with her baskets. The tourists loved them and Abe made a tidy profit, while Louisa was only paid modest wages. Abe's cottage industry ended when Louisa passed away in 1925. Some of those baskets today are valued as high as a quarter of a million dollars each! A substantial increase in their values, when there was a time, when willow baskets were simply traded for a bag of salt.

GO WEST YOUNG WOMAN!

Before they could hold a frontier dance, the men would have to pull straws and decide who this time would have to tie a red handkerchief onto their arm and take the role of a woman. This they did good-naturedly because they had no choice. For there were so few women around the camp, this was the "only" way they could hold a hoe-down. Over time of course, that would change. But just after the gold rush, there was such a shortage that it caught the attention of some enterprising people back east. Motivated by everything from social consciousness, to capitalistic greed, there arose a few schemes to induce, even import more women to the west.

From as far away as Europe, several businesses began to offer a new service to the American frontier: mail order wives. Lonely men could purchase a wife from Paris or from Germany. The mail order companies were sometimes reviled by California newspapers. The "Alta California," for example, compared this enterprise to a form of white slavery. In fact, not all of the young women that were imported to this country were sent as brides-to-be, as their destination was a dance hall, there to serve a term of years as an indentured servant; much as the Chinese laborers had to become, to pay for their transportation to this country from China. But there were others that saw a social opportunity in the west. Catharine Beecher saw a need for more schoolteachers, and more employment potential as the east was well supplied with teachers. Many young qualified women couldn't find a job while the economy out west was booming. She even wrote a book called: "The Duty of American Women to their Country," in which she implored women to head west: "Go west young woman . . . go west." But only a few did at first. Elizabeth Farnham also tried to encourage more women to head west. Her late husband had been there in 1848, and she recalled his letters describing the overwhelming maleness of the population and the demand for marriageable women. So Elizabeth began a crusade, to recruit all that she could to head west. Placing ads in newspapers, and even booking passage on a ship to San Francisco. But in the end, she only found three ladies who were willing to go, not the thousands she'd hoped for. But it was a start, and as the years passed, and more ladies joined the western migration, the men no longer had to assume the role of a woman at the town dance, unless of course they wanted to.

ICE PALACE

As old time "lakers" well know, the Tahoe area can get a lot of snow. And while winter storms can wreak havoc on Tahoe's roadways and driveways, they also bring winter fun. For our snowpacks have had a tremendous impact on the year-round use of this part of the Sierra, and our year-round economy. Tahoe's present status as a major winter sports area didn't come overnight. Things started off slow and then gained momentum as we moved deeper into the twentieth century. One of the very first winter attractions around the area was the Ice Palace that was built smack in the middle of Truckee. It was actually a chicken wire & wood-frame oval ice-skating rink that was big enough to fill an entire football field. They sprayed water on it every night to give the walls a shimmering icy coating. And in the evening, the bright lights of twenty arc lamps reflected against the ice oval so that it could be seen from the hills above it. If you got tired of skating, there was a toboggan slide on one side of it, and on the other end stood a band wearing fur coats who filled the air with their cheery music. During the late years of the 19th and the early years of the 20th centuries, the tourists poured into Truckee by the thousands to enjoy this Palace of Ice.

In the 1930's, "Snowball Special" trains coming out of San Francisco headed to Truckee were running all winter long. They'd leave after midnight returning just before the next midnight, giving people most of a day in the Sierra snowfields. The great skiing boom was just beginning, although at first, a lot of people were content to just spend a day playing in the snow, with or without skis. But that would change. Just before World War I, toboggan rentals were as popular as ski rentals. In 1928, the Tahoe Tavern, a majestic hotel-resort at the time in Tahoe City, hosted a competition of bobsled races, hockey contests and exhibition skating along with ski racing and jumping. By the end of the 1930's, a t-bar lift was opened near Glenbrook, at Spooner Summit, it could move up to 300-people-an-hour up White Hill, when there was enough snow. A few years later, west of Echo Summit at Camp Sacramento, a small resort called "Edelweiss" was opened. Sierra-At-Tahoe opened up in 1946. In the mid-fifties, Heavenly Resort opened up with two rope tows and a chair lift and a winter's ski pass that cost $25. So while all of our present resorts and of course the 1960 Winter Olympics held in Squaw Valley have had a major impact on helping to establish our area as a winter resort destination, it all started a long time ago, with a chicken-wire covered skating rink all covered with ice, up in Truckee.

THEY HAD A BIG HEART

For some, the spirit of Thanksgiving and Christmas lived the whole yearlong. When people today run into hard times like a devastating flood or wildfire, there are some wonderful organizations out there ready to help, like the Red Cross and Salvation Army. They've both been around since the mid 1860's. But in most communities, especially back then, it took time, sometimes a lot of time before these organizations, and even the local churches, could put together enough resources to be of much help. During these times, you had to rely on your neighbor to reach out and help. There was no other safety net out there during hard times.

One of the best examples of old fashioned neighborly generosity took place in Virginia City in 1877, when the giant mine conglomerate, the "Consolidated Virginia," ran into financial trouble, and failed to make its monthly payments, and almost overnight thousands of people; mine employees, were suddenly penniless, and had no choice but to wander the streets begging for food. The jails were quickly filled with vagrants, and the crime rate also soared as some people out of desperation did whatever they had to, to care for their families. Mrs. Mary Mathews, who ran a rooming house with her friend Mrs. Beck, watched this happening around her, and decided "something" had to be done. So the two women ran around to all the restaurants in town, asking for and getting the garbage barrels, which the ladies had noticed often had edible food thrown in them. With this food, along with some wilted vegetables, scraps of meat from the butchers shop, and day-old bread from bakeries, they opened up Virginia City's very first soup kitchen. They even managed to get a local dairy to donate some fresh milk. They also managed to get some cash donations, which helped them even more. And in a matter of days, these two wonderful ladies were feeding 500-people a day! They rose before daylight and often worked until late each night. And before long, others came over to help them, by cutting wood, washing dishes and hauling water. And Mrs. Mathews and Mrs. Beck's soup kitchen kept whole families alive. Eventually the entire town was helping them out. They served three meals each and every day for months, until the churches and charities were up and running and could carry on their work, and the kitchen was closed. But while it operated, that soup kitchen showed that people can make a big difference during rough times, especially when they're good neighbors.

YOUNG COURAGE

Courage, as they say, is resistance to fear, not an absence of fear. You can find it in just about anyone at any given time, but it is especially impressive when you see it in young people. There was the case of fourteen-year old Octavius Pringle. The year was 1846 and his family was in trouble. They had been headed west from Missouri, but had some trouble crossing the plains. Nothing serious, but it caused a delay in their schedule, and similar to the Donner party late that same year, they would be pushing it to complete their journey before the snows of winter trapped them. But their luck was fast running out, as they found themselves low on food, and the weather turning cold, with miles to go. So it was that Virgil and Phernia Pringle turned to their oldest son, Octavius and asked him to ride ahead to a small community 125-miles down the trail, and bring back food. Though scared to death, he left, riding through country he'd never seen before. Trading with Native Americans for his own food, he made the journey, and returned to his waiting family. Together they finished their journey, arriving safely at their new home on Christmas day.

There was also the case of eighteen-year old Moses

Schallenberger, a member of an 1844 wagon train that had attempted to cross the pass above Truckee and into the Sacramento Valley (a pass that was later to become known as Donner's Pass). But it was late November, and the weather had turned brutal, and the members of Schallenberger's wagon train decided they could only manage to get half of the wagons over the pass before another winter storm blew in and threatened to dump another blanket of snow on the pass. So a decision was made to leave some volunteers behind, to watch over the wagons and the personal possessions that were to be left behind until the following spring, when they could then be moved over the pass. There were three volunteers, but in the end only Moses Schallenberger was to stay the winter. For the three men soon realized there wasn't enough food for all three, so they each fashioned some snowshoes and headed off to Sutter's Fort. But Schallenberger was soon exhausted, and suffered from leg cramps, and he soon faltered. He realized he couldn't make it, and so he turned back to the camp at the lake while the other two men went on. Moses was alone. It turned out to be months before a rescue party returned for Moses, but when they did he was both happy and relieved. And he was proud, for he had done his job. Finally, there was the case of fourteen-year old Jackson Ober. A late-night fire had broken out in a Placerville boarding house, and young Jackson had heard the cries of a mother who suddenly realized her child was still inside that burning building. She'd at first thought her child was with her husband, but he wasn't and she'd run to the firemen for help. Without hesitating, Jackson ran into that burning building, found the child (still sleeping), grabbed it from its bed, and barely escaped the flames before the entire building collapsed. Octavius, Moses and Jackson; young men with a lot of courage.

OLD TAHOE CHARACTERS

Our part of the country has had its fair share of colorful characters over the years. Some were known for how they behaved, or didn't behave, and others for what they did. There were people like Yank Clement, a former mountain man, 49er and Tahoe hotel pioneer, was known throughout the area as the "Champeen Lyer of the Sierra," and he worked hard to keep that reputation, for Yank loved pranks and churning out tall tales by the hour to the delight of Tahoe visitors. There was Charles Parrish, a hard-swearing saloonkeeper at Bijou; a man who never minced words and sold a homemade brew of Tahoe whiskey that was guaranteed to drop a burly logger to his knees. It was known as "Tahoe Tarantula Juice," and it sure was popular. There was also at the turn of the century, a fun-loving bear of a man that lived at the lake, Walter Scott Hobart Jr. He was usually found racing boats around the lake at breakneck speed or hosting a lavish banquet at his most favorite place in the world: Sand Harbor. Hobart rarely slimmed down to

300-pounds and became known as the wildest party animal around the lake, earning him the nickname of the "Slapdash Sage of Sand Harbor."

There was another kind of man who was perhaps less of a character, but he was a man WITH character. His name was William Morris Stewart, and it was December of 1861 when a massive flood swept thru the canyons around Virginia City, and overnight, Stewart saw everything he'd worked to build, destroyed. He estimated that he'd lost $500,000 that day. But more importantly, there were hundreds of men on his payrolls, that suddenly had no jobs, and who now looked to him for help. But Stewart had no money, but he did have a good name, and that would get him some emergency credit, if he could only get to San Francisco where a friend could give him a loan to get his mills back in operation. And so he began his trek on snowshoes over the east-slopes of the lake while a winter storm was raging around the Sierras. He made it to Yanks Station in Meyers, where Yank Clement pleaded with Stewart to wait there until the storm blew itself out, but Stewart had a mission, and he pressed on over Echo Summit while hundreds of other men stayed holed up at Yanks, knowing how dangerous the mountains were during a storm. And Stewart staggered through the snowdrifts, until he reached Strawberry where he collapsed for the night. The next day he went on, nearly swept away by avalanches. Finally, he reached the Sacramento Valley where he had to find a boat to get through flooded lowlands. But eventually, finally, Stewart made it all the way to San Francisco, where he got his loan, and then he headed back towards the lake, and to his flooded mills, and the men who waited for him. It was a journey that took him over a week and hundreds of miles, into the history books and into the hearts of those people that depended on him.

TAHOE'S OLD NEWSPAPERS

Nowadays when you want to read a newspaper there's a variety of choices available every day all around the basin. There's the almost daily local and national papers, as well as daily editions from big cities like Reno, Sacramento and San Francisco. And too, there's always the monthlies and weeklies and even specialty news publications covering everything from real estate to garage sales. With multiple printed pages often packed with flyers, advertising the latest sales, food coupons and the weeks' television schedules. In days past, newspapers only covered the barest amount of local news and less often national events. Most were only a few pages of printed type and half of that space was dedicated to advertisements. They were printed perhaps once a month and there were often so few printed that individual editions were generally passed around from person-to-person. And many of them didn't last for very long.

The very first newspaper in the region was a short-lived little paper, called the "Scorpion," and it was born over in

Genoa in 1857, and it was hand-written. The editor, Stephen Kinsey, with only a handful of pencils, produced about a dozen editions of this local paper, full of articles about current events, and some editorials about the importance of honesty and justice. It was considered to be a pretty good little paper at the time, but Kinsey couldn't keep long-handing the paper forever, and the Scorpion quietly disappeared.

Tahoe's first newspaper was the "Tahoe Tattler." It started out over in Tahoe City in July 1881, and was printed on half-sized sheets of paper, and came out every day except Sundays. It focused on Tahoe's social life; who was staying in the hotels, and how great the fishing was, and costing only a dime, it was all the rage for a short while before quietly disappearing for a time. One of the most unusual of the early day papers had only one edition, and was printed in Reno in 1890. It was called the "Snowbound," and was a four-page one-of-a-kind newspaper written by George McCully, who was a paper editor from the east coast. But he had been trapped, like hundreds of others in the train depot in Reno, waiting out a savage snowstorm that had blocked the Sierra passes for days, stranding him until the tracks could be cleared. McCully had even identified himself in his paper as "a prisoner in Car-36." The paper was printed out of boredom and frustration, and was intended to provide his fellow passengers with the latest information on the progress of the snowplows, and poke fun at everyone's predicament. But his paper also blasted the railroad for not having more snowsheds and not putting up the stranded passengers in a better hotel. Shortly after the paper came out, the tracks were cleared, and another small newspaper vanished forever.

LAKE TAHOE
WINTERS

The storms of winter have often created havoc for the people that live in the mountains, and sometimes starvation. The most well known group that has long been identified with the perils of heavy winter snows are of course the members of the Donner Party, who struggled and suffered through the winter of 1846-47 just north of the lake. Over the years, there have been other (though odd) incidents involving winter storms. Drifting snow had blocked roadways into one small pioneer community during the winter of 1852-53 and the residents were on the brink of starvation, and had sent out a relief party to San Francisco, only a few days away, where there were warehouses packed with food supplies. But, the merchants weren't selling, instead they were holding onto their stores of food until the demand pushed prices sky high, and then they expected to make a killing. The relief party returned home empty handed and still hungry. But desperate, the community residents gathered again, and this time passed an emergency resolution that unless they got their food immediately the whole town would go and force their way into the food warehouses and take what they needed if necessary. They got their food.

Even around Lake Tahoe, back in the winter of 1937-38 there was a classic incident involving heavy winter snows and starving residents. At least that was the rumor. Now, accounts vary, but some say the rumors began after a caretaker over at Glenbrook was visiting with the captain of the steamer that made daily trips around the lake in those days, and had jokingly commented that because of the deep snowpacks around Glenbrook, he'd had to put his starving horse down. So if the captain was interested, he'd share some horsemeat with him. That story was soon passed around and it wasn't long before it got twisted a bit and soon people all over the state were hearing shocking stories about the starving residents at Lake Tahoe who were forced to survive on horsemeat. After all, a whole lot of snow had been falling around the Sierras that winter and it was easy to believe. And so an emergency supply of food was gathered up and packed into an airplane and flown over to Tahoe City, and dumped out over the golf course! Of course the Tahoe residents really weren't in any danger of starving as everyone around the lake knew-well that winters up here could be rough, and were stocked-up with plenty of canned goods for the winter. But they sure did appreciate the fresh vegetables and meat, and the thought.

SCHOOL DAYS

There was once a time when bells used to ring out every weekday morning. The sound echoing out over the small settlements of Glenbrook and Lake Valley, beckoning the sons and daughters of the pioneer families who lived and worked around Tahoe's east and south shores; the children of the loggers and mill workers. And each morning, they'd come. Usually on foot, but sometimes they caught rides on local logging trains, to a modest looking little place, but a place filled with lesson books about Shakespeare and Latin and geography. This was the place during the 1880's where the first children of Tahoe would learn addition and subtraction, read poetry and the classics, and learn about the world on the other side of our mountains. It was the schoolhouse, only a single room with sparse furniture, a few wood benches and desks for the children and a potbellied stove for warmth. The walls decorated with students drawings and a few pages from magazines, and some maxims of the time: "Look Before You Leap," and "A Rolling Stone Gathers No Moss." From late spring to early fall, this handful of "young scholars," as they were called in those days, as few as half a dozen, and growing to over twenty during the summer months spent much of their day under the watchful eye of one of Tahoe's first teachers, Harry Goodrich in Lake Valley and Mabel French, at Glenbrook. Tahoe's schoolhouses were closed during the winter months, for the snowdrifts were too deep, the winds too cold, so many of Tahoe's residents went to warmer locations in Carson and Sacramento valleys.

Even by the turn of the last century, Tahoe was still a small collection of settlements. There were no doctors, no drugstores and few people stayed up here all winter, but there was still a need for schooling Tahoe's children, and in 1932 the community established the Lake Valley School District with a total of seven students. Still in a one-room schoolhouse near the "Y," (junction of Hwy 50 and Hwy 89), it served the south shore from Meyers to Stateline from March to June and July through December. But it only went through the eighth grade, and Tahoe's students needed to board in Gardnerville or Carson or in Sacramento to attend high school. But eventually, in 1949 a new high school was established in the small schoolhouse near the "Y," with all of five students and one teacher. But Tahoe was growing, and in just a few years, in 1952 there were sixty-five students enrolled, outgrowing the one-room schoolhouse, so students attended classes in the American Legion Hall until a larger school could be built, and today, there are around 5000 students just in the south shore schools, even during the winter; still learning about Shakespeare and geography. But times have changed, for the one-room schoolhouse is gone, along with the potbellied stove. And too, there's no school-bell to beckon the children of Tahoe, like it once did, so long ago.

TOM POOLE THE BANDIT-PATRIOT

Thomas Bell Poole was a desperado of the Sierras. He ended his days at the hands of justice on September 29, 1865 at the Placerville gallows. Although justice might have been better served if he'd been caught and sentenced a few years earlier. Tom Poole was once a lawman: Undersheriff of Monterey County. He was a strong-minded man, but quite popular with the area's residents, and its likely he could of successfully run for a local political office should he have chosen to do so. But Tom Poole had an independent side to him that was to push him towards the shadowy side of the law. He showed that side during the bizarre case of a bandit named Jose Anastasio. Anastasio had also been recently convicted of a capital crime and sentenced to the gallows by a Monterey Court. But the Governor had some concerns with the proceedings and issued a stay of execution. But the reprieve the Governor sent, inadvertently misspelled the man's name, as the order stated one "Jesus Anastasio" was to be reprieved. But Tom Poole ignored the obvious clerical mistake and went ahead with the sentencing. The Governor was livid and thoroughly chastised the callousness of Poole, but no charges were brought against him, yet. As Tom Poole was soon to run afoul of the law again in another unusual way.

He left Monterey and wandered over to San Francisco, where he soon took up with an organization that supported the Southern Cause, the Confederacy. These were the Civil War years, and the passions of the north and south were also felt out west. Poole, an ardent southern sympathizer, joined the Knights of the Golden Circle, and there joined forces with a man with a plan: Asbury Harpending. Harpending had obtained a commission in the Confederate Navy, and then enlisted the help of several more southern supporters, and purchased a 90-ton schooner that was moored in the Bay. They placed several 12-pound canons on board, some rifles and cutlasses, and recruited twenty sailor-warriors and were about to set sail for Mexico's waters, where they intended on raiding inbound steamers, stealing whatever gold and valuable cargo they could for the south. But they were betrayed, as someone had warned the federal troops, and just before they cast off, a Federal sloop-of-war showed up, and arrested all of the would-be pirates and southern patriots, including Tom Poole. But again, he wasn't charged with any crime. Though he did have to take an oath of allegiance to the Union. Of course, Tom Poole didn't plan on keeping that oath, for his travels were to take him into the Sierras, to a stagecoach robbery site just west of the lake. Once again, he intended to hand over any spoils to the Confederacy. Joining a gang led by Rufus Ingram, Poole waylaid a stage and this time, was to set in motion his own just end. A sheriff's posse tracked the gang and caught up with them in a way station. There was a shootout and Poole was wounded in the foray, bad enough, but not so that he couldn't have escaped with the rest of his gang. But they left him behind, not wanting to be burdened with him, and so it was, that Tom Poole was soon captured, and sentenced, and justice was finally served.

TOM SAWYER AND HANNAH CLAPP

Little did Hannah Clapp know that December day in 1862, that her Carson Valley schoolroom was about to become the inspiration for a chapter in one of the most beloved novels in American history. It was the end of the school term, and examination day was less than a week away. Hannah had been working hard, coaching her young students who were anxiously rehearsing their recitals and penning their compositions. Preparing for the moment when they would stand up before their teacher and parents in a ceremonial display of classroom wisdom and memorization. And while Hannah's students labored, parents throughout the Valley were abuzz with excitement over the coming event. For in those early frontier years, "Examination Day" brought out the whole community. Even those residents without children attended, for they were still neighbors. And so the local newspaper sent over a reporter to the schoolhouse. The reporter took a seat in the back of the classroom and quietly jotted down a few notes, intently watching, impressed by all of the industrious young scholars, as many recited their lines over and over again, polishing their delivery while adding gestures for dramatic flair. Studiously repeating ancient Latin poems, and contemporary sermons about piety, longings of the heart and melancholy love. Other young students were equally engrossed, plying their way through problems in long division or devoting all their attention to absorbing the smallest details of history and geography from their ancient textbooks. After a few hours, the reporter left, writing a few lines for the next edition about all of the preparation that was going on in Hannah's classroom. Though the visit was a short one, that reporter just couldn't forget the image of all those children working so hard doing their very best to pass their examinations, for he admired them. And so, he was to return again, this time "on" Examination Day. There to recapture in his mind that vision, for a book that he was going to write someday. And in chapter twenty-one of that book, the book he called "Tom Sawyer," the reporter described in exaggerated but loving detail the scene he witnessed in Hannah's classroom. The crowded room, the proud parents, the eager young scholars along with a nervous Tom Sawyer, who was fated to suffer stage fright when his turn came to recite his speech "Give Me Liberty or Give Me Death." The reporter of course was Mark Twain (Sam Clemens). He'd initially come to the schoolroom to cover a story for his newspaper, but instead he found inspiration for his own story.

HE WAS CALLED
"COCK-EYE!"

We still consider it challenging, and for some, even a bit intimidating to use, but the route over Echo is still a vast improvement from the first pathways through this part of the Sierras. It's the legacy of an Eldorado County pioneer with a rather odd nickname: "Cock-Eye" his friends good-naturedly called him, although he was also addressed as "Colonel," as a title of respect. He was Jack Calhoun Johnson, and he was credited with being the first wagon road builder in the Tahoe Basin. Johnson was born in Deerville, Ohio in March of 1822. A good student, he was to do something unusual for the times; attend law school (Cincinnati Law School). Being admitted to the Ohio Bar after graduation. But Johnson wasn't content for long with practicing law for a living, for shortly after the word of the gold rush in California reached the Ohio Valley, he packed up and headed west, to an area near today's Camino. There, in 1850 he filed for a half-section of land (320 acres), and built himself a ranch. Johnson it seemed always had an itch for adventure, for he soon signed up for the state militia, and with his exceptional (for the times) education, wrangled himself an appointment as Adjutant. He turned his ranch into a mixed military compound, housing two hundred militiamen at one point, and a trading post. There was also a rumor that Johnson provided a haven for passing immigrants who were beginning to pour into the Sacramento Valley. Allowing hundreds to camp out on his half-section of land while looking for a permanent residence. Meanwhile purchasing necessary supplies from their temporary landlord.

The Colonel, old Cock-Eye, was also an explorer at heart, and it was he that scouted and marked out a route through the Carson Valley, through the south end of the basin, over the summit and westwards to Placerville. His route managed to shave over fifty miles distance between Carson Valley and Placerville, which is quite a savings! His route over Echo was also lower. Today's Highway 50 runs just south of Johnson's original route. Johnson for a time also tried politics, being elected to the state assembly, but that apparently didn't keep his interest either as he wandered over to Arizona. But that was his undoing, as he was done in by Apaches there in 1876. But he did leave a legacy, a western route out of the basin. Even though it is a bit challenging, even today.

WINDS AND GLORY HOLES

Those who lived in the "Comstock Country" (especially the Carson and Washoe Valley) in the 19th century had more than their fair share of challenges to face; the primitive roads, the lack of conveniences. Clothes for example, were often hand-made and everything else it seemed, from sugar and flour to lamp oil had to be shipped in from far away places. There was no such thing as a washing machine or a SUV. But most people took these things in stride, for that's just how things were. However there "were" other things that the old timers often did complain about. One thing was the weather. Those winter blizzards could be rough, but it was the wind that seemed to get on people's nerves; that persistent and sometimes aggravating wind. They called it the "Washoe Zephyr," and it would come blowing up out of the Sierra's and down into the Carson & Washoe Valleys with such a blast of air that some locals claimed they once saw a mule carried a hundred feet up into the air, braying all the way, and then dropped on top of a roof. The sky would be filled with clouds of dust, hats, tin cans, umbrellas, and even furniture. And anybody that was unlucky enough to get caught up in one had better reach for the nearest tree or find themselves blown to the other end of town. At least that's what they used to claim. Especially during the spring and fall months, the wind was a daily part of life on the east-slope and it became a local legend. Our own "Zephyr Cove," was named in honor of that gust of wind, for the word "Zephyr" is just another name for the Greek God of the west wind.

Another complaint of the early day settlers in the foothills east of the lake was also a real hazard. During the first months following the 1859 discovery of the Comstock Lode, the first wave of fortune hunting prospectors dug and abandoned countless worthless mining shafts, or glory holes. They were all over the hillsides, and a person could easily fall into one of these holes after dark, or after a snowstorm covered up the ground. And people did before they finally got all of them boarded over! One man in Virginia City, heading home late one night, very drunk after an evening in the local saloon, didn't notice one old mine shaft until too late, and it was three days before they found him. But he wasn't even aware of what had happened, since he'd just laid there and slept it off for the whole three days. And finally, there was the unbelievable but oft-told story about that team of eight-oxen, still yoked together, that had been staked out on a hillside to graze while the teamster sat down and ate his lunch. And as he sat there munching his food, right in front of his astonished eyes, the whole team suddenly disappeared into the ground. Unknowingly, the teamster had placed his oxen over an old mineshaft. He had a whale of time getting them back out!

EARLY DAY
SOLDIERS

These days they have a slogan: "An Army of One." Before that, there was: "Be All That You Can Be." And long before that, there were patriotic songs and posters that encouraged people to join the Army; to protect freedom, to stop tyranny, to learn new skills, go to exotic places and to face and learn to overcome new challenges. And in the process, become a better person. While the slogans are fairly new, the world of the soldier hasn't changed much over the past century and a half; short periods of excitement and extreme stress and long periods of tedium and routine.

Back in the early days of our region, from Tahoe to Virginia City, the security of the stagelines, the settlements, the miners and ranchers depended upon the troopers stationed at Fort Churchill. Situated on the Carson River, it was built after the 1860 battles with the Paiute Indians. Besides watching over the regions settlements, this army fort was used to protect the Pony Express riders and the westbound immigrants passing through the basin. After the

Civil War, the regular Army was too small to cope with the upsurge in hostile Indian attacks out west, so the War Department actively recruited new soldiers for their frontier forts. And these individuals were a mixed lot. Many had been Civil War veterans, including Confederate Army veterans who'd fought against the Union side for four long years, but who now turned to the other side for the hope of excitement and adventure, or simply for a job. Fort Churchill was full of ex-Rebels. Economic conditions around the country were in a rut and times were tough and many were unemployed. In those days there was no such thing as unemployment compensation; people worked 16-hours a day, in some places for all of fifty cents per day. So Army jobs were very attractive, but the army posts also attracted many shiftless characters; drifters, drunkards and petty criminals, who volunteered for anywhere between three to five years of service for a base pay of thirteen dollars a month. So it was no surprise that during the period between the later 1860's and the early 1890's, that as many as one-third of the men recruited for the frontier, deserted. Remote locations, harsh weather and a mixture of tedium, boredom and military discipline contributed to the problem. It got so bad that the Army even allowed soldiers to purchase a discharge after they'd served three years. As few who did desert ever got caught. But surprisingly, a large number of deserters decided they missed their lives in the Forts and changed their names and reenlisted again somewhere else! But for the most part, even though life in these remote areas was a hardship, rough and certainly not for everyone, most of the common soldiers served faithfully. They were the best they could be. An Army of one, long before there was a slogan.

VELMA COMSTOCK EDEN

Velma Comstock Eden was born September 27, 1900 at a beautiful place: Lake Tahoe. She spent her first years here on the south shore, for her family operated the Hotel Tallac, near today's Camp Richardson. It was a child's paradise, and years later Velma was to write of her treasured memories during those early years at the lake. Velma knew the local legend "Lucky Baldwin," and she met many of the rich and famous that came to visit Lake Tahoe, and was to describe them and the lifestyle that awaited them here. The Tahoe resort was located in the remote Sierras, accessible by most only after a long trip on a train and a ride on a steamship, although a few came by carriage (before the days of the automobile), and later came by Stanley Steamer from Placerville. The "gettin" here was so difficult that those that came brought the kitchen sink with them. Bringing maids, butlers, governesses, and trunks of clothes. Few came to spend a weekend, for these were the days when people commonly stayed for weeks, and even the whole summer.

The men would pack a multitude of suits and gentlemanly apparel, but the ladies were always a sight to see, for they brought the most stylish gowns, parasols, high button shoes, evening slippers, fashionable large hats, and an appropriate supply of jewelry. They were there to enjoy the lake, and as the men, they were there to be seen!

The early day Tahoe resort life wasn't at all as primitive as one might believe. As Velma recounted, that no one today could possibly imagine what such an early day summer resort was like. It was a self-contained small community, with its own power plant, its own water system. The Hotel Tallac had about thirty rooms, steam heat, a nice parlor, bakery, curio shop and a bandstand at the end of a large dining room piled high with elaborate pieces of Tiffany silver. A wine waiter saw to the needs of the patrons. Near the hotel was the "casino." Its thirty-five rooms offered a lounge, a large bar, a bandstand where music was played day and night, four bowling alleys, and also a billiard and card room. And according to Velma (behind locked doors) was a veritable little Monte Carlo. There was also a barber shop, a shoe-shine stand, and even a tent outside the building where a manicurist offered her services for the digitally impaired. There was an ice cream parlor, and for those few who forgot to pack everything they might need, in front of the hotel, was a rental shop, where visitors might obtain a bathing suit. The resort stocked all sizes for men and women. For the active guest, there were a multitude of choices, from packtrips and boating and hiking trips to carriage parties. Fishing trips were a resort specialty, with patrons first being treated to a lavish picnic featuring watermelons, fish chowder and wine, and then boarding a small launch and be whisked off to the hot fishing grounds. But in spite of all the amenities and facilities, Velma recalled there were two activities that were always popular: searching for four-leaf clovers in the meadow grasses and just looking at the beautiful Tahoe scenery.

THEY DESERVED EACH OTHER

They were different, yet in their own ways, they shared similar qualities. They were each highly ambitious, and each were known for a lack of conscience. These traits were to tie their lives together, in a rather bizarre, but fitting way. The first person was a powerful multi-millionaire, William Sharon. Originally just a clerk at a newly founded Bank of California, Sharon was sent to Carson to open up a branch office. There, he offered easy term loans to all kinds of business's; logging and mining mills, refineries and transportation companies at a time when the local economy was temporarily struggling. Cash hungry business owners snapped up the loan offers by the generous bank clerk, many offering their business as collateral. Then, the next year, Sharon moved in, demanding immediate repayments of those loans, and since few could repay, the Bank foreclosed, and took control of scores of mines, sawmills, and other companies. Sharon was a hero to the Bank and went on to make millions in mining stocks and investments, often freely cutting deals and crushing opponents with little conscience or concern. His wealth and position made him a powerful man from Virginia City to San Francisco, and a target for a scandal.

Enter two people, David Terry and Sarah Hill. Terry was a firebrand, hothead California lawyer, who'd terrorized the Comstock a few years earlier, leading an armed group of Confederate supporters during a mining dispute with Union Army supporters, he was long known as a rabble rousing, gun toting bully, and now he was the lawyer for opportunist Sarah Hill, who was suing millionaire William Sharon, claiming they had once been secretly married. That she was his wife and entitled to a part of his fortune. Sharon, who was a widower, denied it, and they went to court, where Terry produced some documents to support the claim. It was a media event, as newspapers throughout the country covered the story. But at last, the state Supreme Court decided the marriage documents were fake and dismissed the trial. Terry went on to marry Sarah Hill, but then he went gunning for the case trial judge. A shootout that was to end with Terry in boothill. Sharon, Terry and Hill, three people that deserved each other!

ONG BIRD

It was actually Tahoe's first love story, and it was a dandy. Containing adventure, suspense and a happy ending. Supposedly the story came from an elderly Washoe woman, though it was printed in an 1924 article in Sunset Magazine. The story began with a description of a monstrous bird that lived inside the basin. It was as big as a house, with long sharp talons. And instead of feathers, it was covered with a thick layer of scales. More like a dragon than a bird, it had a human face, but it was an evil face, full of hate. This monster even had a name, it was called the "Ong." Everyone hid when they saw it flying. Its nest was deep under the waters of Lake Tahoe, placed where currents and eddy's would flow through, bringing with them lake-fish and any poor animals that might have drowned around the lakeshore. A steady supply of food for the Ong.

The story began late one fall, when the Washoe's were finishing up their last hunt of the season, before heading down to Carson Valley for the winter. It was the time for the chief to betroth the hand of his beautiful daughter to the bravest warrior of the tribe. But, it so happened, the daughter loved a young man who'd yet to be tested in battle, and so was unworthy of the young maiden. And as you'd expect, the young man also loved the Chiefs daughter. And he was desperate. Resolving there was only one thing he could do to win his lady, and that was to confront the terrible Ong. So he came up with a plan. He gathered up a sturdy rope of deerhide and some poisoned arrows and jumped out on a boulder overlooking the lake and waited, looking for the Ong. And he didn't have to wait long, as he soon heard the shriek of the monstrous bird and the beat of massive wings. And suddenly he felt the painful grasp of the giant talons, and was being lifted high into the air, above the lake, where the Ong intended on dropping him, where he would end up in the nest; food for the Ong. But the brave managed to lash himself to the great talons, and when the Ong let go, the young brave was still holding on and shooting poisoned arrows into its mouth and body. That drove the monster bird into a frenzy, for he swooped and dived and slammed into the lake time and time again, trying to dislodge his tormentor. But the young brave still hung on. The battle between the young brave and the Ong continued all day long, but then evening came and the sky turned to darkness, and the sounds of the battle stopped. Everyone believed the young brave had been drowned. But this lovestory was to have a happy ending, for there, coming out of the darkness, paddling into shore, was an exhausted but alive young brave. The Ong was dead, killed by the poison arrows, and the Chief of course had no hesitation in granting the heroic young brave the hand of his daughter. And so ended an early day Tahoe lovestory.

V⚡FLUMES AND CAVE⚡INS

If we look back at one the most defining periods in the history of the Lake Tahoe Basin, even though it was the most environmentally impacting period; the mid to later 1800's, several men come to the fore as deserving credit for much of what happened. For their inventions were to make possible much of the logging and mining that took place in the Basin and in the Comstock. The first man was to come up with a relatively easy, inexpensive and ultimately practical way of getting milled timber and cordwood from mills to shipping points; across steep Sierra mountain-slopes. His name was J.W. Haines and he came up with the idea of fastening two twenty-four inch boards together, running water down them, and floating the wood to where it had to go. And it worked! So well that logging companies were able to save the enormous and likely prohibitively expensive costs of building roads around Tahoe's mountainsides. With Haines invention, they didn't have to, and continued to cut trees.

The second man was a pioneering genius. A German engineer named Phillip Deidesheimer, in 1860 was asked by a mine owner to see if he could come up with a solution to a problem that threatened to shut down all of the deep mines in the west, including all of those in the recently discovered Comstock Lode. The mine owner was desperate, for the deeper they dug, the more problems he was having with cave-ins. Men were being trapped and buried alive underground and mines were on the verge of closing. No one else could figure out what to do, until Deidesheimer came. He spent weeks down in the darkness working out and rejecting one idea after another. But finally he struck on the answer to the problem. An innovative square-set method of supporting timbers; kind of like building a honeycomb inside a beehive, would work! He built it, the cave-ins stopped, and soon the whole Comstock adopted his invention. It allowed the mines to stay open; the demand for Tahoe's timbers continued and in fact it increased! Many made millions on his invention, but Deidesheimer didn't have a patent, and he was to die penniless in a San Francisco hotel in 1916. But to the miners who knew him, and his invention, Phillip Deidesheimer was a hero.

TRAIN TUNNELS

Back in the days before the popularity of the automobile, trains were often the most popular means of getting around this country. The nations railway system, always popular in the northeast and south, was to expand westward in the 1860s and 70's, into the great Sierra Nevada and around both sides of the Tahoe Basin. Train passenger service into the Basin was even established for a time beginning in 1900. To construct a railway through this part of the country, railroad engineers had to overcome a multitude of challenges. The most formidable challenges were those mountains and the canyons that characterize this region, and so those engineers relied upon a system of tunnels and trestles, and snowsheds through the Sierra. They worked well enough, and the railroads were completed, and so by the end of the 19th century, the nation was connected by rail.

But while they did the job, those tunnels and trestles and snowsheds were also a continuous maintenance problem for the railroads, and they also had another problem; they tended to catch on fire. For they were all made of wood, and despite the precautions of lining them with zinc or hiring special watchmen to keep an eye on them, time and again, sparks from a passing train would set them afire. Typical was the 1872 tunnel fire near Carson City. The Virginia and Truckee locomotive, the "Reno" pulling both passenger and freight cars, had entered the tunnel before the engineer realized that a previous train had ignited the support timbers and the tunnel was ablaze with fire! It was too late to try to stop the train, so he kicked open the throttle and blasted his way through the tunnel! The caboose just clearing the flames before the burning roof of the tunnel collapsed in a heap. The passengers of course were all in a state of panic and shock, but fortunately no one was hurt. The engineer raced to the nearest depot in Carson and returned with the town fire company, but by then flames were flaring twenty feet out of both ends of the tunnel. The tunnel was a total loss and had to be rebuilt. And many similar such incidents took place on the transcontinental railroad above Truckee in those years. The Central Pacific's snowsheds (built to protect the trains from the vicious Sierra winters) would often catch fire. And there were many eyewitness accounts from Sierra travelers, who were riding a train that came upon a blazing inferno, telling a similar account of an engineer (unexpectedly encountering a fire in the middle of a snowshed) pouring it on and racing through a tunnel if they thought they could make it through safety, or hitting the brakes and screeching to a halt if they thought they couldn't. When that happened, it might take hours, even a few days before the flames were extinguished and repairs made and before the trains could run again. It all made traveling by train in those days, exciting and sometimes, dangerous.

THAT DREADED CORSET

During the 19th century when people came to visit Lake Tahoe resorts for a few weeks, they had to bring along trunks of clothes; especially the ladies. For not only did fashion dictate that people have a different set of clothes for every occasion, ladies dresses were bulky affairs that took up a lot of space. And fashion, although flattering was not always kind to women during the 1800's. Long trailing dresses and those binding corsets could be beguiling and downright miserable at the same time. As early as 1856 some of the doctors out west were finding their waiting rooms filled with women complaining of backaches. That was a natural byproduct of all those cooking, cleaning and gardening chores, but was aggravated by the restrictive clothing that many of the women wore. And so at least a few doctors' prescriptions included wearing fewer clothes! One patient was advised to start wearing a light hooped skirt instead of a heavy one, and within a couple of weeks her backache was gone and never came back.

The most unique apparel for women was a pair of trousers that looked like they came out of ancient Turkey. Created by Amelia Jenks Bloomer, this style of dress was rather outrageous to look at, but it was more comfortable than the hoopskirts and long trailing dresses that were the rage during the mid 1800's. The brave women that tried this dress on were just trying to be practical, even though most of the civilized world didn't quite know what to make of this new attire, and some men couldn't help but break out laughing when they saw someone in bloomers walking down the street. Though after a time, the bloomers were somewhat accepted, more than a few stylish ladies dressed in their finest skirts also had felt the chagrin and embarrassment of having a small parade of curious men following them down the street, intrigued with what they saw. But while the bloomers were a small step towards feminine freedom, the phaseout of the corset was true emancipation for all women. The perfect hourglass figure with a small waist was the unreasonable and elusive goal of this breath-stealing, rib-crunching beauty aid. When all laced up tight, women may have looked their fashionable best, but many suffered from fainting spells, indigestion and shortness of breath until they could free themselves from its lacy grip. During the last century, the men were usually the ones who faced the Indian attacks and endured the 130-degree temperatures of the silver mines, but it was the women who had the worst of it, for they had to wear those hoop skirts, bloomers and the dreaded corset. Proving once again, they really are the stronger sex.

ARCHBOLD
AND GUBA

This tale is a bit of history about a man, an explorer, and a bit of history about his airplane, a classic. The man was Richard Archbold. Born in 1907 in New York City, he was a man born to wealth, being an heir to the Standard Oil Company fortune. But Archbold wasn't content with using his fortune to live a life of comfort. He was also a person born to adventure. Early in his life, he found himself fascinated with the thought of exploring uncharted lands in the remote regions of the world. A biologist by training, Archbold was to take advantage of his wealth to help fund a number of expeditions around the world; expeditions to collect and identify thousands of exotic plants, and explorations to study the lifestyles and habitats of unique and mysterious animals that were only seen in zoos in this country. In a 10-year period, from 1929 to 1939, Archbold was to organize, support and lead four biological expeditions; first to Madagascar and then three more into the interior of New Guinea. There, he was to discover a heretofore, hidden civilization of native peoples, deep in the jungles of New Guinea. By 1941, the world on the edge of a war, he decided to establish a permanent biological research station near Lake Placid. A 1,000-acre preserve where scientists could live, explore and conduct research on plants and animals. This was to be his home for the remainder of his life. His research center is still active today.

Richard Archbold was also a pilot. His love of exploring and research was to embrace a love of aviation; of unique airplanes that enabled him to wing his way around the Indonesian and African islands, exploring. In 1937 one of his expedition airplanes was to bring him to Lake Tahoe. It was in January of that year that the US Navy granted Archbold permission to buy a unique airplane of the times. An airplane with floats, a "PBY Model-28-1." Archbold, by this time a research associate with the American Museum of Natural History, named his floating airplane the "Guba;" a word meaning "sudden storm" in a local dialect of New Guinea. He was planning on another expedition to that country and wanted a sturdy, fuel-efficient aircraft, and in the PBY he had that. But it needed to be tested for high elevation takeoffs, and so Archbold decided he would conduct that test here, at Lake Tahoe. In June, he flew here and landed on the lake. With an additional 1500 pounds of sand loaded into the cargo bay, the Guba revved up its two powerful engines and easily took off. That plane was to set a national air record that month; the largest plane at the time to fly non-stop coast-to-coast. But Archbold wanted even more from his plane, and sold the Guba to the Russian military; replacing it with another PBY with larger fuel tanks. Guba was never to fly to New Guinea, although it was used in a polar rescue attempt. Sadly it ended up being destroyed by a German U-boat in 1942 during a shelling of a Russian airfield. But both Richard Archbold, and an airplane named Guba are forever more a small part of Tahoe's history.

CHIEF NUMAGA

He was a war-chief, a man of courage, of principle. He was also a man who wanted peace, but despite his best efforts, he couldn't stop the unstoppable. It was just of matter of time before his people, the Paiutes would clash with the white settlers. It was 1860, the great Comstock Lode had been discovered just a year earlier and people were streaming through the Tahoe Basin, on their way to Carson and Virginia Cities. His name was "Numaga," but the white settlers called him "Young Winnemucca," for the great medicine chief, the leader of all the regional Paiute Tribes was known as "Old Winnemucca." The old chief was known for his wisdom. A shrewd politician, he was alarmed at the invasion of white settlers into the Carson and Washoe Valleys . . . but preferred to try to live with these strange new people rather than doing battle with them. But, he had growing doubts as to whether that peace would last. But Numaga, the name meant "giver of food," was a capable man, possessed with a keen mind and the gift of eloquence, he too saw what was happening to his people, and also felt the rumblings of discontent among the tribes warriors as the numbers of white settlers increased. Numaga was a statesman for his tribe and he often gave his council to the elders. He'd also lived for a time among the whites in California, and had learned both the English language, and also to appreciate their superior technology and overwhelming numbers. So much so, that Numaga came to believe that in the event of a war with the whites, there was no way his tribe could expect to win. He rode from camp to camp trying to persuade tribal members to not engage in any fights with the settlers, but he found that he was being ignored. He made one last effort to persuade the old chief and his council of elders, telling them that "The white man are like the stars over your heads. You may have great wrongs heaped upon you from those stars, but can you reach up and blot them out? You cannot! If you were to defeat the whites in Nevada, they would send soldiers from California to come to wipe you out." He went on to proclaim: "They will come like sand in a whirlwind and drive you from your homes. Your families would starve and you would listen to the cries of your children . . . for food." Numaga may have, for a moment, stayed the coming conflict with his arguments, but events at Williams Station, a small way station on the Carson River were to make his pleas for peace meaningless as a rider came in to report to the old Chief that a small band of warriors had attacked and burned down the station, killing five men. An act of revenge for the kidnapping of several young Paiute women by the men that worked there. A war was beginning, and the opportunity for peace suddenly vanished. So it was, that Numaga would soon find himself fighting a battle at Pyramid Lake against a ragtag army of Comstock volunteer soldiers. Still in his heart, a man of peace, but also a man when called upon, who would go to war for his people.

CHEAP TAHOE LAND

If you're going to run a logging empire you need to own lots of land with lots of trees. And it doesn't hurt to know how to work the system either. And that was the situation for the Carson and Tahoe Lumber and Fluming Company's owners, Duane Bliss and Henry Yerington, in the 1870's and 1880's here in the Basin. They needed to get as much Tahoe forested lands as possible to support their expanding timber operations. Providing sawtimber, cordwood, posts and braces for the mines of the Comstock. And they took every advantage of the loose government rules. Bliss and Yerington, correctly anticipating the demand for timber actually began to purchase land before they formed the company. Picking up 50,000 acres of land on the east shore alone. But it wasn't enough, and so they began to approach other Tahoe land owners, offering to purchase "their" lands, with some success. Pioneer land owners like Rob Woodburn sold out and so did others. They leased other lands, but it still wasn't enough, and so the company adopted another approach to acquiring

Tahoe land. The government, under several programs, such as the Timber Culture Act, allowed individuals to own public lands. The expectation being that individual settlers would homestead and live on the land, and even plant trees on their 160 acre parcel. The owners of the Carson and Tahoe Lumber and Fluming Company were well aware of this program, and so recruited a score of people who were willing to file on a quarter-section of Tahoe land, promising to live there and plant conifers. Who, after obtaining title, then transferred the title of the newly acquired property to the logging company. They were called "nominee buyers," and the practice was highly questionable, but not entirely illegal, as the laws of the 1870's and 1880's were a bit loose. So it was the Tahoe land status books are filled with the names of men; Foster, Patton, Shanklin, Lockie, and a hundred others, who owned Tahoe lands for all of twenty-four hours and then, for a pocket full of cash, gave it away to a logging empire. And so in this way, nearly one-fifth of all of the land in the Basin was acquired by Bliss and Yerington, so they never ran out of trees for the Comstock.

THE HERMIT OF ECHO LAKES

High up in the mountains overlooking Lake Tahoe are a pair of lakes hidden away from view. Called "Echo Lakes," supposedly because you could hear voices echoing through the canyon when the wind was just right. They were once the home of some hardy pioneers who didn't mind the snow or the remoteness. In fact they savored it. Charles Burnham was the first to settle there in 1875. Finding an island at the far end to be a welcome refuge from the hustle and bustle of the Tahoe Basin. But though Burnham preferred his solitude he wasn't a recluse. A short time after he constructed his cabin, he invited some friends of his; one of them the Governor of California, to spend a few weeks there, to enjoy the mountains, the hunting and the fishing, and a chance for them to get away from their hectic lives to play some poker and enjoy a plentiful supply of cold beer. The Governor came and had a great time. John Becker moved in, in 1886 and not only set up a homestead around the lower lake, as he was a man of some intemperance, Becker also established a first class saloon there. Supposedly, it was for the occasional tourist but it also existed for his own convenience.

The man who was to become known as "Mr. Echo Lakes," and the "Hermit of Echo Lakes," was Hamden Eldorado Cagwin. Cagwin was born on Christmas day of 1850, which was fitting, for to many he was like Santa Claus. He arrived at the lake in 1897, and those who knew him were charmed by his warmth, his caring nature and his humility. He was always bubbling with excitement and good cheer that made everyone around him feel better. Echo Lake children adored him and their parents admired him. For his was a tough life. Living in a simple cabin year-round, often alone during the long winter months, Cagwin though was born to live in these mountains. For he was a mountain-man by inclination; an expert hunter and fisherman and he loved to guide visitors into the Basin backcountry. Whenever anyone needed help, he was there, always lending a hand when needed. Often hiking down to Strawberry to pick up the mail for his fellow "lakers." For nearly twenty years Hamden Cagwin lived on the shores of these remote lakes, passing away quietly in his cabin there in 1914. The "Hermit of Echo Lakes" has long been gone. But nearly a century later, today's lakers still speak of him fondly. He would of been pleased.

MAN BITES DOG?

Somewhere around the 1880's, a saying originated; that when a dog bites a man that's not news, but when a man bites a dog, that "is" news. The more unique, the more unusual the story, the more likely it will be printed. And while that does seem to be the case these days, back in the 1860's, area newspapers often seemed to make little distinction between the mundane and the offbeat, printing both kinds of stories as a matter of routine. The 1860's Truckee paper, the "Truckee Weekly Tribune," typified the style, the content of small-town newspapers, who would cover every happening or non-happening such as listing the names of all of the passengers who had recently taken a sailing tour of Lake Tahoe, or the name of a night watchman that had just been hired to protect a town brewery. Or even the names of the people that won their bets during a recent horse race (fortunately, this took place years before the creation of the IRS). Some of the weeks' news would be about civic affairs. One 1868 article for example, was a story about discussions to create a single county government for all of Lake Tahoe to Truckee (with Truckee as the county seat). Another story focused on the concerns over the limited supply of water that was available should a fire break out. Period papers would also be filled with small news features about the struggles between the law and the lawless. But there was a bit of "man bites dog" flair to some of these stories. Stories for example, about a husband and wife who struck up an argument in the middle of a Truckee saloon, that quickly boiled over into the middle of main street, and that soon had a score of the towns citizens crowded around watching the melee until the wife managed to win the argument with a well placed right hook. There was also that story about the call-out of the town volunteer fire department. The rush down the street with the hand-operated fire engine, responding to a cry of alarm that there was a cloud of smoke pouring out of one of the towns twenty-five saloons only to discover that the smoke had come from the cigars of the saloon patrons.

Sometimes the news stories would be presented in a straightforward manner, but end up with a bit of a "twist" at the end in a mix of straight news and man bites dog story combination. For example, there was a story about a man who had decided to close his business and was planning on leaving the Sierras and moving back east. It wasn't until the reader reached the bottom line of the news story that they were informed as to "why" the man had closed his business. His business partner was a thief, and had run off the week before with all of their money. But then there was the 1868 story about an actor who, getting ready for a play, somehow managed to mix up the gum adhesive he used to hold his stage beard on, with a caustic cleaning compound and now was going to miss a number of performances while he was recovering from a bad case of swollen cheeks. Some stories were strange enough to not need any embellishment, for the truth was strange enough.

TAHOE'S LOOKOUT TOWERS

A wisp of smoke appears above the treetops, and soon begins to thicken into a billowing column of heat. In a remote area of the Basin a wildfire has started, and it's beginning to grow. Flames that began life licking at the trunk of a lightning struck tree have jumped high into its branches, sending red-hot embers swirling skyward, torching its neighbors, setting them ablaze and now threatening to burst out and devour the whole forest. But a lookout has seen the smoke, the flames, and an alarm has gone out: "Smoke Report!" Firefighters around the Basin from a score of agencies and protection districts rush to their trucks and race off to do battle. Guided to the flames yet unnoticed or unseen by most around the Basin. But even before they arrive, they'll have a good idea of what they'll be up against: how big the fire is, what direction it's heading and how fast it's spreading, thanks to the sure eyes of the lookout. And that's how it was for a better part of this last century, when "Angora, Zephyr, Stateline and Martis" Lookout Towers stood guard to protect the forests around the Tahoe Basin. But these days, they're seldom used because of newer detection technologies.

For those of us who knew them, they're full of memories and of exciting times not so long ago. Like the day the Angora lookout was intently watching and reporting the numerous down-strikes and puffs of telltale smoke in the Desolation Wilderness, oblivious to an ominous looking storm cloud drifting his way. Suddenly a white-hot finger of lightning slammed halfway down the ridge below him, and moments later, a second strike, but much closer. He realized in an instant the lightning was coming right over the top of the station and immediately dove into his bunk and pulled a blanket over his head just as a blinding white flash hit the ground outside! All of the windows were shattered and a deafening roar momentarily stunned the lookout. But his blanket and the glass insulators under the legs of his bunk saved him from being cut or injured. Another day, the Stateline lookout was nearly burned as a fast-moving wildfire was threatening, but the fire was stopped at the last moment by an air tanker, creating some exciting and scary moments for a lady lookout. While all of the Tahoe lookouts have moved on, the old towers are still around, and ready to serve again if they're ever needed.

RAY KNISLEY
HAD A MISSION

It was an important deal for Tahoe, and a stereotypical response from clearly well meaning government who wanted to do more but couldn't because of individual agency standards and constraints. Sometimes there's too much of a good thing and sometimes there's too little, as happened with the efforts to transfer the privately held lands of Lucky Baldwin and George Pope to the public. After Baldwin's passing in 1909, his estate was protected from additional commercial development by daughter Anita Baldwin. She wanted to keep the lands around his estate in an undisturbed state. After her passing in 1939, title to these prime lakeshore lands passed again to Anita's heirs, and they too wanted to keep the property free from commercial expansion. After all it was an ideal location to construct a block of condominiums or a private resort or even an exclusive subdivision for the wealthy. But Ray Knisley, both trustee for Anita Baldwin and a close friend of the Pope family, was determined to follow the desires of the Baldwin's. And, since much of the Baldwin holdings were based in southern California, Knisley first approached the president of the Los Angeles Chamber of Commerce, to see if he could interest the State of California in acquiring the Tahoe lands for a state park. But the state wasn't prepared to take over what was to be 3503 acres of land, including 10,000 feet of beachfront on Lake Tahoe, along with an additional 17,600 feet of shoreline on Fallen Leaf Lake. It was just "too big" the state said, and besides, there wasn't any money available. Knisley then tried the National Park Service, proposing that they acquire the Baldwin and Pope lands, and even some acreage around Cascade Lake and combine these lands with the Desolation Wilderness area, and make it into a National Park. But even with all these lands, the land area was too small to be practical as a National Park and the Park Service reluctantly said "No," and suggested Knisley try yet another agency; the Forest Service. As it turned out, the Baldwin and Pope estate lands weren't too big or too small, and a land deal was negotiated. A 3-way $946,464 deal paid for by timber cut by private woodcutters from public lands on the Stanislaus and Modoc National Forests. Called a "tripartite" exchange (no longer being done), this allowed the public to acquire and develop such sites as Pope, Baldwin and Fallen Leaf Campground. Fortunately, for one agency, these beautiful Tahoe lands were just the right size.

MUTTON AT TAHOE

Most reviews of Tahoe history initially focus on the Comstock era, beginning with the search for gold and silver and the logging operations that stripped most of the basin slopes of virgin timbers. And later, the evolution of the tourist-based economy, the steamships, and resorts and later still, the establishment of gaming. But often missing is an important, though less visible phase in the history of the Basin region. Our area was once a significant site for raising and grazing sheep, and so there was also a sheep era in our history! Sheep were first introduced into this region during the 1850s. The flood of people into the California foothills searching for gold generated an immediate demand for mutton and wool. Richens "Uncle Dick" Wootton of Virginia drove nine thousand sheep overland to California in 1852. The next year, Kit Carson led a team of sheepherders into the region. They brought thousands more animals with them.

After the Comstock discovery, there was a second surge in demand, and Sierra and Carson Valley meadows were soon used for small herds of sheep. With the construction of the transcontinental railroad over Donner, our area also had access to eastern markets, and the herds began to grow in size. Over 10,000 sheep were on the Sorensen Ranch just south of the lake. Hope Valley became a summer grazing ground dotted with bands of sheep. Other high mountain meadows around the Basin were also popular grazing sites; from Blackwood to Tahoe Meadows. Not everyone in the region at first was happy about the sheep competing with the cattle that were also grazed here, and there were a few harsh words and lots of competition, as sheep tended to eat closer to the roots than cattle, leaving little behind for cows. They required more tending to make sure they didn't stay too long on one pasture. And there were concerns about the fires that herders intentionally set to encourage the growth of new vegetation. But eventually, cattle ranchers and sheepherders learned to get along, as the 20th century dawned, it was a common sight to see both sheep and cattle on the same range. By the 1930's, changing markets, rising land prices and less available acreage because of developments combined to reduce the sizes and numbers of herds around our area and Tahoe's sheep era was over.

NELLIE AND ANNA

Nellie and Anna, were pioneers living among pioneers. Breaking new ground that some people, mostly men, but some women too, didn't want disturbed. They learned that the world wasn't quite ready for them and they needed to proceed cautiously. But in spite of that, they were to leave their mark on the world of 19th century California and Nevada journalism. Nellie Mighels husband Henry, was the owner and publisher of the "Nevada Appeal," and was a widely respected and capable news editor. When he passed away in 1879, Nellie took over the reins of the paper and began doing what Henry had previously done; cover the regions news where-ever it was happening. In those days, this was something that a woman just didn't do and it took a while for Nellie to learn the skills of a reporter. She learned to develop and polish her skills by taking notes during the Sunday sermons at a Carson City church . . . working to train her mind to only copy down and report on the "high points" of the sermons. But Nellie was a natural and soon gained the respect of other journalists even though she sometimes had to put herself in situations, that in the late 1800's, was decidedly "unladylike." Like covering a boxing match. When she covered the James Corbett-Bob Fitzsimmons fight in Carson in 1897 (for the Chicago Tribune), the only other women in attendance that day, was Fitzsimmons wife and two ladies from the red light district. But instead of using her own name as the article's author, Nellie ended up creating a fictitious name, for she was concerned that some of her friends back East, reading the article, would be embarrassed by her presence at that fight. Nellie was to spend her life in the newspaper business and when she passed away at the age of 100 in 1945, she was a respected, and honored journalist.

Anna Fitch came to Virginia City in 1863 with her husband Thomas to start up a new literary magazine in that Comstock boomtown. Anna was no stranger to the world of journalism, having founded, in 1858, one of the earliest women's magazines in the State of California, the "Hesperian." Although fully aware of the limited role that women were free to play in these early days of frontier journalism, Anna wasn't quite as cautious as Nellie about her chosen profession for she primarily wrote "for" women. Providing a needed woman's perspective in the otherwise male focused press. But although Nellie managed to carve out a small niche for herself in the Comstock era press, she also alienated many women for her staunch resistance to women's suffrage: the right to vote. She wrote, that by giving women the power to vote, that would immerse women into the coarse world of politics, and "that" would threaten their natural sensibilities and damage the role of women in society. Suffragettes blasted her, but Anna kept writing her opinions, even though it cost her the support of many women in Nevada. She became so unpopular in the state that when she passed away in 1904, all of the major California newspapers carried her obituary, but not one paper in Nevada did. It had been difficult for her to express her opinions in the face of so much criticism, but Anna Fitch stood her ground. She was a courageous pioneer journalist.

SLOW NEWS DAY

Just ask any of the editors of any one of the newspapers around the lake, and they'll tell you that some-days the news is more interesting than other days. But every edition requires a headline and on those slow days it can be a scramble to find a lead story that will interest readers and sell papers. It was no different during the early days in this region, but news editors then had more freedom and fewer scruples perhaps, to create stories that were part entertainment, part space filler and part fabrication. Occasionally they were blatant lies, strictly works of fiction. But with a little imagination, a little stretching of the truth, even the mundane could become a news story. For example, one early day Nevada editor was to cover in great (front page) detail, the unwanted intrusion of Mrs. O'Riley's pig into the prized vegetable garden of Mrs. Johnson. Not only did that piggish vandal selfishly stuff itself silly with every carrot, every bit of cabbage, every munchy mouthful of leafy green that it could swallow, that swine left tooth marks in her prized squash, though it apparently was too full to completely devour it. A clear case of pigheaded gluttony. Mrs. O'Riley made up with Mrs. Johnson by giving her a fresh side of bacon, though the story didn't say from where it came from.

There was another such story written in another early day Nevada newspaper. This story told of a woman that had gone into a local mercantile store to make a small purchase, a pick handle. Normally something like this would never make it into the pages of a local newspaper but as there was little else going on in the community, the editor was to embellish the story with the conversation the woman had with the store clerk, who casually asked her what was she going to do with that pick handle; "Go prospecting?" To which the woman replied, that "no," she wasn't going prospecting. She was headed over to where her worthless husband was cavorting with a "carroty-headed cat," and to remind him that he was still married! Finally, there were those news editors that on a quiet news day simply took the bull by the horns and printed that "it may seem that nothing was happening," but in fact something was always going on somewhere, and went on to print such near-happenings. Reporting on the arrival of a stagecoach, the passage of a freight train, the fact that a score of dogs were observed barking at a stray cat stranded in a tree, or that a woman stubbed her toes on a boardwalk plank or that the zephyr winds blew the hats off the heads of a couple of gentlemen. Perhaps it wasn't exciting news, but it was still news, and that's what newspapers were all about.

WILLIAM KENT

Up near Tahoe City, all but hidden away by the Sunnyside Resort as you pass by on Highway 89, and these days surrounded by subdivisions, is a modest sized campground and small public beach known as "William Kent." During the summer, this area is abuzz with people, enjoying the resort, the restaurants and general store that mark the Sunnyside area as one of the west shores most popular locations. But nearly a century ago, this same area was a quiet place as only a few cabins and stores were scattered among undeveloped large tracts of land. No one then could have anticipated how developed and how busy this part of the lakeshore would one-day become. And if it was not for the generosity of one man, William Kent, neither the public campground nor beach would be here. Just more homes, more buildings and less beach access.

William Kent hasn't been an especially well-known Tahoe historic figure but he has earned a place of honor in the hearts of many conservationists. A businessman, rancher, philanthropist and a member of the United States Congress (1911 to 1917), Kent was to play a critical role in the establishment of several important natural preserves in this country, without a lot of personal fanfare. In the early years of the last century, Kent became aware of the extensive logging that was taking place in the California coastal areas. Logging that was removing vast stands of majestic old growth redwoods. So in 1918, he reached deep into his own pockets and donated thousands to the Save-the-Redwoods League to buy and preserve lands, to save these big trees. But this wasn't his first effort at trying to preserve nature's scenic beauty. As, a few years earlier, for the then princely sum of $45,000 he acquired some lands in Marin County that were in danger of being developed and he then gave those lands to the government as a gift to be used as the basis for a new land preserve. They wanted to name the preserve after him, but Kent declined the offer, suggesting that the area be dedicated to a more deserving naturalist. It was, and soon the area was to be known as "Muir Woods," after John Muir. It was soon to be established as a National Monument, thanks to the generosity of William Kent. It was also Kent that in 1916, while a member of Congress, was to introduce the legislation to establish the National Park Service. He championed the ideal that National Parks should be natural land areas and not marred by what he called "artificiality of any avoidable kind."

Lake Tahoe was to benefit from his kindness. He'd come to the lake for a visit during the summer of 1903 in the hopes that his ailing mother would feel better, breathing the mountain air and drinking the mineral waters that were so readily available here. And she did feel better, and so Kent bought some land and built a summer home for his family. But after a few years, as he'd done before, he was to recognize this land may have a greater value as a public asset and was to exchange two acres of land at Tahoe for lands elsewhere, and then he donated nearly twenty-three acres of land to the government, including 100-yards of shoreline.

Characteristically, he didn't ask for his name to be on the site if it was to become a park. But in 1949, the Forest Service did give the campground and beach a name, and appropriately, they called it "William Kent."

YANKS STATION

For decades, it was once a primary destination for Sierra travelers. A welcome port in a snowstorm. A refuge for the weary. A house of good cheer and a hot meal. It was even known as a place of tall tales and hardy laughter. For most of its years, it was known as "Yanks Station," a mini-settlement on the road between Placerville and Virginia City in the area we know today as "Meyers." A rare individual built and operated Yanks Station. Half mountain-man, half-savvy entrepreneur, with a dash of flair and uncommon good sense, was Ephraim "Yank" Clement. He acquired a small way station operation from Tahoe pioneer Martin Smith, who, with partner Jim Muir, had built the basin's first trading post/rustic way station. Muir later sold his interest to another trading post operator (George Douglass) and their small operation was expanded. But it was Yank Clement that was to transform the fledgling resort into a popular and locally legendary operation. Yank set to work, and constructed what became a small settlement, complete with 3-story hotel, merchandise store, two saloons, blacksmith shop, a stable with holding corrals and a massive barn. It wasn't long before a butcher shop, private homes, and various small shops were added by others, drawn to what had become a major stopover point for Sierra travelers.

As Yanks Station was located on the busiest road on the way to and from the Comstock (before the days of the transcontinental railroad), every kind of person dropped by: trappers, traders, teamsters, fortune-seekers, bandits, thieves, whiskey-peddlers and traveling preachers. Yanks Station was the host to them all. Yank and his wife ("Aunt Liddy" they called her), were there to greet and care for each one. Yank spun his wild stories and Aunt Liddy oversaw the cooking and cleaning chores and provided a welcome touch of home. An 1860's eyewitness to the scene reported seeing an almost uninterrupted caravan of travelers stopping by, as "Yanks Station" was practically a household word to all who passed that way. It was, at the time (before the days of the lavish resorts) "the" place to stay while traveling through the Lake Tahoe Basin. The crowds dwindled during the winter months, though never fully disappeared. The summer months were a blur of activity. Yanks was also a regular stop on the stageline, and passengers all hours of day or night would be deposited at the front door. Passengers would quench their thirst at the station saloon and/or enjoy a hot meal and some steaming coffee. After the railroad was built, road traffic dropped, but the station still remained busy, if not as hectic. Yank and Aunt Liddy's friendly manner continued to draw customers. Enough that business was stable, and eventually another area hotel-keeper, George Meyers, expressed interest in the operation, in 1873 coming to terms with Yank to sell, George purchased Yanks Station and resolved to continue the old traditions of hospitality, though without Yank and Aunt Liddy it wasn't quite the same. But still, he did a fine job and for thirty more years Yanks Station (now being called "Meyers Station"), served Sierra travelers. The old hotel burned down in 1938, but the legend of Yanks Station lives on today.

GO WEST YOUNG HORACE

He was an enormously powerful and influential man in the mid-1800s in this country, and the founding editor of the New York Tribune. A newspaper, that even during his heyday reached over a million readers. But all that power and influence wasn't going to help him one bit during a memorable stagecoach ride through the Tahoe Basin. A ride that was to forever make him the brunt of an oft-told tale and also elevate a local stage driver to near legendary status during his own time. Horace Greeley was an accomplished writer and debater, and an impassioned believer in social reforms, crusading in print and in person for more workers rights, women's temperance and the abolishment of slavery. He was also a staunch supporter of expanding western civilization (though it wasn't Greeley that actually coined the phrase "Go west young man," he was credited with the phrase).

During 1859 he was to travel to California to help drum up interest for a railroad to the Pacific. His trip west (by way of a stagecoach, since that's all there was in those days) was to be marked by a lot of dust, bouncing around and some accidents, a few fairly serious. Onetime his stagecoach rolled over on a steep hill and Greeley found himself trapped inside, bruised and cut. But Greeley was a veteran of the stagelines and well used to the rigors of this method of travel. Another time, on this same trip, the stage in which he was riding over-turned in a stream and he got a thorough soaking. He may have been battered and sore or wet, but he never gave thought to giving up and returning home. By the time he arrived in Carson City, Greeley was quite prepared for his stage ride through the Sierras. After all, he'd made it across the Plains and through the Rockies, and only a few more miles remained. He'd been through the worst, he thought. He'd arranged to give a speech to the citizens of Placerville, and just needed to get there in time for his presentation and so booked the Carson to Placerville stage for this journey that would take him through the South Shore over Echo Summit. So it was that Greeley casually asked the driver of his stage to do his best to get him there on time. The driver of his stage, Hank Monk however, was an unusual man. A man of local fame for his prowess with his team, and for his wild character, and for his determination to stay on schedule. Mythology has long since obscured the true facts of this trip as the likes of Mark Twain have spun various versions of what really happened. But for certain, when Hank raced up the summit, Greeley was all white knuckles, as Hank was racing all out, his four horses running as fast as they could, a thousand foot drop just a few feet away! And it wasn't just over the summit they charged all-out. For, according to Greeley, they ran like that for 40-miles! Legend says that Greeley screamed to "Slow down!" But Hank just yelled that "You told me to get you there on time, and that's what I'm going to do." And he did, though when Horace Greeley stepped from the stage at Placerville, he was a mess. His clothes were rumpled, and he was covered in dust and shaken up. He managed to give his speech. But for sure, that was one ride he was never to forget!

THAT ONE⚡ARMED MACHINE

They're a part of Tahoe's contemporary history. Sometimes cursed, and sometimes generous, they have come to represent one of the most unique attractions of both of our stateline areas. They're those infamously famous though entertaining one-armed bandits: slot machines. They got their start back east in the latter 1800's. Evolving out of a mishmash of coin-operated machines that were originally designed just for amusement, or for vending, usually cigars or chewing gum. But these mechanical boxes with their spinning wheels and colorful reels were soon to be adapted by several enterprising inventors to provide a new novelty to a nation that seemed to have a hunger for wagering and adventure.

Gustav Schultz was credited with inventing the first primitive slot machine. It was actually a combination slot machine and a nickel-a-try strength tester machine. You dropped your coin in the slot, and then did your best to pull a couple of levers apart. The machine would then let you know if you were a "wimp" or a "brute." Schultz was soon joined by several other slot pioneers, like Charlie Fey, who created the Liberty Bell slots, and Herbert Mills; a manufacturer that turned out slot machines like Henry Ford did cars. His marketing and promotion skills at the turn of the century fostered such a demand for these fascinating little gizmos that he alone, managed to sell 15,000 of them within a few years.

It seemed like everyone loved to play! In the early 20's they found their way all across the country in hotels, motels, gas stations, drug stores, soda fountains and of course in every neighborhood saloon. Their popularity came to a smashing halt during the prohibition era, when slot machines went underground; into the speak-easy's. But then, enterprising slot companies then made some creative and slightly deceptive changes to convert these pure gaming machines into "amusement devices;" gum dispensing machines. For every nickel you dropped into the slot, you'd get a packet of gum, and if you were lucky, you'd receive a token you could trade for a cash prize. It was a ploy, but it made slots legal until prohibition was repealed. In fact the symbols on slots today: the plums, cherries, oranges come from the gum flavors. The bells are a legacy of the original "Liberty Bell brand" slot machines of Charlie Fey. But while most slots today are more microprocessor than gears and levers, and not all even have "arms" on them anymore, they're still popular, and are a part of the Tahoe heritage.

WAY STATIONS

The coffee was hot, and it was strong. Grounds were left in the pot and re-boiled again and again until it had the consistency of tar, and then they'd toss it out and start over again. But no-body seemed to mind, for that was the universal drink at all the way stations that dotted the roadsides between Lake Tahoe and Placerville. And besides it was free, and back in the 1800's there were a lot more things to worry about than scalding black coffee. These way stations offered the only food and shelter a traveler to the lake and beyond could get but these weren't five-star hotels. The nicer ones like Friday's Station, and Strawberry's at least offered beds for the lucky visitors. But many of these so-called inns were little more than a shed with straw on the ground, or sometimes huge barns with rows and rows of bunkbeds built-in to them, and on a typical day during the early years of the rush to the Comstock Lode, these places were not only jam-packed, they were over-flowing with people. During cold and stormy nights especially, half-frozen travelers paid just for the privilege of getting inside a building. And though every bed may have been taken, they at least could find a post or a wall to lean up against where they'd sleep standing up.

A traveler named Steven Massett wrote in his diary about his experiences at a way station while on his way up to the lake from Sacramento: "The heat was insufferable, mosquitoes were buzzing about, and fleas and bedbugs were just about everywhere," to greet him on his arrival at his sleeping quarters; a lodging house that he was about to share with 20 other men; packed in together on a straw covered floor. For most of the night he was kept awake by the scratching, itching, the snoring, the barking of dogs and the unmistakable odor of sweat, and soiled clothes and old socks. But finally, from sheer exhaustion, Massett managed to drop off to sleep, before he was eventually awakened by the cold wet snout of an ox that somehow had managed to stick its head through a window and into his face. And most travelers had the same experiences as Massett.

But there was another lake visitor that was to write about the great time he had at Tahoe's Logan House Hotel. None other than Mark Twain, who wrote about his December 1863 visit there. He gushed over the great food (a trout dinner every day), the comfortable furniture and the grand scenery of the Logan Hotel. Bachelor Twain declaring that staying there was as good a thing as he could ever want, other than having a wife. Strangely though, the Logan House Hotel was to fail, closing its doors a few years later while lesser way stations prospered. Perhaps it was because they had better coffee.

SECRET CODES

Almost as long as people have been talking to and about one another, people have been keeping secrets. Certainly the importance of secrecy has been obvious to the military. Civil War generals used secret codes to mask their movements and battle plans, and even President Thomas Jefferson used secret codes to keep in touch with Meriwether Lewis when he was exploring the Pacific Northwest, to ensure that if any messages sent by Lewis were intercepted by the Spanish, they would stay confidential. Secrecy has also been used in our region to protect business interests. There was a great rivalry between the two companies building the transcontinental railroad, the Union Pacific and the Central Pacific, especially during the last months of construction. Both companies regularly eavesdropped on the telegraph messages of the other railroad company. It was so easy for wire-tapers to simply climb a pole and listen in on the conversations taking place between their headquarters and field crews, learning about their plans and strategies, that both the Union & Central Pacific soon adopted secret codes. Code words that would "hide" real numbers, the identity of individuals, profits & costs and time schedules. And it helped to maintain the confidentiality both companies needed to compete with each other.

Even around the Comstock country, the importance of secret codes was obvious, as literally millions of dollars of mining stocks were owned and traded throughout the west and the nation. One 19th century periodical (the "Alta California") commented that everyone it seemed owned mining shares. Not only the capitalist and the banker, but the wholesale and retail merchant, the lawyer and the physician, the preacher and the editor, the carpenter and the blacksmith, the jeweler and the hotel keeper, the tailor and the shoemaker, even the servant and the laborer owned shares in some silver mine. And the slightest rumor would send the values sky-high or tumbling, and so it became common-place for speculators, for mine owners and investors to use code words to keep the truth secret until they could preserve profits or enhance them. Again, the telegraph was most often the primary mechanism for communication between the Virginia City mines and the financial center of San Francisco. Around 45,000 code words were adopted to convey a wide spectrum of phrases and market conditions. For instance, the phrase "buy before the news gets out," or "sell, before they find out the vein disappeared," were code phrases that would actually mean do the opposite! The owners of the Crown Point mine would refer to themselves as "mutton stew," in their telegraph messages, while the Ophir Mine would refer to itself as "chuck steak." Each mining company or conglomerate kept its own codebooks, which was carefully stored in a safe. One such codebook had ten pages just dealing with silver ore and 200-pages dealing with mining operations. Oh, there still was eavesdropping and spying going on, about the latest discovery or of a vein that had petered out. But through the use of these secret codes, promoters, speculators and mine owners managed to confuse their competitors and optimize their profits.

JARAD CRANDALL AND HIGHWAY 50

The road that had the greatest influence, the greatest impact on the development of the Tahoe Basin had several different names over the years. Once it was called the "Placerville-Carson Valley Wagon Road." It was also known as the "Lake Tahoe Wagon Road," and for a time as "Johnson's Cutoff." Today we call it Highway 50. And while these days, we can find the two plus hour drive between Carson and Placerville a challenge, the road is nothing like it was a century and a half ago when it was considered to be a notable accomplishment to make that same journey in less than twenty-four hours! In fact, there was a time when one such trip between these two communities was to be such a special occasion that when it was completed, it was celebrated with a brass band, a town parade and a 100-gun salute. It wouldn't seem like a big deal by today's standards, but prior to that June day in 1857, no one had ever managed to get a stagecoach over and through the Sierras, only pack-mules and horses and a few small but sturdy freight wagons were able to navigate the steep, winding, boulder-strewn route. But no passenger services were available. Over the years, some improvements to the route would be made as funds from several California counties were made available. For the economic development of the region depended upon improved transportation systems, especially for the growing settlements around Genoa and the Carson Valley, who needed better access into California for its markets and its supply linkages to the east coast.

One man who recognized the need to establish a passenger and freight line between the Carson and Sacramento Valley's was Jarad Crandall. A partner in a Placerville to Sacramento stage line he decided it was time to challenge the road and see if "he" could manage to get a loaded stagecoach over Echo and into the Basin over to Genoa. It was less a test of time, than a test to see if it could be done at all. For the road was terrible, and downright scary in a few places like Slippery Ford (near today's Twin Bridges). There, raging waters could easily block a stagecoach from crossing over and even getting to the western foot of the Sierra Crest. Crandall selected his best, strongest horses and loaded his stage with dignitaries, and a reporter from the "Sacramento Daily Union," and 500 pounds of freight and headed off from Placerville towards Nevada. Somehow they made it past Slippery Ford, and charged ahead, or rather crept ahead. For the road was often little more than a path. But after a number of stops to eat, rest and a few changes of horse-teams they pulled into Genoa, twenty-seven and a half-hours later where they were met by a cheering crowd. This was a stunning accomplishment at the time, as Crandall was declared to be a hero in all of the area newspapers. It wasn't long after this trip that he initiated regular stagecoach service between Placerville and Carson Valley. And it was none too soon, for just two years later, the discovery of the Comstock

Lode would bring tens of thousands of people into the area. But at least some of these people had it lucky for they didn't have to walk or ride a horse. For now, thanks to Jarad Crandall, they could sit back and ride in a stagecoach.

HE WAS NO QUITTER!

There's an old saying that "a quitter never wins, while a winner never quits." But then, sometimes there's a fine line between persistence and just plain stubbornness. Such was the case of a tenacious fellow by the name of Mike Maroney. It was back in the heady days of the California gold rush, in an area a few miles northwest of the lake. Mike was a miner. A pretty good one, for he'd had some success panning around the American River, but now he'd discovered an old stream channel that to Mike, seemed to hold the promise of a bonanza. For overlooking that ancient streambed was a massive boulder. A mountain of stone that was as big as a 2-story house. And Mike just knew . . . knew in his heart that under that mountain of rock was a vein of gold.

Realizing that it would take a long time to blast away that mountain of stone, he first decided to build himself a cabin . . . but when that was done he set to work, gathering up all the blasting powder he could find, and then drilling into that rock and blasting away a piece of it. The rock was hard and the work went slowly, but Mike kept at it . . . the days passing into weeks and the weeks became months. But Mike was determined for he was no "quitter," and kept blasting away day after day. Others would come by and see how he was doing, and Mike would show them the growing pile of rubble, But although there was no trace of gold yet, Mike's confidence was strong (a bit strained perhaps, but still strong). A whole year went by, and then a second year came and went, and Mike was still at it, when suddenly it happened! He'd placed an unusually large charge of blasting powder under a boulder protruding from the rock mountain, and lit it off. The concussion blew him off his feet and into the stream channel, where he was swept downstream. It was when he was scrambling back upstream to his work-site that Mike spotted it! A massive nugget of solid gold was exposed under that mountain of rock. It weighed a whopping twenty pounds (worth nearly $4000 in those days). Mike grabbed that big nugget and raced off towards the nearest town to let the world know about his discovery. After over two-years of hard, backbreaking work, he now believed he'd uncovered that vein of gold he'd always believed was waiting for him. But as it turned out, there was no rich vein of gold. There would be no bonanza. In fact, that single nugget was all that was ever found under that mountain of stone. But Mike Maroney couldn't walk away from his dream of that bonanza. And so a year after his discovery of that single nugget he was still at it, drilling and blasting. After all, he was no quitter.

THE POMIN'S

Theirs is one of the pioneer family names of early day Tahoe. Like the Bliss's, the Kehlet's, the Hobart's, the Clement's and the Glimores, they were among the very first basin residents following the boom-days of the discovery of the Comstock Lode. The Pomin's presence at the lake began in the early 1870's when 4 brothers arrived here fresh from Europe; northern France. A place, that in those days was in the middle of turmoil. A war was beginning, the Franco-Prussian War, and every young man over the age of fourteen was being conscripted to fight. It was from here the brothers journeyed, none of them yet fifteen, to shun a useless war and seek the adventurous life of America. Eventually, looking for work and a future, they migrated to the Tahoe Basin where they found a home. Two of the brothers in particular, were to become local personages because of their fondness for the great blue lake. Joseph Pomin and Ernest John had a talent for sailing, and they soon became dashing figures as captain of several small steamers that plowed the waves during the summer months carrying passengers, freight and the mail in the late 1800's. They called Joseph "Captain Joe" or sometimes just "Cappy Joe," and he became a beloved figure around Tahoe's lakeshores. His brother was to become a Tahoe legend as the longest serving lake captain. As master of steamships like the "Meteor," and the even more legendary "Tahoe." From 1876 to 1919, he stood in the pilothouse, in all kinds of weather, and expertly guided the big steamers around the lake. There must have been lake water in his bloodline, as his son was also to follow in his wake as a Tahoe steamship captain. Ernest Henry Pomin was born in 1878 over in Glenbrook. Spending his early years there, Ernest's first job was in a local grocery store, but that wasn't particularly exciting for a young man who was used to going out with his father on a steamship. So when he reached sixteen, he got a job working with his father on that steamship, eventually getting his own Masters license to become engineer and captain. In his later years he too became a beloved figure, passing at the age of ninety-two. He was known as Tahoe's "grand old man," but his family name lives on today. The Pomin's are a proud pioneer Tahoe family.

A BAD LOAN?

During the earliest days of the California gold rush, merchants selling supplies to hopeful Argonauts were often quite generous with credit; trusting their customers to make good on their purchases. Money wasn't essential because there was a general attitude that a poor man today, may well strike it rich and be wealthy tomorrow. At least rich enough to pay off his debt to a trusting merchant. Perhaps even adding a nice tip out of gratitude for the "grubstake." This is what Sierra merchant William Pike thought when two men entered his small general mercantile store and asked for credit to purchase a mule-loads worth of picks, shovels, blankets, canned goods and what-not for their new mining claim. William gladly filled the order, and granted them credit. For he believed this was a sound business decision, with little risk since there had been recent reports of some gold strikes in the area. The two men, with plenty of supplies set to work. Toiling from sun-up to sun-down; digging, digging. The days began to slip by, and the two kept at their task. Repeatedly journeying back to Williams store to re-supply themselves. William at first, happily obliging them, simply adding their new purchases to his credit book.

However, the dollars were beginning to add up and William began to worry. For he could ill afford to lose the money now owed him. Williams wife, Beverly was soon pressing him to cut the men off, for they'd been stuck before. But William had a hunch and warily but willingly decided to continue to supply them, and so the two men continued to work their claim. But as time went by, it was increasingly evident, they seemed to be wasting their time, as the hard ground yet revealed no riches, and one of the men decided to quit. But, he did agree to spend one last day with his partner; digging. It was then that the unlikely happened. The partner was deep in a hole, beating away with his pickaxe, and about ready to quit for good, and feeling discouraged at his bad luck. He made one last swing of the pick, and there in the previously barren dirt, was a golden nugget. A seven and a half pound nugget! They'd done it! And after their celebration, their first stop was Williams store, where they not only paid off their bill in full, just as he'd hoped, William also received a handsome bonus, a thousand dollars! Even Beverly had to agree that her husband had made the right decision, for once.

A DECENT MEAL

Certainly Mark Twain had his share of problems with the food he found in the mining camps and during his travels across the country on a stagecoach. Even in later life, he was to comment from time-to-time about his bad experiences with food. Deciding in his 70's to give up eating mince pie after midnight, for it would haunt him the rest of the night. Twain well knew that food could be loaded. Oft-times it was clearly the fault of the eater, consuming too much. Sometimes though it was the fault of the cook. Another period writer; a friend of Twain's while he was in San Francisco, was to record in his journals, his mixed experience with the mining camp cooks that he encountered during his travels in the Sierra foothills. His name was Prentice Mulford. Born in Long Island in 1834 he arrived in California's gold country at the young age of twenty-two. Over the next few years, Mulford was to be a gold miner, a writer, a schoolteacher and a cook. A keen observer of human nature, he was to write a score of stories for local periodicals of the day. Referring to himself as "Dogberry," Mulford penned an article in 1869 called "California Culinary Experiences," in which he recounted his experience with various camp cooks. Actually, he called himself a "survivor." And that was probably an accurate description for he was to somehow find himself partnered-up with a variety of men that did the cooking and camp chores while he did the digging. He was to spend one winter with what he called a "fickle and unmethodical cook." A man who would vacillate between the extremes of being meticulous to being outright careless and indifferent. His coffee was either too weak, or too strong. His biscuits either half raw or half burnt. His steaks either nearly raw or almost cooked to a burnt crisp. Everything it seemed, he cooked to one extreme or another. Meals were either cold or piping hot. But somehow Mulford managed to survive this cook and went on to another camp and another cook. This cook was what Mulford called "an experimenter." A cook who was constantly trying out new dishes. Mixing up different recipes with abandon and a certain recklessness, assuring Mulford of a tummy ache. But the cook was undaunted, always searching for the perfect meal. And in fact he did have a few culinary successes, but not often; about one time in ten Mulford figured. So it was that in desperation that Prentice Mulford left this camp and cook and struck out on his own. Finally realizing that the only way he might get a dependably good meal was to cook it himself. So he began to prepare his own camp meals. It took him awhile to learn the art of flipping a flapjack, brewing a tasty cup of coffee, baking hot biscuits and mouth-watering apple pie. But over time he'd polished his cooking skills, and so finally, was able to enjoy a decent meal.

ONE STEP AHEAD OF THE TAX MAN

Like the grand Tahoe Tavern in Tahoe City, and the Tallac Hotel near Camp Richardson, the north shores "Brockway Hotel," also had its moments of grandeur and glory. Vacationers would flock to the lake to enjoy the hotel's hot mineral springs. Both to soak in, and after they were chilled in ice, to drink; believing they were a wonderful natural cure for all that ailed you. William Campbell was the first to build a hotel above the lakeshore. The year was 1869, and when he spotted hot water bubbling out of the ground near a granite boulder, he spotted an opportunity. Soon constructing a bathing house, that later expanded into a full resort. It had a great run, for one hundred years later, in 1969, that resort was still operating. Although the next year it finally gave way to modern condominiums and a heated swimming pool.

But this venerable Tahoe hotel was also to have some rough years. There was a time it couldn't even stay in business. For 1881 was a rough year for Brockway. It didn't help that a poker game there got out of hand, and two locals, one a muleskinner, the other a north shore railroader, working for the local logging company, got into a nasty fight. And that made its way into all the local papers. It didn't help either that the buildings weren't being maintained very well, or the winter snows were especially slow to melt that year, or the fact that fewer tourists seemed to come to the lake that season. So it was that by the end of the 1881 season, the sheriff walked up to the main door of the resort and chained it closed with a padlock. The resorts owners hadn't paid their taxes, and now they were shut-up tight. It was to be several years before those delinquent taxes were paid, and the resort re-opened, with new proprietors. But here again, bad luck struck. About a year after the Brockway Resort was back in business, it had another unprofitable year, and the taxes fell past due again. But this time the resort manager, one Joe Short, was determined to beat the sheriff to the front door. Short loaded up a wagon with everything in sight, including all of the mailboxes that were part of the post office that was housed inside the resort! And off he drove down the road. With yet another new proprietor, the resort was to re-open once again the next year, but it was years before they reopened the post office.

UNEXPECTED PROBLEMS FOR TAHOE VISITORS

Over the years there's been untold millions of visitors to Lake Tahoe. People who came here to have a little fun and perhaps a little excitement. Inevitably too, over the years, from time-to-time, something unusual happened to a few of these recreationists and they ended up getting a bit more excitement than they expected; or wanted. For instance there was that turn of the century couple that was simply taking a hike along the east shore, just exploring, enjoying the scenery of the rocky lakeshore, the bright colors of the lake, when they encountered a four-footed Tahoe local with a white stripe down its back who gave them an exuberant though odoriferous greeting. They ended up throwing their clothes away; never could get that smell out. But then, they should have expected something like that could happen as they "were" hiking in the area known as "Skunk Harbor."

But those 1920's strollers who were enjoying the view of the lake from the open field above Tahoe City (someday to become a golf course) couldn't have anticipated what happened to them that April day. The field offered a panoramic view of the Basin skyline and in the distance they could see an approaching bi-plane. Aircraft were still a bit of a curiosity in those days, and the approaching Curtis held their attention. Which was probably a good thing, for it suddenly started to sputter and misfire, and a small stream of white smoke began to trail behind the tiny craft, which was now headed their way. It was coming down! The strollers had barely enough time to get out of harms way when the bi-plane slammed into the field and skidded to a halt. The pilot was ok, and so were the strollers. However, the poor airplane was ruined and needed to be trucked out of the Basin to be repaired. It was a day to remember for those visitors. But then, there was another Tahoe visitor that would never forget her day recreating at the lake. It was 1875 when Mrs. Virden was enjoying the Brockway Hotel's steambaths, that she happened to walk over a board covering a hot spring, and it broke, and poor Mrs. Virden plunged into a hot springs pool. Fortunately she just managed to grab the side of the board to keep from completely going in! She was rescued in moments by her husband, but not before feeling like a "baked Alaska." She remarked later that when asked how she felt when they pulled her out, the only thing she could say was: "well-done."

DR. CHURCH'S
SNOWPACK

It has become a ritual of winter, for all winter long we routinely listen to their proclamations. Sometimes, it's "the snowpack to date is only 50% of normal for this time of year." Not good. Other times, better times, we hear reports that tell us it's already 120% of normal and there's another storm headed in." Drought years, and heavy snow years, the specialists from the water resources board and staff hydrologists dutifully go out to measure the snowpack and report what nature has brought us "this" year. And we listen as the abundance or lack of snow has serious implications for all of us: how much water will be available for our farmers, for fisheries, or for people. The potential threat of wildfires, the amount of water that downstream reservoirs will be holding this summer, and how much water will be available for boaters and marinas. Watermasters and hydrologists throughout the country depend upon snow sampling to help predict, as early as possible, what to expect when the spring runoff begins. Whether to expect downstream flooding or a water shortage.

Researchers in this country have been tracking the levels of rivers and snowpacks since the mid 1800's, but it was a man from our area that was to develop the worlds first scientific methodology for accurately calculating the amount of water in a snowpack. The water content of snow can vary substantially. In Colorado for example, 20-inches of snow might only yield an inch of water. Dry powder snow, which is great for skiers, but is not so good for water yield. Even in the same storm, the water content of snow can vary and vary even more with changes in aspect and elevation. The world needed a simple but effective system for measuring the snowpack. James Church, a Professor of Latin and Greek from the University of Nevada at Reno, was to create that system. An amateur meteorologist, Dr. Church saw Lake Tahoe as an ideal laboratory to test and perfect his invention, a long cylinder that was pushed into a snowpack and its contents weighed to provide a snow-water equivalent; how much water was in the snow. Near the turn of the last century, Tahoe's waters were critical to a score of entities: farmers, a power company, residents of the lake, and the Paiute Indians for Pyramid Lake. By 1911 Church and a US Weather Bureau observer by the name of Cecil Alter, were regularly stomping their way through blizzard and gale to places like Mt. Rose conducting snow surveys; trying to establish a critical baseline for data, comparing one year to the next and one area to another. Dr. Church's snow sampler became "the" standard throughout the world for sampling snowpacks. Now there's over 1600 mountain snow courses that are monitored by federal and state agencies, and another 500 snow telemetry sites. Many of Dr. Church's original snowcourses are still being monitored around our area each winter. Today, we get an early warning report about our most valuable natural resource, fresh water, thanks to a professor of Latin & Greek.

FINAL LINK
AROUND TAHOE

For years, Tahoe travelers had enjoyed a primitive but functional road system that linked Placerville with the Carson Valley, but there was no road that ran around the lake. In the early 1850's, a road connected Washoe Valley with Auburn. It ran across the north end of the lake before crossing the Carson Range at a point south of today's Incline Village, at a place called Tunnel Creek. After the 1859 discovery of the Comstock Lode, an immigrant road was developed to accommodate the freight and passenger traffic that was now flowing through the Basin. By 1861, the route over Kingsbury Grade had been improved by David Kingsbury and by 1913, the scenic Emerald Bay area was opened to vehicle traffic.

But by the 1920's one last segment remained. A segment of shoreline that had been ignored because until then, it hadn't been necessary for the regions or even the Basins transportation system. For years, freight and passenger traffic had been successfully routed over the Basin mountain passes, and there was little need for a connection route along

Tahoe's east shore. Especially since there was a perfectly good road on the west shore, and a convenient steamship transit service that could pick up and deliver people and freight anywhere along the lakes shoreline. And only a few hardy souls lived during the summer months in the area between Spooner and Incline. A road just wasn't deemed essential. But with the advent and enormous popularity of the automobile, the demand for a road system that circumvented Lake Tahoe would grow. The numbers of people coming to the lake during the "roaring twenties" by way of automobile was challenging the numbers of those who came by train. So it was, that engineers from the Bureau of Public Roads, the Forest Service, and the Nevada Department of Transportation began to lay out plans for this final link in Tahoe's road system. But, while the engineers envisioned and designed a road system that hugged the shoreline, allowing drivers a world-class unobstructed view of Lake Tahoe as they journeyed between Glenbrook and Incline, one man, William S. Bliss, wanted to preserve the last undeveloped shoreline. Fortunately he welded a great deal of influence, since part of the proposed highway would have had to cross his lands, and he wasn't about to grant a right-of-way for a road that degraded that natural shoreline. This wasn't the only controversy, as there arose a debate over where to find the needed funds for constructing this new road. The state alone didn't have sufficient highway funds available and expected to find additional funding support from the counties around the lake, but in the 1920's, there were still some Tahoe area county officials that didn't see much value to their residents from this new road. Fortunately other funds were found and construction commenced (far away from the lakeshore). It took a few years, but by 1933 the base grading was completed, and on one pretty day, a ribbon-cutting ceremony was held. Actress Carol Lombard was to do the honors. The final link in Tahoe's road system, today's Highway 28 was completed.

WASHOE CANARIES

They called them "Washoe Canaries," for although they didn't have wings, they did have hooves and a sharp wit. For some pioneer prospectors, their wit was too sharp! They were those four-legged, ungainly beasts known as donkeys or burro's, and many a time these sturdy little beasts of burden got the upper hand on their owners; the prospectors and miners that used to work the diggings throughout the Sierra. There was the tale of Mark Wallace, who'd spent years prospecting up and down California and Nevada with no luck. But one day he unexpectedly stumbled across a small streak of gold in some rocks. He'd found a small vein that was going to make him wealthy. But on this day he was content to pick and shovel out enough to fill a couple of packbags of that gold ore, which he carefully loaded onto his burro; making sure it was securely tied down with some sturdy rope. When that was done, Wallace headed for the nearest town, and after a long days walk, long after sunset, he reached the outskirts of a small mining town. It wasn't much of a town, but at least here he could file his claim. But the hour was getting late and Wallace was both thirsty and in a mood to celebrate his discovery, so he tied his trusty burro up outside of a local saloon; still loaded down with the gold ore and he went inside. Hours later, just before sunrise, Wallace staggered out of the saloon to gather up his burro and head over to the claims office. But his burro was gone! Oh it wasn't stolen! Bored with just standing there, it had just walked away. Wallace spent days looking for it, but he never did catch up with it again. Though he did spot it once running with a wild band of burros with that load of gold still tied to its back.

Sometimes, these wily little critters would get their comeuppance. Especially deserved when they started to raid the mining camps, as wild burros sometimes became a nuisance, for they could be accomplished thieves. They would hang out on the slopes overlooking these camps, quietly grazing; watching and waiting until the miners headed out for the day to work their claims, and then they'd run into the deserted camps and eat everything in sight; sugar, flour, bacon and even gunny sacks and the sides of the tents. When the miners returned in the evening, the burros would be back up on the hillsides, quietly grazing away, and the miners could never catch them. One camp solved the problem though, by setting out a batch of yeast and salt mixed in with some flour, which the cagey burros greedily ate. But now thirsty, they went to the nearest spring and filled themselves with lots of water; and the yeast began to rise. And all the four-legged thieves blew up so big that they all looked like a balloon with legs! But they never did raid that camp again. Poor things . . .

SQUAW VALLEY
OLYMPICS

It wasn't that long ago, that the eyes of the world were focused on the winter games at Salt Lake City. But years ago, in 1960, those eyes were focused on a small mountain valley, just north of Lake Tahoe. It had been a quiet place, the first inhabitants were only summer visitors, the Washoe. While the men hunted the ridges above the canyon, the women stayed on the valley floor, gathering pineseeds and grinding huckleberry oak acorns into meal for bread; giving the meadow the name "Squaw Valley." By 1955 there still wasn't much development, only some dairy farming and ranching and a small ski area with a single chair lift, a rope tow and a small lodge. But that was about to change. New York socialite and promoter Alex Cushing, along with developer Wayne Poulson saw potential in this mountain canyon. If only they could get the support of California legislators and drum up some financial backing. So Cushing set to work, persuading both Governor Edmund G. "Pat" Brown and a number of US Senators to support his goal to bring the worlds 8th Winter Olympic Games to Squaw Valley. With their backing, Cushing was able to obtain a million dollars from the State of California to start constructing the Olympic Village, new skating rinks, ski jump areas, parking lots and dormitories. But first, Cushing must convince the International Olympic Committee to pick Squaw Valley as their site for the 1960 games. After a number of close ballots, Squaw edged out Innsbruck 32-30 and the games were on!

One of the first major obstacles was the limited parking capacity in the valley. Early plans to bus spectators in from the Truckee area were scrapped in favor of an innovative scheme that involved the US Navy, as a team of eighteen naval specialists from Antarctica were brought in to convert the meadow area to a parking lot by dumping tons of sawdust and compacting it with a mantle of ice; it worked! But while construction moved along at a steady pace, the one thing that worried everyone that winter was the lack of snow. Just weeks before the games were scheduled to begin, the valley floor was summer brown and the mountain snowpack thin. And so, urgent plans were made to truck in the necessary snow, and move some of the events to another location. But Mom Nature stepped in and dumped a thick layer of snow just before opening day. So much so, that the director of pageantry, Walt Disney feared his opening ceremony would be lost in the swirling snow. But the skies cleared, not only for the opening pageantry, but for the duration of the events, making conditions in Squaw Valley just perfect for the 8th Winter Olympic Games. Which was ideal since the whole world was watching.

SHE WAS NO LADY

Our region has had its share of tough people. People who lived hard lives, and people who themselves, were hard. And while many that have been written about were men, there were also a few of the fair sex that captured the attention of early day historians. Charlotte (Charley) Parkhurst was one that quickly comes to mind. A woman that, dressed like a man, drove a stagecoach through the Sierras for 15-years. Charlotte was a cigar-chomping, hard drinking and scrappy individual that took no lip from anyone, least of all, road bandits, and she became a legend.

Another lady, who lived up in the Truckee area in the late 1860's wasn't to gain the widespread fame Charlotte did, but she was in her own way, no less a formidable individual. Tough, rough and in this case, dangerous. Her name was Carrie Smith, but few ever called her by that name. Her unusual handle, her professional nom de plume was "Spring Chicken." She was the companion of a notorious town bully by the name of George Prior, but she was more feared, and by some, more admired than Prior ever was. For Carrie was not only a professional, working in the town red light district, she was one wild individual; never seen without a derringer and knife. For she seemed to savor making enemies; being arrested for assault and battery on a regular basis; usually against men. But she wasn't selective, stirring up a fight with about anyone, and woe be the man that slighted her, for Carrie was a vindictive soul, as one man found out. He'd stupidly insulted her, and she flew into a rage. The man prudently ran into a local hotel for shelter, but Carrie ran after him, screaming she was going to do him in (and she intended to!). Fortunately for him, inside the hotel, Carrie was restrained by a couple of men, barely. But she continued to shout, and running outside, grabbing any rock she could find, proceeded to pummel the outside of the building and broke every window. Finally she stormed away, but she planned to catch up with the man later. But fortunately for the man and for the town, Carrie was soon arrested for yet another crime and sentenced to a long term in jail. But even there, she didn't lose any of her steam, as she managed to set her bunk on fire. What a character!

TAHOE'S COULD=OF=BEEN's

What if . . . What if some of the things that were proposed to be built here, actually were? Tahoe would certainly be different. Perhaps for the better, but not in every case. It would have been interesting if the planned world class observatory envisioned by James Lick at today's "Dollar Point" had been constructed in the 1870's. Tahoe during the last century would have been a research center for the heavens. But it wasn't to be. Another plan that would have significantly impacted the lake was devised in the 1860s by engineer Alexis Von Schmidt. He proposed that water be pumped out of the lake and sent to San Francisco. About twenty million gallons a day was his target, and it wasn't literally just a "pipe dream," as Von Schmidt aggressively pursued the needed financing, constructed a small dam at Tahoe City and completed surveys for the needed waterline. He nearly succeeded, but was to fail, largely because the mayor of the City by the Bay decided at the last moment to not enter into a contract with Von Schmidt, as he didn't like the idea of a privately owned water company supplying the city's water as he correctly suspected there were legal debates ahead over Tahoe's water rights. Our water stayed in the lake.

More recently another "almost was," but ultimately "wasn't:" a planned bridge over Emerald Bay. In the late 1950's State Senator Swift Berry of Eldorado County, the local Chamber of Commerce, County Supervisors and concerned highway engineers championed a bridge across the entrance of Emerald Bay for improved winter (west shore) access. Alternatives were identified, tunnels and snowsheds, but while the bridge was deemed as the most reliable and safest choice, it generated a storm of controversy and debates over the impacts of the bridge to the Bay and the planned highway route through Bliss State Park and the project eventually was dropped. And there were other "coulda beens:" a small airport near Pope Beach, a planned 50,000 resident subdivision in Meyers, a 206-foot high steel tower "fun-ride" over by Kingsbury Grade. If any of these projects had actually come to be, Tahoe today would be different, especially if they'd built that "fun-ride."

SHE BEAT SOME JUSTICE OUT OF HIM...

Being a newspaper editor in the 19th century had a measure of prestige to it, and even more satisfaction, as you could enlighten your readers, and perhaps entertain them while sowing a few grains of truth and wisdom. And possibly even make some money while you were at it. But, it wasn't all without some risk, as many early day editors found out. Mark Twain found himself challenged to a duel for what he had written once, and Dan De Quille once had to grab a knife off of a local thug because the man didn't like having his name mentioned in the local papers, and he was threatening De Quille. There was also the time an actress from Pipers Opera House in Virginia City stormed over to the local editors office and beat a little justice out of him after his paper had printed a highly critical review. The paper had gone so far as to proclaim that the actress had about as much talent as a packmule! But since the actress didn't have much of a sense of humor, the paper ended up missing a few editions, for that editor found it hard to write with bandages on his hand.

Sometimes though, the editor tried to turn the table by attempting his own thrashing. As happened to Major John Dennis, an editor and publisher of a small newspaper in rural Nevada in the late 1800's. Dennis had been walking down the street after his morning edition was out, when he was confronted by an angry reader, who didn't like what was written about him, so he hauled off and started a scrap with the editor. But the constable happened to be nearby and threw the reader in jail. But Dennis was mad, and he wanted to finish the fight, so he put up the man's bail. But unfortunately, he was the one who got licked! And on top of that, the man also jumped bail and left town, so Dennis also got stuck with the tab. And once in a while, an editor would get suckered into printing a story that would back-fire on him and put him in harms way. That happened one time to a local editor who was approached by a man that identified himself as "John Smith." Smith told the editor a light-hearted tale, supposedly about a make-believe character. A tale about a buffoon with the odd name of "Slasher." So it being a slow news week, the editor copied down all the details of Smiths story and printed it in his next edition, expecting it would amuse his readers. But instead, the next day, he had a knock on his door and standing there was a hulk of a man; with bowie knife and six-gun, and a scowl on his face. And sure enough, he announced that his name was "Slasher," and he was howling mad. The editor knew right then and there, he'd been had by John Smith, or whoever he really was. Clearly, he decided, it was time to give up the newspaper business and find a new profession! And with that, he jumped out the back window, and ran for his life!

THE CHURCH
BLEW AWAY

Early day churches around the eastslope of the Sierras sure didn't get much help from Mother Nature. In fact, it seemed like there was almost a conspiracy against religion. During the summer of 1860 Tahoe was just a sparsely populated mountain community, only a few small settlements, nothing big enough to call a town. But just over the hill, was that bustling and sinful Virginia City. And if there was anywhere in the western half of the country that needed a few good churches it was the gambling, drinking and carousing Virginia City. So it was that summer, that first the Catholics resolved to move out of the mine tunnels where they had been holding services. Constructing a chapel out of wood timbers hauled over from the east slopes of the lake. But they hadn't reckoned on the powerful winds that roared down from the mountain slopes: the "Great Washoe Zephyr," and their chapel was blown over. So, they scratched their heads a bit, and selected a more secluded spot down near the Carson River, and built a very imposing new chapel.

But they'd barely finished pounding the last nail when the winds flared up again, and absolutely demolished it. Only scraps were left. But they weren't about to give up, and called in another man to oversee the construction of the Catholic Church. A former miner from Grass Valley, who had just joined the priesthood: Father Patrick Manogue. And with his mining experience figured out a way to whip the wind, thru a strong rock foundation. And he built a church that didn't blow away.

So now it was the Methodists turn, as they decided they too needed a real church, for they'd been holding services in a blacksmiths shop. But they'd been watching all the problems the Catholics were having with the wind. So right off they placed an order for bricks. Enough bricks to build themselves a fine church. And they hauled in wagonload after wagonload of bricks all the way from the Sacramento Valley through the Tahoe Basin to Virginia City, and constructed their church. But something must of been wrong, for it wasn't up but a short time when that terrible valley wind, the "Zephyr" roared up out of the west and blew it apart; just as it had done to the other churches. So they cleaned up the mess and rebuilt it, but then a fire broke out and the insides were burnt up. And the Methodists were discouraged all right, but they had a mission, and set back to work again, but first they traded some of the bricks for bigger timbers and this time, finally, they had themselves a church that stood no matter how hard the wind blew.

But perhaps both the Catholics and the Methodists could have saved themselves a lot of heartaches if they'd adopted what a small Presbyterian Church did in San Jose in the 1850's. Their church wasn't much more than blue jeans sewed together to make a tent, and inside there were a few wood benches. It sure wasn't fancy, but it did the job, and if the wind blew their tent away, why they'd simply grab some needle and thread and sew some more blue-jeans together, and they were back in business.

LIFE-SAVING
DOGS AND CATS

Most days, a dog is clearly man's best friend. And some go beyond that, becoming a hero. One such tale of canine heroism took place near here in 1870. The route between the lake and Carson was narrow and winding and accidents weren't uncommon. A man by the name of Frank Osborne was driving a freight wagon to Placerville. Behind his wagon, trotted his small dog. The journey had been going smoothly at first, but on a steep grade his brakes suddenly failed and it wasn't long before his wagon began to pick up speed. Frank tried his best to keep control, but he couldn't, and his wagon ran off the road and down a ravine. His mules continued to run on, but Frank was thrown off, right under the wheels of his wagon and both of Franks legs were badly broken. He lay where he was the rest of the day, hoping that someone would come along and find him . . . but no one did. His only company was his little dog. But he was also to become Franks guardian. As Frank drifted into and out of consciousness, the dog sat and watched over him. Evening came, and a band of coyotes appeared, and that small animal defended Frank from them. Sometimes growling; sometimes fighting, and always protecting his helpless master. Finally dawn came and Frank was spotted by a teamster from the road above, and he was rescued. Frank was taken to a doctor where he had his legs set and bandaged. From that day on, Frank never failed to appreciate what his furry best friend had done for him. A little dog with a big heart; a canine hero.

But historic animal heroes weren't just limited to dogs as there was an 1850's tale of a life-saving feline. James Filly, his wife and three children were headed to California; to Dutch Flat in Placer County. James and his wife had intended on leaving their cat behind, with neighbors, but the children were distraught at the idea of leaving their beloved pet behind, so the parents relented, and "Jip" the cat was taken along. That proved to be a providential decision as by the time the family reached the Humboldt River, their wagon train was on the brink of starvation. Disease and poor grass along the way had left many cattle sick or weak, and the family had no luck in finding any game for food. The children were struggling, (and there was no food for Jip), when a most unusual thing began to happen. A freshly killed rabbit appeared one morning by their wagon! No one knew where it had come from, but the family soon made themselves a meal. The next morning, there was another rabbit, and for the next two weeks there was a fresh supply of rabbits each day! Enough to keep the family fed until they reached the Carson Valley where there was food. The family eventually figured out that it was Jip that had been the successful hunter, catching the rabbits in the willows by the river. Later offered a hundred dollars for the cat, James Filly refused, for he wouldn't have taken a thousand dollars for Jip, the helpful kitty.

JOHN MUIR'S MOUNTAINS

His words and insights were to shape the American conservation movement three quarters of a century after his passing. And much of his passion was to be shaped by his many visits here. His days at Cascade Lake, McKinney's on the west shore, and his journeys into the Sierras fed his love of the mountains, and his growing fears that civilization would eventually destroy the wilderness he saw from here to Yosemite and beyond. John Muir, between 1872 and 1875 spent many of his days hiking throughout the region, climbing scores of Sierra Peaks, both exploring and studying; learning and eventually teaching. An extremely shy man, he at first found it painfully difficult to stand before even a few people and share what he had learned after his years in the mountains. The glacial history, the regional geology, the wondrous beauty of the Sierras.

His first lecture was in Sacramento, in 1876. Sponsored by the Sacramento Literary Institute, he was extremely nervous about lecturing. So much so, he walked around the block a few times to muster up enough courage to go inside the lecture hall, a church. The standing-room-only crowd he saw there scared him even more, but he managed to contain his stage fright and slowly began his lecture. He stumbled a bit at first, but gained confidence as he began to focus on his subject, which came from both his memory, and from his heart. The audience sat quietly as Muir spun his tale of how the mighty Sierras were formed, of the powerful forces of nature that created them and continued to shape them and he was a success! Both entertaining and informative, he described in a simple, almost casual tone his first hand understanding of the Sierras. The multitude of mountain ranges, valleys, majestic waterfalls and lush meadows that were, in the 1870's thought as little more than sources for timber, mineral riches and grazing lands. Clearly his past trips to the Tahoe Basin during the logging years must of been fresh in his mind. John Muir also managed to stimulate a passion as he was to sow the seeds of the present conservation movement. And in one small but important way, his visits here were to convince him of the importance of preserving the Sierras.

PAIUTE INDIAN WAR ... COMSTOCK BATTLE

We don't usually think of the Washoe and Carson Valleys as historical battlegrounds, but in fact they were for a few difficult weeks back in 1860. The Paiute Indians, desperate to preserve their way of life in the face of an overwhelming onslaught of their lands; first by the 49'ers and then a decade later, by the thousands of adventurers who poured into this region looking for silver and their fortunes, struck back.

It was early May when a large group rode down on a place called Williams Station, near Virginia City and killed the five-men that were there at the time. Within a day a panic swept through Virginia City, Carson City and down to Genoa. Everyone was thrown into a frenzy, the Indians were coming! So men in every community grabbed whatever rifles and ammunition they could find and volunteered to go out and meet this new threat. So it came to be, that 105 men, untrained and inexperienced in Indian warfare set off down the Carson River under Major Ormsby, to pick up the trail of the offending Paiutes. After a few days march they reached the Truckee River and headed off towards Pyramid Lake, above Reno, still following the trail. What they didn't know at the time, and it was to cost them dearly, was that the Paiutes were waiting for them, and they were ambushed and out-fought and lost 46 men before they could escape, including Major Ormsby. All the next day the survivors straggled back towards Virginia City. And now everyone was really in a panic! People everywhere were simply scared out of their wits. Virginia City was even placed under martial law.

It was now that the final and inevitable chapter of the Paiute Indian War was to be played out, for massive forces were organized, both infantry, calvary and artillery companies. Nearly a thousand men were sent out from all over California to face the Paiutes and the outcome was never in doubt. In early June, these regular army soldiers and trained militia once again tracked down the warring Paiutes, but this time, following a three hour long battle, the Indians were over-run, and those that were left were driven into the desert, no longer a threat. And the Washoe and Carson Valleys were no longer a battleground.

LUCKY BALDWIN

He was one of Tahoe's pioneers; an impulsive man of mixed reputation that deserved to be admired for his industriousness and entrepreneurial spirit if not for his excessiveness with the ladies and devotion to games of chance. Elias Jackson Baldwin was to build, in the late 19th century, a luxury hotel resort complex on Tahoe's south shore (at a location we know today as Kiva Beach, located near the Tallac Historic Sites). The centerpiece, a three and one-half story white palace. E.J. Baldwin's Tallac House had rooms for a hundred guests, with accommodations for 150 more guests in the resort's cottages. It was a Tahoe wonder, built on a grand scale with a covered veranda that ran the length of the building. Its guests were fed and treated like kings and queens. The Tallac House even featured faro and poker tables and slot machines, reflecting Baldwin's sporting nature. For Lake Tahoe was only a part of his personal grand empire, and he was a man that thrived on luxury, ladies and horse racing. For one of Baldwin's early estates was in southern California. And "there," he immersed himself in the world of the racetrack and breeding thoroughbreds. He always had a love for fine horses, but a stroke of good fortune was to give him the opportunity to indulge himself in this and his other passions.

In the 1860's, following years of odd jobs and careers (as a teamster, a trader, a peddler and livery stable operator) Baldwin had managed to save some money and he was able to acquire a large block of shares of stocks in several Comstock mines. While the Virginia City mines went through periods of boom and bust, Baldwin held on to his stock holdings. In 1867 though, he sold a few shares of stock that seemed to him to have peaked in their value. But he held on to a block of other shares that had actually lost some of their value. But Baldwin believed he would at least try to recoup his original investment, for the depressed stocks might yet increase. So he stuck them in his safe, hoping for the best. He then decided to take off on an extended vacation to the orient, but not before instructing his broker to sell his stocks if & when their market price equaled that original purchase price while he was away. Baldwin was gone for a year and when he returned he learned that his broker had failed to dispose of those stocks as he'd been instructed, for Baldwin in his haste to prepare for his vacation, had neglected to give his broker a key to his safe! The price of the shares did rise as Baldwin had hoped. They rose and kept climbing as news of the discovery of a new silver vein caused the value of the shares to skyrocket! So that turned out to be quite a stroke of good luck for Baldwin, for he was now a multi-millionaire. Not only did Baldwin use his money to purchase an 8,000-acre estate at Rancho Santa Anita, he was able to purchase several prize mares and stallions and begin a horse breeding and racing stable. And one-day, buy land at Lake Tahoe. He also was to acquire a lifelong sobriquet, a nickname . . . "Lucky" Baldwin.

MODERATION
WAS THE KEY

Some of our regions, in fact many, of our regions first businesses involved saloons. Every early-day mining or logging town had their tavern. Places where people went after a long days work, to socialize, to unwind and to imbibe. In 1867 in Virginia City alone, there were a hundred licensed saloons, or about one for every 150-residents! They served some pretty potent drinks to their patrons, and it was strictly "buyer beware," for more than a few of those drinks were little more than cheap alcohol mixed with anything handy, and some drinks were only a step away from being liquid poison. But of course, the colorful names of many of the early day drinks should have given the buyer some warning about what they were about to pour down their parched throats; with names like Red Dynamite, Nockemstiff, Stagger-Soup, and the ever popular Coffin Varnish. And too, there was also the ever-present whiskey and beer on the menu. In 1880, it was calculated that the average resident living in the Carson & Washoe area consumed around fifteen gallons of beer a year, and that was in addition to the roughly five gallons of hard liquor that they were downing that same year! That's about a glass a day of liquor, though some suggest the Comstocker's put down as much as a quart a day per person!

News editor Wells Drury recounted in 1876, that he believed some people felt it essential to visit the saloon each and every day, as he recalled the story about one Brutus Blinkenberry, who groaned when his wife accused him of being drunk twenty-seven nights in a row during the preceding month. But Brutus responded by lamenting that somehow he'd missed three-days in that month! And there was Patrick Harrington, who at the ripe old age of 104, was still enjoying his daily flask of Irish whiskey. His only sorrow was, that during an earlier period in his life; a period that lasted 50-years, he had sworn off the drink, thinking then it would shorten his life. A customer in Virginia City's Sazerac House was to comment: "This Sir, is my sixty-fourth drink today. I must put on the brakes, or the first thing I know I shall degenerate into excess. Moderation Sir, the grand secret of health, has been the rule of my life;" so was denial. Another man, flaunting his drinking prowess to a temperance worker, responded to the question: "Young man, what would your father have thought about your drinking two-quarts of whiskey a day," by answering: "Why, he would have called me a sissy." But even though the amount of drinking could be excessive, there were few problems with drunkenness. Partially because there was a social pride in being able to "hold" your liquor, and more importantly, if you had a job in a mining or logging camp, they'd keep you off the job if you reported under the influence. So for most people in our neck of the woods, there were some constraints. Though, there was that legendary binge of Mark Twain and humorist Artemus Ward. Their bar-bill came to $237 at a time when a good steak dinner cost all of three dollars and a shot of red-eye all of fifteen cents. That, was some drinking!

JOHN MACKAY...
AN UNUSUAL MAN

He was perhaps the richest man of his day to walk the Comstock Country. He was certainly one of the most unique of men. Obviously a capable businessman, he was also a daring man, a caring man and a complex man. His name was John Mackay, one of the so-called Silver Kings of the Comstock era. He was to become a Nevada legend, making $10,000 a day. Quite an accomplishment for an uneducated man, who was barely able to read beyond a fifth grade level. Born in Dublin, Ireland in 1831, he immigrated to this country only a few years later. Typical of the times he came out west to California and tried his hand at mining over in Downieville. After the discovery of silver and gold in Nevada, he migrated into this area. Mackay and a mining partner, Jack O'Brien reached the outskirts of Virginia City, at a place called the "Divide." There they stood looking down the road, into an uncertain future. It was there that Mackay asked O'Brien if he had any money in his pocket. "Not a penny," O'Brien answered . . ."not a single cent, I'm flat busted."

"Why, how much do YOU have," O'Brien asked Mackay. "I have fifty cents," Mackay responded. But then he stuck his hand deep into his pocket . . . pulled out his meager fortune and tossed it into the bushes. "Now, let's go into town like gentlemen." So it was that Mackay entered Virginia City penniless and proud of it. Both he and his partner got jobs digging in the mines. Using pick and shovel they earned their living as hardrock miners, for wages.

But fortune was to smile on Mackay, encouraged by some wily speculation by Mackay. Taking some of his salary in mining stock instead of money, John Mackay began to acquire stock that was to earn him a good $50-million in revenues. One story even had Mackay braving the Civil War battlefields to track down a soldier who owned some mining stock he wanted to purchase, Mackay sneaking through the Confederate Army lines at Chattanooga to find his man. He made his purchase while bullets were flying through the air. And it turned out, those mining shares were to jump in value a short while later, from a few hundred a share to over $20,000 a share! Typical of the people with great wealth, John Mackay found himself deluged by hundreds of people. But he believed that by just giving people money, it took away their pride, and so constantly turned a deaf ear to the greedy. But he was a compassionate man to those who truly needed his help, giving away millions of dollars to individuals and real charities during his lifetime. Though a multi-millionaire, Mackay also distinguished himself during his Comstock years by daily inspecting his mines. Each morning at 6am he went down to each level, talking to his men, his family of miners, handling problems, giving pats on the back. There's a statue of him at the University of Nevada, but the greatest praise of the man came from a former business partner, that following Mackay's passing in 1902 stated that Mackay's primary interest was people, not making money, for Mackay only had a rough idea of how much money he actually had; an unusual man.

PAYING FOR
LAW AND ORDER

Tahoe lawmen Harry Johanson, Carl Bechdoldt and Robert Montgomery Watson had a tough enough job in the early years of the last century; dealing with the occasional rowdy, the unruly. But at least when they were enforcing the law as town constable or sheriff, they didn't have to worry about having to personally pay the costs to keep the peace. But their predecessors did. The early-day lawmen that used to protect and serve the Basin needed to have the financial resources to do their jobs. And those costs could be considerable. 1860's Constable William O'Connor's activities underscored the various elements of the job that lawmen were expected to subsidize, if not pay for. He listed all the services he'd performed as constable for the area around Carson and Virginia City's: During a five month period, he'd financed the costs of putting together eight juries; including the costs for subpoenaing, finding and bringing to court sixty-four witnesses. He'd served five warrants of arrest and made scores of arrests on the streets. For a capital crime, he'd needed to hire some armed guards, and a stagecoach and transport a prisoner from Virginia to Carson City. Constable O'Conner petitioned the county to refund his costs to him. But they decided to only refund about a third of his claimed expenses. It wasn't long after, O'Connor resigned his office, declaring among other things, that the office didn't pay enough for him to stay.

Early-day Tahoe area Sheriff John Blackburn went one better with his out of pocket expenses, for he personally paid to feed and house his prisoners. His $1560 bill to the county for several months of service was greeted with indifference, and concern, for the county didn't have the money. They did realize however, that the sheriff could help them with their cash problem, and so decided to levy a new tax on the operators of the Kingsbury toll road and the sheriff would collect those taxes from which Sheriff Blackburn would be paid; in county script instead of cash. Fortunately for the lake and the Washoe region, Blackburn had the resources to pay the bills and the desire to keep his job as lawman. The basic problem for these early-day lawmen was the perceptions of the times that while some jobs like judge and commissioner were essential year-round, to look after the civil affairs of the county, there wasn't that need for a steady sheriff or constable. The job was viewed as being part-time, and not worthy of a regular monthly wage paid by the county. Crime, after all, wasn't seen as necessarily being a daily problem. Lawmen were required to find their own sources of income, or at least "front" their expenses and file a claim later, hoping for a full refund. Some, in lieu of a regular salary, received a percentage of the fines that were levied against lawbreakers by the courts, and others a percentage of the take on the towns poker tables. Finally, by the end of the 19th century, attitudes had changed and the regions lawmen were placed on a steady salary. No longer dependent upon their own pocketbooks to enforce the law.

SANDY AND ELLIE...
RICHES TO RAGS

Their story is often told when regional historians need a good example of a rags to riches to rags story. For the tale of Sandy and Ellie is truly a classic example of good luck, poor judgment and money. Ellie had met Sandy when she was operating a boarding house east of Carson City. A mule skinner and miner, Sandy was an Irish charmer and it wasn't long before they decided to marry. Neither had much at first, just their love, but that was about to change as before they'd met, each had acquired a mining claim, and those claims were to make them millionaires; six times over. Overnight they were wealthy, when gold and silver were discovered on their claims. Ellie especially found herself overwhelmed with her new fortune, and resolved to embrace a life of extravagance and excess as soon as she could. They constructed a mansion in the middle of Washoe Valley and ordered expensive and ornate furniture, carpets and lavish decorations, chandeliers and even a magnificent library of 2,200 books . . . all of the finest leather and lettered in gold . . . even though, neither Sandy nor Ellie knew how to read. They also acquired oil paintings from Europe, hand-painted china, marble statues and a huge grand piano, with a keyboard made of mother-of-pearl. And even that wasn't enough, for Sandy and Ellie departed for a shopping tour in Europe. They paid top dollar for everything, often careless about their money, for after all, they thought they had an endless supply of it from their mines in the Comstock. That wasn't to be, as eventually these mines would play out and Sandy and Ellie would be bankrupt.

Their path from riches to ruin was partially due to their excess, to their poor judgment and of course, to their mines playing out. They spent their millions with abandon. But they were also victims of some of their friends. Friends who took advantage of Sandy and Ellie's generosity and poor financial management. One of the worst was a man who they'd trusted implicitly . . . an advisor and a friend. J. Neely Johnson was their attorney, a man of supposed integrity. After all, he'd served as the 4th Governor of the State of California (1856-1858). Ex-Governor Johnson was managing Sandy and Ellie's affairs for them while they were busy shopping and touring in Europe. Johnson saw in their absence, an opportunity to help himself with his own home construction expenses. He recently moved to Carson City and was setting up his own mansion. So not only did Johnson charge an inordinately high amount of money for watching after Sandy and Ellie's estates while they were away, he had wagons full of construction materials and furniture delivered to his home, paid for by Sandy and Ellie unbeknownst to them. But even without Johnson's help, Sandy and Ellie would have eventually spent themselves into the poorhouse; it was just a matter of time.

ECOLOGICAL
NIGHTMARE

Normally when we look back at the years of the California gold rush, we focus on the colorful and exciting times, the unique people, the hardships and the dreams of a nation being formed and manifest destiny. But the gold rush also left a legacy that wasn't so endearing or positive. The search for wealth from the Sierras and their foothills also created a great deal of environmental destruction that endures today. One University of California geographer likened the impacts of the gold rush to a hydrogen bomb going off in the wilderness. For after the first flakes of gold were panned out during the earliest days, miners needed to adopt other methods to find the elusive gold. One was river mining, in which streams were rerouted so people could get at the gold lying on the bottom. And that was bad enough, but another mining technique was to ravage the Sierra slopes.

Called hydraulic mining, water was diverted into ditches and wooden flumes, then fed into a iron pipe, and with the help of gravity, water exploded out of a nozzle with a force of 5000 pounds per square inch; enough pressure to wash away whole hillsides to expose any gold that may be buried. Over 1.5 billion cubic yards of soil and rocks were washed away from the Sierras by these hydraulic miners (equivalent to 8x the material that was excavated to build the Panama Canal!). All that gravel went downstream, destroying the streams that used to support teeming populations of trout, salmon and other wildlife. As the debris moved downstream, major tributaries such as the Sacramento River began to clog with sediment and even turned yellow for a time. Flooding increased throughout the central valley because marsh and estuary areas were filling with gravel. Even San Francisco Bay is from three to six feet shallower today as a direct result of hydraulic mining. Another legacy of the period was the mercury residue used in gold recovery. Nearly 4000 tons of the noxious liquid was dumped into the Sierra's streams, and you can still find traces of it in fish living in coastal waters that drain out of the mountains. So while the gold rush was clearly a significant historical event, it was also a ecological nightmare.

STAGE ROBBERS
BEWARE

When stage robberies became too frequent, the stage companies tried all kinds of preventative methods of stopping the bandits. They hired armed guards, used reinforced strong-boxes, and coyly hid them in concealed compartments in their stages. They had employees carry large sums of money on money-belts, acting as passengers, while the stage money-box was stuffed with phony bills. One company even placed live rattlesnakes in the strong-boxes. Yet another would bite the bullet and actually hire the bandits to not rob their stagecoaches. Figuring that this was cheap insurance, since they'd failed to catch the bandits and stick them in the pokey. And it worked, so long as the bandit in question remained honest; kind of a contradiction in logic.

One of the most unusual approaches used by a stage company to ward off stage robberies came from a stage company that operated in the 1880's. The idea originating with a Carson City pioneer, Oliver Roberts, who reasoned that if you can't stop the bandits from preying on the stagecoaches, you could at least beef up the stage to make it more difficult for them. Roberts plan was to take an old stage and make it bullet proof. Much like an old John Wayne movie called the "War Wagon," the stage was converted to be a moving pillbox. Several well-armed guards would be inside. A dummy would be placed on the front, replacing the driver, who would safely be inside the stage, working his team from a protected open-slot, the reins feeding in through another slot. There were portholes on each corner, and one in front and back. A stage was actually converted and a plan was hatched to attract some highwaymen. A rumor was spread around the area that a rich shipment of bullion was about to be transported over to the Placerville area. An especially large amount of money was to be moved in a special stagecoach with no external guards. The bait was cast and a trap was set. And as hoped, the rumor attracted some interest. The reinforced stagecoach set out on its inaugural run; supposedly packed with money. It was around dark that the bandits struck. Figuring this was going to be a simple robbery, they planned accordingly . . . not suspecting they were being set up. A half dozen hid themselves behind a rocky outcrop while their leader stepped out into the road, signaling for the stage to stop. The stage stopped, and the moment the bandit was yelling for the driver to throw out the strongbox, he realized it was a dummy that was sitting atop the drivers box. Something was wrong, he knew, but not what. He signaled, and his fellow bandits began to fire at the stage, thinking this would convince the hidden driver to give up his valuable cargo. But instead they were shocked to find themselves targeted by a stage full of sharpshooters, and the bandits had to scurry for their lives. Several were wounded, and the stage went on its way. This unusual stage was never used again, as it wasn't practical for day-to-day use. But clearly, it had done its job.

CAPTAIN WHITTELL

He was one of Lake Tahoe's most influential people, and was also one of its most mysterious residents; for to many, he was a recluse. At one time he owned most of the Nevada side of the lake; more than 20,000 acres of land. His name was "George B. Whittell Jr.," but he was generally addressed as "Captain." His father, "George Sr." a successful San Francisco businessman made a fortune in banking, real estate and in railroading. A fortune that George Jr. inherited and was to use to purchase land at the lake, and construct two majestic estates: the Thunderbird Lodge Estate near Sand Harbor, and the 50-acre Woodside Estate, near San Francisco. He filled them with art objects and wondrous bric-a-brac: first edition books from Kipling and Hemingway, art deco desks, tapestries, a Louis 16th mahogany bureau and a crystal mantle clock.

Whittell was to earn his title of "Captain," during World War I. First he'd volunteered to drive ambulances for the Italian Red Cross, braving the battlefields and earning a decoration from Italy for his service. Then, Whittell enlisted in the US Army while still in Europe, and became a pilot in the aircorp, serving with Eddie Rickenbacker, eventually attaining the rank of "Captain," a title he was proud of his entire life. Just after the war he met and married Elia Pascal, in Paris. He'd married before, and had divorced, but Elia was to be his life's companion. While the Captain enjoyed a score of diversions: driving power boats, viewing sports contests, gambling and occasionally drinking and carousing, he held a special passion and fascination for animals, especially exotic animals. Whittell maintained a zoo of sorts at both the lake and at his Woodside Estate, a sanctuary for lions, Bengal Tigers, giraffes and elephants. He often was in court defending himself from claims that one of his lions mauled a visitor. He was guilty of turning loose a pack of dogs once on a process server. For while Whittell loved animals, and he loved the land, especially the beautiful Tahoe shoreline, he didn't care much for people. He avoided visitors whenever possible. Even the Governor of Nevada Grant Sawyer was to recount how he unsuccessfully tried to contact Whittell a number of times to discuss a land purchase for a state park at the lake, but the Captain ignored him as he did most officials. The State of Nevada finally had to give up trying to talk with Whittell but ended up suing him in court. Obtaining thru their powers of eminent domain for the public interest, some of his lands which would become today's "Lake Tahoe State Park."

George Whittell however, could also be generous, as he did donate some of his land for a high school site, to the University of Nevada, to St. Mary's Hospital in Reno, and after his passing in 1969 at the age of 87, to the SPCA and wildlife protection groups. Captain George Whittell, was a private man, an eccentric man, who once made Lake Tahoe his home.

BREYFOGLE'S GOLD

The discovery of gold has always brought with it a promise of fortune. But not everyone that found it prospered from it. There was the case of Snowshoe Thompson, a Tahoe regional legend. A man who in the 1850's and early 1860's carried the mail from Nevada into Placerville and back, during the dead of winter, for free. But legend goes, that on his last trip through the Sierras, he happened to stop to rest on a small ledge near a place known as Diamond Valley. There, he spotted a glimmering piece of quartz. He couldn't believe his eyes, but that rock was full of gold! So he filled his pockets with the gold quartz and went on to Genoa to drop off the mail, planning on coming back during his next trip thru the area. But fate dealt him a harsh hand, as soon afterwards, Snowshoe Thompson was to fall ill and he was to pass away before he could tell anyone where he had found the gold. People looked, but that gold-filled ledge has never been found.

There was another man that was to find (according to legend anyways) the richest vein of pure gold ever uncovered in the world, but he was to lose track of where he found it. A prospector by the name of Charles Breyfogle.

Breyfogle came to California during the gold rush to try his luck, but when he didn't strike it rich he settled down for a time in the Bay Area. But the lure of gold was still running in his veins, so by 1864 Breyfogle had taken off for central Nevada where he could run a hotel and on the side, do a little prospecting. Sometime late that same year wanderlust caught up with him and he joined up with a group of other men for one last search for that vein of gold. Somewhere around the southern end of Death Valley, Breyfogle's group was ambushed by a band of Paiute Indians, killing everyone but him. But while Breyfogle managed to escape, he was left with no food, weapons, or water. So now he set out on an odyssey, at first only finding brackish water which he greedily drank even though it had a foul taste, and stumbled and crawled his way toward the northeast. It was somewhere around here that Breyfogle spotted an outcropping of reddish soil from which he uncovered a fragment of brittle quartz, and a massive vein of glistening gold. Ever the prospector, he stuck a chunk of gold rock in his pocket and continued on; eventually he was found by a passing rancher. In all, Charles Breyfogle had journeyed over 200-miles since his group had been ambushed. And, as you might guess, he later went back, again and again, retracing his route looking for that lost vein. Others went with him, but he had been in a daze most of the time, and the ground looked different to him. For most of the remaining years of his life Charles Breyfogle continued to look with no success, and that rich vein of gold is still out there somewhere, waiting to be found.

BRIBERY WAS
A WAY OF LIFE

Justice in early day Nevada was well-known. Well-known for its flexibility. For it often went to the highest bidder, the greatest bribe. It could be so obvious, that it might of reached some rather comical proportions if it wasn't for the miscarriage of true justice. Perjury was conceded to be common, and briberies of both judges and witnesses were notorious. All judges weren't necessarily corrupt, though a few were clearly opportunists.

One high profile case was to underscore the seriousness of the problem and the pains lawyers would go to, to obtain a favorable verdict and ruling. It involved a lawsuit between two large Comstock mine owners, and a large sum of money was at stake, so it was a given that operatives from both mines were soon at work, jury and judge tampering. It was soon apparent who paid the largest bribe as on the first day of the trial, the judge stepped down from the bench, walked over to the just selected jury and made an eloquent plea for one of the mine owners. His bias made clear, he then walked back to the Court Bench and commenced the trial. Of course, he didn't have to worry over who it was the jury would support, for they too had been well bribed by the same mine owner! The judge already knew that, but he was hamming it up to "earn" his illicit fee. It was immediately evident to the lawyers for the other mine owner, that they would clearly lose their case unless they did something soon. They quickly came up with a counter-plan that did the trick for them. First, they hired some witnesses to appear on behalf of their client, full of wild claims and wilder accusations against the "other" mine owner. These so-called witnesses were led in and took the stand, one after another. All sincere and full of stories about the illegal activities of that despicable other mine owner. But that alone wasn't enough to ensure a favorable verdict, so they took a next step.

When the jury was excused to deliberate their verdict, sequestered on the second floor of a local hotel, those same lawyers waited until the coast was clear, then tossed a small stone against the window of the jury-room, attracting the attention of one of the jurors, who stuck his head out, looking down at the lawyers. One lawyer then tossed up a rope, telling the juror, to pull it up. He did, and up came a boot filled with gold coins AND the name of the lawyers client on a slip of paper! The jury quickly realized what was being offered, and being greedy, they emptied the boot, and dropped it out the window where it was dutifully refilled with gold coins and then pulled back up; again with the name of the lawyers client on a slip of paper. This was repeated a number of times, but after a time, the gold coins were replaced with silver coins and finally it came up empty; the lawyers having decided they'd bribed the jury enough. And sure enough, when the jury got back to the courtroom, they came in with a verdict that gave those lawyers client the victory. Even though the judge was surprised, he had to accept it. Never knowing the greedy jury had been swayed, again, by an old leather boot filled with money.

CHILDREN'S DIARIES

More than a quarter of a million people came west in the twenty-year period before the Civil War. Mostly all men at first, but it wasn't long before they were joined by their wives and their children. Now many of those pioneers kept a dairy or recounted their trip in journals after their long cross-country trip on a wagon train was over. So the history books brim-over with stories about these intrepid men and women. But here and there, the children of these pioneers also kept diaries. And they tell us that the 4-6 month journey across the country, through deserts, Indian country, and mountain ranges was not only a child's life of adventure, it was a period of learning, of growing up. Sometimes years before they should of had to.

Most children on the wagon trains felt the journey was a lark, for it was fun and different and oh what an experience! They kept busy doing all the essential chores, helping out their parents by fetching water and gathering firewood when there was some and buffalo chips when there wasn't. And they helped herd the livestock, cooked, and cared for babies and helped to clean and mend the clothes. With a child's eyes they wrote about how wonderful everything seemed to be, though often complained about the poor food they were required to eat. An eleven year old noted that he was only getting to eat but one meal a day, only a few dried apples that made his tummy swell up, and how he missed those fresh fruits and vegetables that he always had back home! A lot of the children recorded they were afraid of the plains Indians, because they'd been fed wild stories all their young lives about "savages" who kidnapped babies, and many ran screaming at their first sight of a Pawnee or Osage Indian.

And while most children's journeys were (aside from the hardships) relatively uneventful, circumstances required that at least a few had to suddenly take on an adult's responsibilities, to instantly grow up. Eleven-year-old Elisha Brooks had to take charge driving the wagon and standing guard at night when his widowed mother's hired hand deserted the Brooks family halfway to Sacramento. Octavius Pringle at the age of fourteen was sent alone on a 125-mile ride to bring back food to his starving family. One young girl, barely in her teens was to take charge of her entire twelve member family and somehow managed to get them all safely to California after her parents, overcome by all of the hardships of the journey had just given up. But despite their different experiences, and difficulties on the trail, historians did find there was a common thread that ran through all of the diaries of those young pioneers. And that was, that 19th century children were by nature both optimistic and very resilient, even when their parents were not. And that it seems, is still the way things are today.

DON'T BOTHER
THE DOCTOR

During the mid-years of the 19th century, most of the doctors practicing medicine were more experienced with nursing farm animals than people. The lack of formal medical schools was part of the reason, and the relatively primitive state of medical technology was another. Doctors of the day had few remedies that worked against the numerous contagious diseases of the times, offering pseudo-medications as camphor, calomel, castor oil, and opiates in alcohol. A few of the wiser ones also adopted some of the herbal and natural medications used by the local Native Americans. Most could set a broken bone, were competent with childbirth (midwives were usually better though) and in the wilder towns, were adept at treating gunshot wounds. But at least, they were relatively cheap. Though sometimes you didn't get much for your money.

One 1880's era English doctor was paid by a mining company to tend to the injuries and ills of the company employees, for which he charged each miner a flat rate of

50-cents a month for his services. This particular doctor used to love to play poker late into the night. One night, just after he'd gotten to bed after losing a tidy sum, he was awakened by a pair of miners, one of which had a nasty little cut on his hand; he'd snagged it on a rusty nail, and was hoping for some medical care. But, already in a foul mood because of his poker losses, the doctor took one look at what he considered to be a minor injury and in a fit of anger, decked the miner! Telling him to never come and wake him again in the middle of the night, unless he "really" was hurt. Mumbling that "What did they expect for fifty-cents a month? A hospital bed?" But even fifty-cents was a nice piece of pocket change in those days, when a person was lucky to make five dollars a day, and western doctors could make themselves a comfortable living, even at these low rates, especially if they were the only doctor in a town. A classic local tale involved Dr. Edward Willis. When he arrived in Placerville during the gold rush era, he discovered that another physician had already set up his practice there. Upset that he suddenly had a competitor, the other physician demanded to see Dr. Willis's diploma and medical credentials. When Willis handed them to him, the angry doctor tore them up, and spat in Willis's face. That would lead to a duel; a duel that Dr. Willis was to win. Becoming in that way, the only practicing physician in Placerville.

But still, he didn't get rich, as he often gave away his medical advice for free. He did however, charge for his medical treatments. Extirpating tumors ranged from three to ten dollars. For delivering a baby the charge was five dollars. Twins though, cost ten dollars! For many treatments the nominal rate was a dollar. You'd plunk your dollar down and for that amount you could get a tooth pulled, or an arm set, or even an enema. But you did need to make sure you told the doctor what it was you wanted done for that dollar "before" he started his treatment!

HE COULD THANK
HIS DENTIST

One of the enduring tales of Americana is that our first President, George Washington, had false teeth made out of wood. Now it's true that he did have his problems with his teeth, and he did need to wear dentures, but they weren't made out of wood. Most historians believe they were fashioned out of ivory or animal bone, but never wood. For even in George's days, the 1700's, when the practice of dentistry was still focused more on extraction than prevention, they commonly used materials such as silver, gold and even mother of pearl for false teeth, so they looked natural. People were concerned about their appearances even back then.

But this leads us to an odd tale of Harmanus Van Vleck, or rather a tale about his false teeth. About a 130-years ago, near where the City of Reno now stands, a small wagon train of westbound immigrants settled in for the night. They'd circled their wagons for security, and had finished up their dinners and most were looking forward to a good nights rest after their exhausting day. But one member of the little group, a man by the name of Harmanus Van Vleck, was too nervous to sleep, for he'd seen some campfires in the distance. Fires from a Paiute Indian camp, and he became worried about a possible attack! Although the rest of his group thought he was a little crazy, he saddled up his horse and rode out into the night to scout out that Indian camp. For if they were planning an attack, his wagon train was in real danger. Harmanus took his time, circling down wind to avoid any dogs that might be in the camp, he quietly tied up his horse and worked his way behind some sagebrush to where he could look into the camp. And it was even worse than he had feared. There were a lot more Indians than he had expected, and they were wearing war paint, and were dancing around their campfires working up to an attack on the sleeping wagon train. Harmanus realized there was no time to get back to warn his friends, and even if he did there was a chance they'd be overwhelmed anyway by the large numbers of warriors. Sitting there he reasoned, there was only one thing he could do, and that was to try to stop the attack before it started. So he took a deep breath, jumped on his horse and headed straight into the Indian camp, yelling and screaming and firing his gun over his head, Harmanus sounded like a group of 10 men and surprised everyone! But what scared the warriors the most was when he pulled out his false teeth, stuck them out in front of him as he snapped them open and shut at the stunned Indians and let out a piercing screech. These warriors had never seen a man pull his teeth out of his mouth before, and that was simply too much for them and in a fright they took off running through the desert! The wagon train was saved and could thank Harmanus Van Vleck for what he had done, and Harmanus, could thank his dentist.

A TAHOE SOCIAL EVENT!

When novelist-humorist John Ross Browne first came through the south end of Lake Tahoe just after the 1859 discovery of the Comstock, he happened to spend a night at a hotel near the lakeshore. Then called the "Lakehouse," it wasn't much of a place, and when Browne wrote about his adventures, he went to great lengths to point out how bad it was. Cramped, noisy, filthy and woefully short of food and good whiskey, the Lakehouse, in Browne's estimation, was clearly a place to avoid. So it was probably no surprise that the hapless hotel was destined to change hands and change names a number of times within a few short years following Browne's visit.

One of the new owners, Thomas Benton Rowland, called the two-story way station after himself: "Rowland's Lakehouse." And fully aware of its past reputation, was determined to make it "the" place to stay, a regular five-star Tahoe hostelry. To help make that happen Rowland decided he needed both a center-piece, and an annual event to draw people to his doorstep. And so he constructed a two and one-half story dance pavilion and tavern. Even before it was finished, Rowland was planning a grand opening dance extravaganza. Sending out thousands of invitations to anyone and everyone within a days travel from the lake, and rounding up every available stagecoach, surrey and steamship, Rowland knocked on the doors of every guesthouse and resort around the lake, and extended an invitation to his big bash. That done, Rowland then sat back and crossed his fingers. And they came! The Great Rowland's Dance Ball was on, as people poured into the south shore. They came from as far away as Reno and Virginia City. Entertained by a string and organ quartet specially brought in from Sacramento, the bash began in the evening and continued all night long; ending up when the sun rose the next morning. Revelers lay exhausted all over the lakeshore, and some were so plastered they could barely move. This 1870's event was such a success that Rowland held another dance the next year and for years afterwards, and it was to be known as "the" social event of Lake Tahoe. Even when John Ross Browne happened by, he had to admit that the Lakehouse had indeed, gotten a whole lot better, thanks to Thomas Rowland.

EARLY DAY VOTING

The first polling sites on the California side of Lake Tahoe were established just after the 1860 general election, and people back then took their voting privileges very seriously. Regularly voting for the candidates of their choice whenever they could, and as often as they could. In the election between Republican Abe Lincoln and Democrat Stephen A. Douglas, over 7000 Eldorado County residents cast their votes. Which is interesting since there weren't that many people registered in the county at that time! So it appears that someone voted more than once. Douglas, by the way, beat Lincoln by about 500 votes, but four years later, Honest Abe won the local vote.

One pioneer area resident, William Gibbs recalled that, back in the 1850's, when California first got to vote in national elections, there were many places around the state, especially in the smaller Sierra towns, where no one really knew how many people lived there, let alone who was an American citizen and allowed to cast a vote. Or, sometimes, if the voter was actually old enough to legally cast a vote. According to Gibbs, it wasn't unusual to see a boy, barely tall enough to look over the top of a bar, pick up some extra pocket money from any unscrupulous politician who was on the ballot. The young man would get in a voting line and cast his ballot for that politician, then go outside and get back in line again, and vote again, and no one it seems complained! According to Gibbs, most of the polling areas were so poorly supervised, this was easy to do. So, it was possible that several hundred men and boys could easily generate several thousand votes.

Things were no better on the Nevada side of the lake, for voting abuse was frequent. For example, in those Comstock era days, each political party had their own tickets, and it was common to see voters handed a pre-marked ballot by a party's supporters, and then they would be watched closely to see that he didn't change his vote. It wasn't difficult to see how people cast their votes in these early days because there was no such thing as a secret voting booth as it was all out in the open. Pioneer editor Sam Davis wrote that in the balmy days of the Comstock there was always more or less rough work connected with politics. An election was frequently an affair with all the elements of a riot. Toughs (bullies) were hired by one political party supposedly to "preserve order," but then the other party also hired their own "toughs" to keep their opponents orderly. And too, Davis reported, the use of the departed was always a problem during elections, for it was not unusual to see the names of people listed on cemetery monuments showing up on voter rolls, as having cast ballots. Davis did say that if they were going to do that, the least the election crooks could do is to make sure the lifetime politics of the departed were respected. A lifelong Republican for example, not having his name showing up as having cast a vote for a Democratic candidate. Clearly, voter reforms were needed and one-day they would come, but it would take time.

A PINCH OF
GOLD DUST

For a while, about a 150-years ago, a primary currency around the Sierras and foothills was gold dust. These were the days when just about no one used paper money, and pocket change was still fairly scarce around many of the small settlements and mining camps. But a pinch of gold (the amount someone could hold between their thumb and forefinger) was universally considered to be worth about a dollar. It was actually more widely accepted than paper currency, as many things were paid by the pinch: a drink at a bar, potatoes from a vendor or a steak dinner. Most business owners accepted that since peoples hands were of different sizes, and some "pinches" would be a bit bigger, and some a bit smaller, but overall, it would all average out. And most of the time everyone was honest, but where there's opportunity, there's temptation, and a few merchants came up with some creative ways to skim more money and a bit more profit. Such as the merchant or bartender that grew his fingernails a mite longer than normal, so his "pinch" of gold might be a touch larger when he reached into a miners small pouch of gold dust, his "poke" to take payment for an item, or a drink; a few extra cents here and there added up.

And then there were those opportunistic bartenders who picked up extra "tips" for themselves by slapping some extra grease on their hair to make it sticky. For after dutifully grabbing a pinch of gold from a customers poke, and dropping it into the boss's cash-box, he'd then wipe his hand on the back of his head, and any small flakes still sticking to his finger would of course now stick to his hair, which he would carefully shampoo out each night to recover any gold. This scam might even produce a few extra dollars a day. There were also those bartenders who made a daily practice of rubbing small pebbles between their fingers, trying to create a small impression in their thumb and finger that would hold just a little more gold dust and more money. Some of the miners countered this bit of larceny by taking some brass, and filing it down to get the shavings, and then adding that to their "pokes," and it looked just like gold dust; a great way to even up the thievery. And too, there were the totally honest tavern-keepers that wouldn't take unfair advantage of their customers, but they weren't fools either, making it a point to carefully mop the floors around the bar every evening, washing out every flake of gold dust they might find in the wash bucket. And the really sharp ones in some of the mining camps had small gaps or spaces built into their floors by the bar, where a few errant gold flakes might fall and they'd regularly pry up the flooring to recover the gold (after the customers were gone of course).

Since no one pays their bills with gold dust anymore, there's little opportunity these days for squeezing out a bit more profit, but if the old timers were around today, they'd probably say that collecting payment from a customer just isn't as much fun as it used to be.

BLUE LANGUAGE
AND SUCCESS

Their language was deplorable, but they were proud of every blue colored word they uttered. For this was not only a symbol of their profession, it took a lot of study and constant practice to become fluent in the profane language that gave them their identity. For 1800's era teamsters, all depended on the cuss word to get the attention of their charge of oxen, mules or horses; the more blasphemous the better! The air would be filled with the sounds of the cracks of their leather whips, and their cries of profanity. And according to one 1870's Sierra visitor, (who'd just arrived from a trip to civilized Europe) it wasn't just the teamsters that were guilty of continual swearing. For the visitor, who kept a detailed journal of his travels from Placerville thru Tahoe to Virginia City, was first shocked, then appalled at the apparent widespread use of colorful and off-color language. It just seemed that every other word he heard was a cuss word. Hardly a sentence was expressed without the inclusion of a string of expletives! And it appeared that many a man couldn't express himself or be understood unless he incorporated a sprinkling of obscenities into each sentence. Why in fact, it appeared to the Sierra visitor that the English language had been replaced by a local dialect that you needed to use to communicate. Even educated and nominally civilized people were using strong and shocking words as an elemental part of their daily vocabulary.

But at least the Sierra visitor did have a sense of humor, for he noted that the constant cursing and the use of slang and profanity wasn't just a temporary affliction for the regions residents (fostered by the earthy people and rough characters that inhabited the then relatively primitive communities of Placerville, Tahoe and Virginia City); why then, all of the schools in the region shouldn't waste their students time teaching the words of Shakespeare, or bother to wash out their pupils mouths with a bar of soap for swearing. No, the teachers would better serve their students by teaching them to cuss; properly and with enthusiasm! So they might express themselves correctly, and one day become pillars of their community.

BRAVE MEN

People in the robbery business during the 19th century, usually had the upper hand. Catching their victims unaware, and then running off with their booty long before the local sheriff could get a posse rounded up and headed after them. But sometimes things didn't work out the way they'd planned because their victims didn't want to be held-up. One of the more amusing incidents took place at the general store in Truckee in the 1880's where a man named Charlie Atwood was sitting in a rocking chair smoking his cigar and visiting with the store clerks when two men burst in with their shotguns and demanded all the money from the store's till. But old Charlie started laughing, for he thought this was all just a joke! But then another man came in from the back of the store and poked Charlie in the stomach and told him to shut up, that this "was" a robbery. Charlie didn't like being poked in the stomach, so he grabbed his rocking chair and smashed it over the head of the man and jumped after the other two would-be robbers who quickly decided there were easier places to steal money from, so they dropped their shotguns and took off running; Charlie was just too much for them.

There was another man, about the same time, the 1880's, whose bravery in the face of robbers made him a legend in his time. His name was Aaron Ross, and he worked for the Wells Fargo Company as a guard. Aaron was riding in the railroad express car, watching after a $600 payroll shipment that had been loaded on at Reno by Wells Fargo. A few hours out of Reno, the train was stopped and held up by a band of robbers, who then walked over to the express car where Aaron quietly waited. One of the bandits pounded on the heavy express car door and told Aaron to open the door and get out, or else suffer the consequences. Aaron wasn't going to come out, so they unhooked his railcar and sent the rest of the train down the line a short way and then started shooting. Shots began ripping through the walls of the express car! Aaron kept shooting back, and so they tried to set it on fire with sagebrush. But it didn't catch on fire, and Aaron kept on shooting! Four long hours they battled, Aaron catching several rounds in his hip, and one in his hand, but still firing back. The robbers even tried to ram his express car with the train locomotive and a mail car still attached to it. Time and again, they slammed into the express car, but Aaron held on. Finally, another train approached from the west, and the robbers reluctantly had to give up, leaving Aaron exhausted and bleeding but alive. The robbers were eventually caught, and put in prison. Aaron Ross lived to the age of ninety-three, a tough man and a brave man. Both he and Charlie Atwood were men who refused to be a victim. They were also lucky men.

IT WAS ONLY A
FLIMSY WIRE

It put the Pony Express out of business, and eventually was replaced by another technological innovation: the telephone. But while it lasted, the telegraph was, for a time, this nation's primary means of communication. And the Tahoe Basin was part of the great transcontinental telegraph system. It began with Samuel Morse. His 1844 invention was to be embraced by a nation that didn't want to wait for the pony express, as fast as they were, or the slower stagecoaches to carry messages for news about world events or receive a simple but important personal note. In 1853, telegraph lines were being constructed, connecting Sacramento with the Central Valley and the Bay Area. The Alta Telegraph Company in 1854 extended the lines to Placerville. Fred Bee formed yet another company, the "Placerville, Humboldt and Salt Lake Telegraph Company," and soon pioneered the first lines connecting such communities as Genoa with Placerville. Constructing the line, though not as complex as building the railroads through the Sierras, it still had its own challenges. One crew would do the surveying, laying out the line, and a follow-up crew would install the poles, while a third crew would string the wires. Yet a fourth crew would be required to operate the construction camps, feed the work crews and care for the required packstock.

In the Nevada desert country, poles needed to be hauled in; shipped from forested areas. Around the Sierras, and the Basin area, the extensive granite outcrops created another kind of barrier to the thin wire system, and here both poles were used as well as tree branches. It wasn't especially tidy and the wires tended to break when the winds blew too hard, but it worked! Actually quite well, for by 1861 the nation had a transcontinental telegraph system, and it revolutionized communications from coast-to-coast. Tapping out Morse Code, using a small spring-loaded brass lever, the telegrapher became an indispensable member of the mountain community, translating the dots and dashes into meaning. Bringing to Tahoe word of a prize fight, or the results of an election, or perhaps a birthday greeting from an old friend. So it was that for years, a flimsy little wire helped to keep us in touch with the nation, and with the world.

IT WAS A ONE-RING CIRCUS

Back in our pioneer days, before there was such a thing as radio, television, movies, CDs, or the world wide web, people would temporarily escape the drudgery of the work week by attending community socials such as dances or picnics. The less restrained might head for a nearby saloon or gambling hall. The sporting might also go to see a contest, any would do! A boxing match, or a wrestling match, perhaps a badger fight or even a rifle-shooting or a drinking contest (hopefully with different contestants). But for everyone, one form of entertainment seemed to have a universal appeal: attending a circus. During the late 1850's circuses began visiting mining towns all around the Sierras.

Joseph Andrew Rowe's Pioneer Circus played in Placerville for two days in April of 1857, with one performance a day. Miners dropped what they were doing to attend the grand show. To watch Miss Mary Ann Whittaker ride around a small ring performing amazing acrobatics from the back of a white stallion, or perhaps William Franklin;

who billed himself as the "Greatest Equestrian Artist in the World." And for the children, or young at heart, there was Hiram Franklin, a trapeze artist who could also wow the crowd with his funny faces and wild antics; a clown. During their first performance in Placerville, the Rowe Circus took in over $700. But then, this was a working town, and the miners had to go back to their diggings, as the next day only $331 was taken in . . . but then the miners had a lot of exciting memories to carry them through the long days ahead; of jugglers, of acrobats, of exotic animals and of Mary Ann Whittaker, until the next circus came to town.

For the circus performers, theirs was a life of excitement and endless days on the open road. When they weren't traveling between shows, they were practicing their art; their tumbling, their tight-rope dancing, and their trick-riding. And they were constantly trying to come up with acts that would pack the house. A few of the early day circus's resorted to a bit of trickery to attract customers. One clever showman advertised what he called a "gowrow." A so-called monster that was trapped and caged and was now on display in his circus. His tents were painted with a vivid mural of a wild-eyed beast in the act of devouring a family of mountaineers. But he had reasoned, while that would bring in the curious for one night, to keep them coming, he needed a ploy . . . and so created a wonderful bit of chicanery. After the audience had taken their seats, waiting to see the horrible "gowrow," at the right moment, the showman would kick off his act. Starting off with behind the curtain screams and shots! Then an apparently bloodied man (it was actually catsup), would appear from the behind the curtain screaming "Run . . . run for your life . . . the gowrow has broken loose!" And at that moment, the back end of the tent would collapse and there would be more screaming, and invariably the audience would take off in a panic. Running for their lives! Never knowing they'd been had by a creative showman.

DONNER PARTY
DECISION

Of all the poignant moments surrounding the plight of the Donner Party during the winter of 1846/47, few could compare to the heart-wrenching moment when Margaret Reed had to make a terrible decision. Should she go ahead with the rescue party? But that meant leaving her two youngest children behind; three-year old Tommy, and eight-year old Patty. At stake were the lives of her other two children; five-year old James and Virginia, who was the oldest at twelve. They too needed to be evacuated from the winter camp, the camp where people were still starving. But after just two miles, both Tommy and Patty were too weak from hunger to continue walking with the rescue party, and Margaret couldn't let James and Virginia go on alone. This was an impossible choice for any mother, and likely she would not have gone on with the rescue party, but for one of the rescuers, Aquilla Glover. For it was he that volunteered to take the two struggling Reed children, Tommy and Patty back to Donner Lake, to the cabin where the Breen family still waited for "their" rescue.

Margaret Reed was agonizing over what to do, reluctant to continue westward when she looked intently at Glover and a glimmer of hope came to her, as she asked him if he happened to be a "Mason," for her husband was. Glover replied that "why yes, he was." Instantly Margaret Reed demanded a vow, a promise as a Mason, that Glover would, as soon as he could, return to Donner Lake with another rescue party to save Tommy and Patty. Glover agreed, and after a tearful farewell, Margaret headed west with James and Virginia, believing now her children would not be abandoned. Her trust in Glover keeping his word was absolute. Glover was to keep his word, returning with a second rescue party, although it was Tommy and Patty's father, James Reed that was to reach them first, and bring them to safety. This faith that Margaret Reed had in Glover's word, came from her belief in the traditions of Freemasonry. Possibly the world's oldest fraternal society, its members stood for philanthropy, virtue, civic participation, personal dignity, and the rights of an individual to be free. Masons in the 1800s were known for their support of orphanages, schools and homes for the elderly, and a members word to help someone in need was a sacred promise. A promise that Margaret Reed was to depend on when she made the most difficult decision of her life. It turned out to be the right one.

DON'T STOP
THE PRESSES!

Some of the old time newspaper editors were dedicated professionals. What was the code for mailmen: neither rain, nor sleet, nor dark of night would stay the successful completion of their appointed rounds, also went for them. As foul weather, and a lack of daylight not only didn't deter them from getting the paper out on time, they sometimes represented opportunities to these fearless journalists. After all, news was still being made long after the sun went down and a raging storm was always a good story. Early day editors though had to face at least one challenge that the mailman didn't. That was a rip snorting fire that might sweep through the town, burning out their whole operation, turning the newsprint and the printing press into charcoal! The lucky ones would have enough time to carry out all of their equipment into the streets, where as often as not, they'd just set up shop and print their paper while watching their building burn down. If they couldn't save their equipment, these hardy souls were known to sit down and handwrite a special edition, just to stay in business. For missing a scheduled edition was the last thing a news editor wanted to see happen.

Sometimes these fires necessitated that a burned-out newspaper, faced with that situation went to a competitor paper and paid "them" to print the news on their behalf. Enterprise editor George Daly faced one of those situations in a classic way once when he found his ground floor newspaper office being threatened by a wildfire that was sweeping through the town. Though the flames were getting closer, George was oblivious of the approaching danger, he was so preoccupied with writing out his special edition telling all about the town burning down! When the flames finally reached his building, they first torched the upper stories, sending hot ashes down to the bottom floor where George was now busy printing his news bulletin. As soon as the papers had been inked on his presses he grabbed an arm-full and ran out of the building, which was now sending up a column of smoke from top to bottom, and ran out into the streets, where he sold his special edition to news-hungry onlookers. Never giving a thought to just how close he'd come to becoming as charred as his printing press! But that was the code of a newsman.

VIGILANTE DAYS

During the 1850's western miners setting up camps along the uninhabited frontier were plunged into an environment where government didn't exist, and since it was necessary for them to live together peaceably, for as long as it took to strike it rich, they had to generate some kind of legal system, and that came to be known as "Miners Law." It was an imperfect form of justice, but it was direct. While certainly the capital crime of murder was serious, theft and assault were also considered to be significant, and the accused would quickly find themselves standing before a group of 12 true men or perhaps even the whole mining town to answer to their charges. And if the verdict was guilty, punishment was direct, with no appeals, as the individual was either immediately branded, flogged, executed or banished from the region, depending upon the crime.

One of the elements of Miners Law, was that every person in the community had the opportunity to participate in handing out justice, and this was pretty intoxicating stuff for the average miner who, back home, never had this kind of power before. So quite often, "Miners Law" was close to being illegal, barely allowing for "due process," or protection for the rights of the accused, and sometimes, would evolve into the shortcut version of law and order called "Vigilante Law." Here, although judgment and punishment was clearly swift, justice was seldom served. This happened in the spring of 1871 in Virginia City, when the numbers of homicides and robberies jumped dramatically and the residents were frightened, but also determined, that something needed to be done about the rampant crime, and almost overnight there sprang up a secret organization that came to be known as the "Six Hundred and One," or simply "601." Near midnight one March evening, masked men, vigilantes, spread out through the city rounding up known thieves and gunslingers and either invited them to leave Virginia City at once, or end up being permanent residents . . . and most chose to leave on their own, but there were several that ended up staying, victims of the vigilantes. And when this sweep was over, the members of the 601 took off their masks and became good citizens of Virginia City again. The town was a safer place now, but even some of those who took part in the activities recognized that this was not the way for a civilized town to behave, and through their efforts, the life of the Virginia City vigilantes, the 601, was happily short-lived, although similar vigilante organizations were to reappear in other communities around the Sierras, including Truckee, Placerville and even in quiet Genoa!

EARLY DAY TWAIN

If we want to take a close look at a local character, there is none better to talk about than Sam Clemens. When he joined the writing staff of the "Territorial Enterprise" back in 1862, he was a careless, abrasive Missourian who only took the job because he preferred to push a pencil over a shovel. While he first used the pen name of "Josh," Sam adopted the more famous nom de plume of "Mark Twain" after a few months on the job. On his first day as a reporter, Mark visited a wagon train of immigrants that had just come across some hostile Indian country and they'd had a little (although not much) trouble getting through. Deciding that the more color he could put into his first real news story, the more interesting it would be for everyone to read, so Mark jotted down the names of a few of those immigrants. Knowing full well, that wagon train would be heading on west early the next day, and that no one on that train would be around to read the paper when it came out later in the day, he wrote up a wild story fabricating an Indian attack on that same wagon train (also adding the names of the departed immigrants to a list of killed and wounded). It was all a lie, but no one but Mark ever knew the truth.

Some of his best satire came a few years later, when he worked up a fake ad offering all of the Nevada state officials for sale or for rent. The Governor, Mark wrote, was almost entirely new . . . and had attended Sunday-school in his youth, and still remembered his lessons. The Governor never drank, but his other habits were otherwise good. And the Governor would make a wonderful ornament for special events and displays, particularly if there was a speech to be given. The Lieutenant Governor, according to Mark Twain, was also new, and he too had a few good merits to his credit . . . he especially liked to travel about anywhere as long as it was at the public's expense. The "for sale or for rent" ad described the Secretary of State as an old experienced hand, that according to Mark was very capable, although the Secretary wasn't weighed down by any particular principles, religious or otherwise. And continuing his way through the organization chart, although Mark characterized the state Treasurer as "Second Hand," he did take excellent care of the public funds. In fact he treated the public's money just like he would his own money. As for the various state legislators, judges and comptrollers, Mark let it be known they were all for sale or for rent for practically nothing, after all, they weren't of any value to him, and anyone interested could contact Mark Twain c/o Carson, of the Nevada Territory. Mark's comments were a little irreverent, a little true and clearly help to explain why he spent most of his adult life in Missouri.

SUMMER DAYS AT CAMP RICHARDSON

Just down the road from the "Y," along Highway 89 as you are heading towards Emerald Bay, is a historic old resort called "Camp Richardson." Compared to some of the newer hotels that have been constructed around the lake in recent years, Camp Richardson is clearly more rustic and relatively modest in appearance. But that, is its charm. The resort also serves as a rare reminder of what the Tahoe area looked like during the early to mid-years of the twentieth century. The site itself was originally used as a ready source of timber by the Comstock era logging companies, as well as by early-day settler Yank Clement. In 1898 M.H. Lawrence acquired the land from Yanks wife, Lydia. And he was to develop a simple resort there.

But it was the Richardson family that was to make the resort into a popular vacation resort. Alonzo LeRoy Richardson was a trucking operator from Placerville in 1921 when he decided to lease some land from Lawrence, and start up a summer camping resort. And, to Richardson's mild surprise, it managed to do well, even though a nearby major resort complex, the Tallac House, had been struggling to stay open. "Al" Richardson, as he was usually called, soon added a pier, a café and a curio shop, and he began to attract a loyal clientele of family campers. Campers that would return year-after-year to his charming Lake Tahoe resort. While other resorts of the time often had guided tours around the Basin, Al had no "social directors," as campers were totally on their own to entertain themselves, and that worked just fine. For there was still lots to see and do around Camp Richardson. Every evening during the summer, a huge bonfire was built, and campers would often improvise, as there was no set routine. Sometimes they'd sing songs (staff and visitors together), sometimes they'd put on a skit. Other times, someone would throw a bed sheet over a tree limb, so there would be an improvised theater, and someone would show a movie. And for sure, there would often be a dance, and people from all over South Shore would flock to Camp Richardson to join in. Everyone was welcome, for you didn't have to be a camper. The resort staff was normally hired from universities in California or Nevada, with the numbers varying from twenty to thirty. And many also played a musical instrument; working in the campground during the days and playing in the Camp Richardson orchestra during the evenings. A fun place to work and a great place to visit.

The Richardson family was to pass the resort to the federal government in 1964. Today it's operated under a special use permit from the Forest Service, still striving to retain the old Tahoe charm that made it popular for so many years to so many people.

FERRIS AND HIS WHEEL

He didn't exactly invent fun, but he sure brought a lot of fun into people's lives. His name was George Washington Gale Ferris Junior. We remember him for his invention, the Ferris Wheel. In 1864, when Ferris was just five years old, his family moved out west; coming from Galesbury, Illinois and settling in the valley just south of Carson. Here he spent his boyhood years playing hide and seek or a game of "tag" with his friends. But Ferris also had a fascination for mechanical things. He especially loved to ride his pony down to the river and there, spend hours watching a giant water wheel spin around and around; carrying water a bucket at a time, to a massive water trough, where it would be used by livestock. That image of the waterwheel seemed to find a home in his imagination. Even as he grew up, when he went away to college, to study engineering, that waterwheel just seemed to come to mind. And it came to Ferris that perhaps he could build a contraption that would carry people instead of water; a "fun-machine." So he set to work drawing up plans for a giant wheel for the upcoming Chicago Worlds Fair.

His first version wasn't quite heavy-duty enough to satisfy the fairs promoters, so he modified the design to beef it up, and it worked! His giant wheel for people was 250 feet in diameter, and could hold up to 1440 passengers at one time! Steel cars were fastened to the giant wheel; weighing thirteen tons each and carrying about forty people each. They would look out through thick plate glass windows as they were carried high in the air, around and around in a slow circle that took ten minutes to complete. It was an immediate success. The first day it operated at the Worlds Fair, Ferris even had a forty piece band packed into several of the cars and they played their cheery music while they warily watched the world spinning outside their windows. By the time the fair had ended, nearly one and a half million people had ridden on the Ferris Wheel, paying three quarters of a million dollars for the opportunity to be carried high in the sky. Then Ferris simply dismantled his wheel, and moved it to another Chicago site where he operated it for a number of years. His wheel was clearly a success for updated versions of his Ferris Wheel were also included in the St. Louis and the Paris World Fairs. And of course today they're an icon of every county and state fair across the country. And it all came out of the mind of a young boy who spent his days dreaming on the banks of the Carson River.

FIRST MILLIONAIRE

One historian was to call him the Bill Gates of the Gold Rush. A pioneering entrepreneur, a wheeler-dealer who knew how to create great wealth, how to promote a product and how to make himself a profit. Sam Brannan in fact became the first and the wealthiest millionaire during the early days of the gold rush. Not by getting his hands dirty, prospecting or digging for the Mother Lode, Sam Brannan was to make his fortune by speculating and risk-taking and effectively marketing his product: gold. Sam was a thirty-two year old New Yorker that in the late 1840's was a combination merchant and newspaper publisher for the "California Star." After James Marshall and John Sutter realized they had made their golden discovery at Sutter's sawmill in Coloma, they tried to keep the discovery quiet. Sutter was clearly worried, and he should of been, that once word got around, people would swarm over his lands, threatening his empire. Though in fact, there is question today over whether John Sutter even held legal title to the Coloma millsite.

But despite their efforts at secrecy, word inevitably leaked out. And so enter onto the scene one Sam Brannan. Rumors began to fly in far away San Francisco about gold in Coloma, and that was enough to catch Sam's ear. Though at first he was a bit skeptical, but as rumors persisted, and bits of gold began to show up round town Sam decided to go up to the foothills himself and see what was going on. After all, he was in the news business, and hoped the story might sell him some more papers. Once there, he saw there really was something to the rumors. Deciding that time was short, returning to the Bay City, he quickly ran around buying up all the pans, shovels and pick axes he could find, cornering the market. His next marketing move was simple, yet pure genius. Sam ran down the main street waving a bottle of gold dust and shouting "Gold . . . Gold from the American River!" The ensuing furor was instantly gratifying to Sam and rewarding, for the crowds rushed first to his store, purchasing pans for fifteen dollars each; pans that Sam just paid all of thirty-cents each for, and then they ran off to the foothills. But though Sam for a time was the richest man in all of California, he died broke in Escondido forty years later. The victim of bad investments and a costly divorce, but for a time, he had the world by the tail!

FLOUR AND CHARITY

Watching a man pushing a peanut down the street with his nose isn't something you see everyday, or would even care to see, but it wasn't that unusual back in the 19th century after an election. For that was commonly the outcome of a lost bet between two opposing candidates or their supporters. And this ritual of public embarrassment has long been a part of the American tradition, with many variations. Often involving wheelbarrows; the winner catching a free ride down the center of town at the expense of the loser. One supporter of Millard Fillmore in 1856 lost a bet to a supporter of John C. Fremont during a primary election for the presidency. And for his penance he ended up pushing a wheelbarrow loaded down with apples; near 200 pounds worth, from one part of the county to another; a distance of over thirty-six miles. He did it, although he lost about twelve pounds in weight by the time he ended his journey!

In 1884 another bet loser had to put on a suit of armor, and wear it for at least thirty days. He did, but he also lost a lot of weight in the process. Another loser had to put on his bright-red underwear and parade down the street pushing a wheelbarrow with the bet winner comfortably being carried while sitting on a big cushion and waving a flag. He actually got off easier than did a man from Kansas by the name of Charles Taylor, who also had to push a winning politician down the street in a wheelbarrow. But Taylor had to wear a ladies house-dress and slippers while he paid off his wager. That must of been quite a bet!

And finally, in 1864 there was the bet between Nevada miner Reuel Gridley (a Democrat),and the town doctor (a Republican), over who was going to win the office of town mayor. Gridley's man lost, and as he had wagered, he had to hoist up a 50-pound sack of flour onto his shoulder and carry it through the middle of town; accompanied by a brass band and a crowd of onlookers. But as it turned out, this particular bet led to the making of history as Gridley, after he'd carried that sack of flour as promised, decided to auction it off to the highest bidder, with the money going towards charity. At first try he received $250 for that sack, with the bidder telling Gridley to keep the flour and sell it again; and he did, and eventually all of Washoe County and people from as far away as San Francisco & New York got into the act and before they retired that sack of flour Gridley had collected nearly $250,000 for charity! And it all started with a lost bet.

EQUALITY WAS YET TO COME

It was never fair, but it happened more often than not. Men treating women like a second-class citizen. A mix of Victorian ideals and a dose of male chauvinism combined to either minimize the contributions of women, or simply ignore them during the last century. This was most evident in the writings of the local and regional newspapers of the period. Newspapermen around the west seemed to struggle with the new freedoms and expanded roles of women in the frontier as women began to break-out of their traditional stereotypical roles and were venturing into the previously all "mans world" as educator, doctor, lawyer and business owner. News editors, nearly always a male, especially from the smaller communities, didn't quite know how to cope with this new prominence of women in their community. Oh, the ladies were always to be admired for who they were, but only when they lived within the frameworks of the old social norms that rigidly confined their activities. Because of this well developed sense of male superiority, women were often criticized in print for the social changes that made the men uncomfortable; seeing a woman running a business; controlling her own destiny; making her own decisions instead of deferring to a man. One newspaper even went so far as to suggest that women should be banished, as they were behind the problems of the community! Few women were ever mentioned publicly in the early day papers. Even when they did unusually brave things that should have been heralded on the front page, in bold face type!

A classic example involved Mrs. John Garrish, who, along with her young daughter, had been riding a stage down the east slopes of the Sierra, headed towards Virginia City, when it was attacked by a band of Indians. The driver and a lead horse shot, Mrs. Garrish jumped out of the coach; cut the wounded horse loose; climbed into the drivers seat, and raced off down the road with bullets flying around her! True to the traditions of a western novel, she encountered a garrison patrol that fortunately had been heading her way. She'd made it to safety! But this was no tale, and yet, Mrs. Garrish only received a bare mention for her actions in the local newspaper. The editors were clearly uncomfortable with making a woman a public figure. Eventually, things would change. Especially, when women began to enter the newspaper business, and events such as those were no longer ignored by the papers.

EARLY DAY MEDICINE?

For a time, it was a medicine of choice, widely prescribed by medical practitioners of the 18th and 19th centuries. For not only weren't there that many effective medicines to choose from, this remedy actually worked. For it contained alkaloids; organic bases of such modern medicines as morphine, and codeine. But it came with a high price, for it was addicting. The medication was opium, and it is not only a part of our medical history, it's a part of the local and regional history too. Opium soothed pain, and relieved the intensity of diarrhea. But it was also dispensed to help ease bouts of coughing. But often, it was just used to help patients relax, and that had a value too. When mixed into an alcoholic solution like laudanum, it was easy to take, just like cough medicine. But this medication was much stronger.

Opium gained most of its well-deserved notoriety from its use as an inhalant; when it was stuffed into small pipes and smoked like tobacco. This habit was first introduced into our region by those hard-working laborers of the Central

Pacific Railroad; Chinese immigrants who'd relied on this practice in their home country to ease their aches and pains, and to help them cope with an often unfriendly new country who needed their backs but treated them with indifference or worse.

In his classic 1876 work "The Big Bonanza," Comstock writer Dan De Quille described a visit to one of the typical opium dens that dotted Virginia City and was found in many of the period mining and logging camps, including San Francisco, where-ever there was a Chinese population. De Quille described a dark room, illuminated only by a single dull red lamp. Small boxes of opium, and scales for weighing and pipes were lying about, as were scores of dimly lit bunks, all filled with smokers in various stages of stupor. A heavy sweetish-bitter odor of the burning opium fills the air. And all's one can hear is the quiet breathing of the den's customers; lost in their individual dream worlds. And they weren't all Chinese customers either, for here and there were Irish and English and Germans and Italians; mostly men, but a few women. The opium dens ran day and night, with the same customers returning two or three times each week. Even around the Basin, where-ever 19th century Chinese woodcutters camps are discovered, the odds are there'll be small opium bottles scattered about. Testifying to the popularity of this early day effective, but insidious, "over-the counter" medication.

BOOM⚡BOOM HOLLINGSWORTH

There's a few scattered old bottles now, but not many. Collectors have scoured the area many times, so little is left. The site itself is grown over by tall clumps of sagebrush, having been swept by wildfires and ravaged by floods. But one time, back in the 1860's, it was a wild and wooly boomtown. Packed with this regions liveliest, noisiest, hardest-drinking miners, merchants and loggers. It was called "Galena" and was located east of Mt. Rose, northwest of Washoe Lake. Galena's hardy residents earned a footnote in the history books by their reaction to the mule train that broke its way through the snowpacks to bring food to the town, as its residents were on the brink of starvation. For a blizzard had closed the only road into town for over a month and Galena was desperately short of everything. But despite their obvious hunger, when the Galena residents discovered that ONLY food and NO supplies of beer or whiskey were in the packbags, they were disgusted! Now, a town with that kind of thirst resolved never to be caught flat footed again, so the residents all chipped-in and they built their own still.

But the towns real fame came from the way it treated a new-comer named Hollingsworth. He came to town to operate a bakery and a candy store. A pleasant-enough fellow, there was one thing though about Hollingsworth that his fellow residents felt was a bit odd: he didn't like to drink. He'd been in business for nearly a week and not once had set foot in one of the towns bustling saloons. Before long it was quite apparent that Hollingsworth didn't drink. Well, that sort of behavior just wasn't to be tolerated in this town for it had an image to maintain. So a town meeting was held, where it was decided that no man would be allowed to remain in business unless he was a supporter of the local saloons. After all, something had to be done to protect the town from this deplorable individual. So the Galena founding fathers rounded up two kegs of gunpowder, and in the middle of the night, stuck them under Hollingsworth's store, and lit a fuse. There were two resounding booms, and the front end of his store was gone. Hollingsworth wasn't hurt, but he did get the message, and packed up and left town that same day. The residents cheered, and headed off to the nearest bar to celebrate. Galena must have been quite a town!

CAVE ROCK TEMPLE

The correspondent from the Placerville Herald spun a colorful tale that ended up in a score of history books. But it was at best, an old Washoe legend, and at worst, a complete fabrication. But it did have the ring of sincerity to it, and so it became a part of the Tahoe legacy of ancient tales.

It was back in 1853, that the correspondent was exploring the Rubicon River area west of the lake with an old friend, a Tahoe pioneer by the name of John Johnson; though his friends always called him "Cock-Eye." They had worked their way to the lakeshore, eventually reaching Lake Tahoe in the area of Meeks Bay. From there, they gazed out across the lake, to the Nevada side, where they caught sight of a most interesting feature on the far shores: a massive rocky outcrop that rose up out of the lakes waters. And it appeared to have a cavern reaching into its interior. That night they camped with a band of around 70 Washoe Indians. The correspondent proceeded to ask them scores of questions about the lake, and particularly about that mysterious looking cavern across the lake. An especially old and wise Indian elder began to tell them of the legend of Cave Rock; of the story of the water demon; during the ancient days when there were no mountains here yet, just a flat plain that ran to the ocean. There lived a peaceful tribe that would never harm anyone. But one day they were suddenly invaded by a fierce tribe from the north who beat them and forced them to build a giant temple from where their conquerors could worship the sun. They had just completed it, when the God of the World, angry over what had happened, caused a great wave to rise from the ocean to sweep across the land. Everyone, from both tribes ran to the temple for safety. But there, the invaders drove out the members of the peaceful tribe, who quickly raced away to their canoes and freedom. Soon after they had escaped, the high waters receded, but now there was a deafening roar, as the ground heaved and fire blew out of newly opened vents in the ground. Mountains began to form, and then snow began to fall, and in the heat it turned into water; a lake began to form. At the same time the great temple began to sink into the ground and the Indians from the fierce tribe had to climb onto the top of the temple. But the God of the World was still angry, and walked out onto the lake and grabbed them, one-by-one and threw them into the cave, where to this day, you can hear them cry when the water is high.

The next day the correspondent and Johnson then rowed over to Cave Rock to see the cave for themselves, and they reported that it really DID resound with low moaning sounds. They must have made "that" part of their story up . . . or did they? We'll never know.

CHIEF TRUCKEE...
A MAN OF PEACE

The wide river that drains the waters of our big blue lake carries the name of a man who might be called a visionary, though others, during his lifetime may have criticized him for departing from traditions, from his culture. But he was arguably, the most influential Native American in the history of the Tahoe Region, exceeded perhaps, only by his granddaughter, Sarah Winnemucca.

He was Chief Truckee; the undisputed leader of the northern Paiute tribes, whose lands stretched through western Nevada, including those lands north of the lake. During the 1840s and 50's this chieftain was to play an important role in the exploration of the region, and in the survival of the first immigrants to pass through the Sierras near what would become Donner Summit. Explorer John Fremont's party were among the first to discover that this Paiute Chief, was not only friendly and generous to Euro-Americans, he seemed to welcome their presence on his lands. Feeding them and providing guides. Often, it was the Chief himself, to help the whites find their way through the mountains. For the Chief believed that all men were sons of a common ancestor, that the people with the red hair and the blue eyes were still brothers. Others in his tribe weren't so happy to see the explorers and the early day settlers pass through their country, and there had been skirmishes in eastern Nevada, and people injured, but the Chief passionately argued against a war, and there was only friendship during his years as head of the tribe.

There was no record of the number of immigrant groups that he had helped through the mountain pass down to Sutter's Fort, but he was to become a legend. In 1846, the United States went to war with Mexico over the future of Texas, and Fremont organized a militia of volunteers, even enlisting the support of Chief Truckee, who became an officer of scouts; proudly wearing a blue officers coat with shinny brass buttons, he was to be known as "Captain" Truckee. After the war, he was awarded a commendation by Fremont for his services, which he treasured for the remainder of his life. Chief Truckee passed away in 1860, respected by all those who knew him. A man of peace. His name, some believe is the Paiute word for "everything's all right," fittingly honors the only river that flows out of our lake, the Truckee River.

COMMON SENSE AND HARD WORK

There was an old song that proclaimed "what do you get when you work your fingers to the bone? Why, you get bony fingers." Or put another way, just because you work hard doesn't guarantee you'll become a success. And things were no different a century ago, as people found out that even in a lovely place like Lake Tahoe, where it seemed like anyone with enough sweat and effort could make it. Especially to a person who wanted to be in the logging business. William Harmer in the late 1870's was an aspiring capitalist; a man with a vision of greatness and richness. He figured that wealth would come running his way and all's he needed to do was to start up his own logging company here at the lake. He had a right to be encouraged, for it seemed that everywhere he looked there was a mill or a log deck, or a camp of woodcutters, working six plus days a week and still not able to satisfy the demand of the Comstock for Tahoe timbers. Harmer hocked everything, contracted with one of the giant Basin timber corporations to supply timbers from the north shore, and set to work. He chopped down trees from dawn to dusk; limbed them, and chained them and drug them with his team of horses to a decking area. And with block and tackle and a lot of back breaking effort, loaded the timbers onto a transport wagon, and delivered his load to the nearest shipping point; most often a loading-chute on the lakeshore, where a steamer waited to pull these logs to the company mill.

Harmer soon hired more men to help him, and bought more equipment, and flushed with excitement over how smoothly things were going, he entered into more contracts with the big companies, and committed his small company to the increased production expectations. All his hard work was paying off, but he was soon to learn a lesson of life: that hard work without some common sense, and perhaps a touch of good luck, wasn't enough. He soon was to overextend himself, for it was getting harder to meet his timber quotas, for trees were increasingly further up the mountain slopes and he'd already cut the biggest ones. Harmer worked even harder, but his impetuousness, his passion to make money, had settled his fate and he had to declare bankruptcy. And he ended up in 1886 selling everything to another would-be capitalist named Spooner, and quietly left the lake. He left behind a pile of unpaid bills, but took with him the hard won knowledge that success DOES take more than hard work.

COURAGE WAS SOMETIMES NECESSARY

At first, they weren't known as brave men, just honest men. But there was much that people were to learn about these two early day Nevada residents. Both had a bit more courage that surprised even those that had known them for years. The first man was a quiet Carson City lawyer. His job was to take to task an area rowdy who'd started up a fight and was now in court answering for his actions. But it so happened the rowdy was a good friend of one of the regions most notorious gunslingers; none other than that Tahoe legend "Long-Haired Sam Brown" himself. And when Brown found out his friend was standing trial, he grabbed up his six-guns and headed off to disrupt the court; expecting to intimidate everyone there to let his friend go. But Brown hadn't reckoned on the mild mannered Carson lawyer, one William Stewart. For when Brown strutted in to the court room, and most people scurried out the doors, Stewart grabbed his own colt revolvers and forced Brown to sit down in the witness chair. There, still at gunpoint, Stewart got Brown to further incriminate his friend, telling the judge how he and his friend loved to pick fights and shoot-up saloons. That did it, and Browns friend was declared "guilty as charged" and sent off to jail. Brown angrily left the courtroom, but wasn't about to challenge Stewart to a fight of his own, for Stewart, he realized, had too much courage.

The other man was long known as a mild, timid person. A person that rarely spoke above a whisper. Someone who'd go out of his way to not harm anyone or anything. Which seemed appropriate since he was the town doctor. In 1870, Dr. Gaily was also elected to be the towns Justice of the Peace. It was only then that people became aware of another side of his character. A local trouble-maker and loud-mouth named Newton had gotten into an argument with rancher Alex McKey and pulled a gun on him. That case ended up in front of the meek doctor, but the moment both Newton and McKey entered the courtroom, words began flying, and Newton charged at McKey! But to everyone's surprise, Gaily let out a scream for Newton to stop, and let loose with a blast from a shotgun he held, and Newton froze in his tracks. And, keeping him under guard, Gaily commenced the trial. Newton was found guilty and fined $1000 but he refused to pay it, and attempted to walk out of the courtroom. But Dr. Gaily quickly blocked his path, and with his still-loaded shotgun leveled at Newton told him to pay up. Newton was angry, but he did as he was told. Surprised as everyone else was, at the doctor who'd he previously thought was only a meek man. But he'd been wrong for Dr. Gaily clearly knew when to prescribe some courage for himself when he needed it.

A WHITE LIE

Few people would likely question the value of honesty. Clearly it is both a virtue and a defining quality of good character. The standards we live under are tight. Always telling the truth is the ideal, while just usually telling the truth isn't at all an acceptable practice. But given the obvious imperfections of us humans, fueled by our vivid imaginations, our fondness for embellishment, for exaggeration and enjoyment of a good laugh, we may sometimes, not often, slip just a tiny bit into telling a "white lie," or a simple tale. Mark Twain was a man that also valued honesty, but he clearly believed it was often a rare commodity. Remarking that the only absolutely honest man he'd known had only been so for a short time, as Mark had just come from the man's funeral. And when he was asked how he viewed himself on the same subject, Mark thought a bit then declared that "Yes, even I am dishonest. Not in many ways, but in some. Forty-one I think it is."

Our region was to even glorify the art of lying. For being a good liar is something that doesn't come naturally to everyone. It takes practice, a certain logic and it's absolutely essential to have a believable delivery. The master of the art of lying lived in Nevada during the later half of the 19th century: Fred Hart. Fred started out as a clerk in a Virginia City dry goods store at the same time Mark Twain lived there, though he barely knew the soon-to-be great writer. Fred though, was a good writer of his own, and yearned to start up his own newspaper. And so he migrated over to a small Nevada community and wrote for and edited that town's paper. But Fred loved the tall tale, and decided to bring more attention to the locals tendency for stretching the truth. Perhaps getting himself a news story at the same time. So he created what became known as the "Sazerac Lying Club." All of the towns leading citizens joined, swapping stories and telling lies. Stories that were required to be believable, and entertaining, or they wouldn't be acceptable. The club was an enormous success and membership was anxiously sought by aspiring liars, eagerly polishing their skills. After all, learning to tell a good lie just might come in handy someday; like telling your wife you really do like her experimental new hairdo.

WILD NIGHT
AT GLENBROOK

There was one time when a dinner at the lake was to lead to the resignation of the top judges in the region known as Nevada. The year was 1864, and Nevada hadn't attained statehood quite yet. It was still a territory, but it had a government, a territorial governor, and legislature and a judiciary; essentially a three man Supreme Court. And in those early days of government, corruption, while still the exception, was for some, a way of life. Votes were quietly bought and sold, and fairness was a matter of price. This corruption was to be exposed one night in Glenbrook. Two mining companies were disputing in court over "who" owned a rich vein of Comstock silver ore: the Collar Mining Company & the Potosi Mining Company. Millions of dollars were at stake, so one of the rival companies, the Potosi, decided it would try to stack the deck a bit in its favor.

The Chief Justice of the Territorial Court, Judge George Turner, wasn't known as a beacon of honesty, however his sympathies tended to lean towards the Collar Company. But there were two other judges on the court that might be influenced by the Potosi owners. First they managed to "persuade" one of those judges to retire from the bench, Judge Mott. He couldn't be bought outright it seemed, but he was susceptible to the offer of a fat retirement fund! Mott was replaced by another judge; John North, who happened to be very sympathetic to the Potosi mining interests. They then bribed the third judge, P.B.Locke. Locke it seemed never met a bribe he didn't like! So the Potosi Mining Company managed to get its hands in the pockets of two of the three judges as their lawsuit with the Collar Company began to be heard. But although there was still a need to be discreet about the manipulations of the bench; after all, bribery was still frowned upon, Judge North got a little careless. The court had been in session for weeks and North was getting impatient. After all he knew what the outcome was going to be without even listening to the lawyers from the Collar Company. And so in the middle of their arguments, he suddenly announced he was sick, and the court was adjourned for the day. But instead of heading home, he, along with Judge Locke rode over to the Glenbrook House at Tahoe & spent the night partying with the owners of the Potosi Company. Unfortunately for them, they were followed by the lawyers for the Collar Company. Their corruption exposed, both Judge North & Locke were forced to resign. And following a general outcry for a cleanup of the Nevada bench; people were tired of the dishonesty, even Judge Turner was forced to resign. So it was that a wild night at Glenbrook was to help bring honest men to the Nevada courts.

BAD LUCK OR FATE?

For some reason, good fortune did not shine upon those who discovered the great gold and silver bonanzas of the last century. Both James Marshall, and John Sutter ended up in poverty, and so did their Comstock counterparts, Henry T. Comstock, and his lesser known partners Peter O'Riley and Patrick McLaughlin. For a dark twist of fate seems to have followed all of them, when by all rights, each should have been set for life. And before these men, there were two others. Two brothers, who were also on the verge of striking the biggest bonanza in the history of this country. But the same fate was waiting for them too, and it still hasn't been explained by historians.

They were the Grosh Brothers; Allen and Hosea. Sons of a Pennsylvania preacher, both young men had come out west during the 1848 Gold Rush, to strike it rich for their families back home. For the first few years, they doggedly kept at it, finding just enough gold to pay their expenses and keep their hopes up, and eventually they wandered into the Sierra range, through the Tahoe Basin and into western Nevada. But here in 1857 they discovered a large quartz vein that they believed contained silver, and lots of it!

So they made notes about it and moved on, still prospecting. But it was then that an accident happened. Hosea had struck his foot with a pickaxe while checking out an outcrop of rock, and the foot was soon infected, and within days, tetanus and lockjaw set in, and Hosea Grosh was dead at age 31. So after seeing to his brothers affairs, the heartbroken older brother, Allen set out for California with another miner, Richard Bucke. The secret of their potential silver bonanza; their notes, were left behind in a cache of rocks. They had only gotten as far as Lake Tahoe when their burro broke its hobbles one night and took off. And that cost them a precious four days, since winter was coming on. When they reached Squaw Valley, a blizzard hit them and they had to hole up in a tent, and soon it became a race for life. The burro died and they roasted it for food. But the snow kept falling, so they struck out into the wind and spent the next two weeks, wading in waist deep snow, half-frozen and lost before they were found by a group of miners who pulled the two men into camp on sleds. But their legs were badly frost-bitten, and Bucke had to have both his legs amputated. Somehow, he lived through the ordeal, but Allen refused to have his legs operated on, and on December 19th, he died. And a short two years later, the large quartz vein the Grosh Brothers had discovered turned out to be a bonanza. A part of the great Comstock Lode. But none of that fortune in silver was destined to end up in their hands. We'll never know if it was fate, or just bad luck.

A STAND-UP COMEDIAN

Standup comedians are a unique breed of individual. A good one is someone blessed with a uncommon blend of wit, talent, timing and showmanship. And, a penchant for finding humor in commonplace life and the ability to point it out. One of the finest standup comedians of the 19th century was a charming character by the name of "Charles Farrar Brown," though he went by his stage name of "Artemis Ward." And he was "the" acknowledged master of wit back in the 1860's when he first visited the west. A close friend of Mark Twain when Mark lived in Virginia City, Artemis once told him: "Seriously, I've done too much fooling around, doing unimportant things, so I'm going to do something that will live." "What's that?" Mark asked. Artemis looked hard at Mark and said "Tell lies!" Mark had to agree that a lie well told, was immortal! And Artemis Ward told a bunch of them, on stage. But his one-liners were so entertaining, his stories so outrageous, his delivery so engaging, people everywhere loved him, and could care less if he was fabricating a lie or actually telling the truth, as long as it was funny.

He dependably packed the house wherever he went, performing for entertainment starved audiences throughout the region. His popularity though was bound to expose him to some good-natured pranksters. Artemis had booked himself into a remote mining camp, where the entire population of 150 miners turned out, eagerly paying the two dollars charged to hear him speak. He as usual, was a great hit and they all loved him, and laughter filled the impromptu theater-house, a local saloon. The grateful audience decided to give Artemis a going-away surprise, one that he would never forget! After escorting him to the stage for his return trip to Carson, they made sure to advise him that he needed to be aware of a reported sighting of a rogue band of Paiute Warriors that were in the area. They'd set him up of course, and sure enough, a few miles out of town there was a whoop and a holler, and the stage-driver screamed they were being chased by a band of warriors. Artemis was unaware of the hoax and scared to death as the stagecoach pulled to a stop, surrounded by war-painted raiders. They of course played their role to a hilt, and had the comedian petrified before the miners decided to let him know it was just a prank. After a few nervous moments Artemis relaxed and let out a big sigh of relief and then began to laugh. He even invited the men to the nearest saloon, to buy them all a free round of drinks. Recognizing that a good joke, even if it's on him, was to be enjoyed!

SPOONER JUNCTION: MILLED LUMBER IS UNLOADED FROM
THE GLENBROOK

TRAIN -1882

LUNCH BREAK ON A FALLEN TAHOE YELLOW PINE - 1880

MASSIVE LOGS WERE SKIDDED DOWN THESE WOOD CHUTES
TO THE MILLS

- 1880's

BROCKWAY HOTEL - LAKE VIEWS AND A HOT SPRING!
-1880

LOADED WAGON OF TAHOE TIMBERS HEADED TO THE
MILLS - 1880's

A MORNING'S CATCH IN LAKE TAHOE - 1890

GLENBROOK INN - A VACATIONER'S DREAM - 1913

Note: All photos provided courtesy of
"Nevada Historical Society"

PAPERS, EDITORS, AND POLITICIANS

During our regions pioneer days, it was often the custom for the editor of one newspaper to lambaste the editor of another newspaper. It was not only sport, it provided bored editors with a chance to flex their literary talents and perhaps stimulate sales of their own papers. Two pioneer California newsmen, Walter Colton and Robert Semple, found themselves roasted by a rival paper, the "Star" of San Francisco. The Star editor described Colton and Semple as "a lying sycophant(a flattering toad), and the other, as "an overgrown lickspittle (a fawning underling). Another news editor of the period was to describe the editor of his local competing paper, as an underhanded sneak, a liar, a ruffian, and a two-faced scarecrow whose whiskers are leaking for a need of a bath." Whatever that meant! But that wasn't so bad as the nastyisms that another editor flung at his competitor, for he called him ignorant, scrawny, miserable, contemptible, disgusting, blear-eyed, and depraved. But this mudslinging was taken in stride, and there were only a few accounts of the insults generating a fight between the affronted editors. That was simply a part of their business.

But as bad as these traded barbs were, they were only child's play to what some early day editors would unleash against politicians. They were always fair game for the poison pen, and those few corrupt or overbearing politicians deserved their bashings. Deserving or not, they were commonly a source of derision and entertainment for newspaper editors. Politicians found themselves derided, slandered and belittled in the press. Mocked and demeaned, most politicians tried to court the news editors and sometimes that worked, but not always. One 1886 Nevada Governor (Jewett Adams) was running for re-election, and unfortunately locked horns with the editor of a Virginia City paper called "The Occasional." Adams thought he was going to win in a runaway, but just before his party's caucus, that paper came out with a scathing editorial that called him ignorant of the law and blatantly unworthy of that office. His unofficial polls showed his nomination was suddenly in trouble. Shocked but savvy after his years in public office, Adams had learned the power of the press . . . so he put out his own newspaper, which of course praised his record as Governor, and he won his party's nomination . . . though he was to lose the general election.

Another powerful individual of our area was to go one better. William Sharon, a multi-millionaire Comstock mining and banking baron, decided to run for the US Senate. He was instantly blasted by the most influential newspaper in our region, the "Territorial Enterprise." An occasionally ruthless banker, he wasn't well liked by anyone, and was both feared and despised. But he was also a smart man, knowing that if you can't beat them, buy them out, and he purchased the Enterprise and instantly its editorials were flowing with words of support for his candidacy. He won his Senate seat, with the help of the press and lots of money.

CONCORD COACHES AND PROGRESS

They were the clipper ships of the great oceans, the greyhounds of the prairie, and they were also works of art. During their day, the mid-to late 1800's, they were often called the "Queens of the Road." They were the Rolls Royce of stagecoaches. Known as the "Concord Coach," these nine-passenger horse-drawn vehicles were considered to be the best. The most comfortable and the most reliable means of getting from here to there (before the days of the railroads and the later automobile), these beauties stood eight feet tall and weighed 2500 pounds. While other stagecoaches of the time used steel braces to dampen the bouncing and bumps that made traveling in these things so miserable, the Concords were made with thick leather thorough-braces that acted like shock absorbers. And that made them a lot more comfortable, even though by today's standards, a long ride in one was still grueling, but even the curmudgeonly Mark Twain was to express his admiration for a Concord coach he rode in, in 1861 while coming out west with his brother, describing his coach as an imposing cradle on wheels. Drawn by six handsome horses, this swinging and swaying stagecoach fairly flew over the hard, level ground.

In remote communities throughout the country, the stagecoach was the best and sometimes the only means of transportation, and our local history has its share of tales about famous stage drivers. People like Hank Monk, Baldy Green, Mustang Al, Big Jake, Curly Bill and that (knight of the lash) Charlotte Parkhurst (a stage driver who dressed and acted like a man). But despite the relative comfort of the Concords, and the skills of the drivers, progress was to slowly replace the stagecoaches. By the early 1900's, the railroad had become the major mover of people and materials through much of the urbanized portions of the country, and a few years later, the motor vehicle would take center stage as the preferred mode of transportation in our region. But during those first years of the 20th Century, trucks had their limits. Mountain roads were steep and unimproved and they were full of dust in the summers and turned to mud in the winters, when they were open. But people were in a hurry to push progress, and so an experiment was tried. It was 1906 when a transit-freighting company decided to purchase the latest newfangled internal-combustion powered truck and have it shipped to Reno. It was intended to replace horse-drawn coaches that had been in use, to haul both people and supplies around the Carson Valley. The new truck arrived on a train in Reno, and was greeted with great fanfare. It was unloaded and fired-up, and followed by a group of curious onlookers, the driver headed south. But barely a few miles down the road that marvelous mechanical contraption got stuck in a sandy stretch of road. And it stayed stuck, for the driver broke an axle trying to get it out. So, in the end they hitched up a team of horses to pull the truck out of the sand, and then they sent it back to Reno to be shipped back east where it was made. The roads would need to be improved before it could ever be practical. Sometimes progress is a little too far ahead of its time.

HELLMAN
AND TEVIS

Tahoe certainly seemed to attract its share of wealthy people over the years, especially in the early 1900's. Mark Twain was to call this "the gilded age." The big lake and the beautiful mountains made this area a preferred destination for those born with silver spoons in their mouths or those with just lots of dirty old cash in their pockets. For this area was relatively remote for most visitors before the day of the automobile and it cost a fair amount of money to journey here from such places as New York and Chicago and even San Francisco. And the resorts at the dawn of the last century tended to cater to those who made more than the "average" wages of the day. Oh, there were some places for the so-called "middle-class," but it wasn't at the larger Tahoe resorts. They had to book at the lakes more rustic cabins and camping grounds. Those with a great deal of money could enjoy all the big city amenities: fine food, fine wines, luxurious surroundings, all the comforts of home, complete with servants, even up here in the Sierras. Some enjoyed this lake so much they built private estates here for themselves. Places where they could relax and entertain their business friends. Many of the wealthy of the day were successful industrialists, entrepreneurs, businessmen and quite a few were bankers. Two such men that had a common attraction to the lake, also had something else in common. They were, at one time, presidents of the same large company, Wells Fargo. Isaias W. Hellman was a leading capitalist on the west coast. A man with financial interests up and down the state, he purchased over 2,000 acres of land on Tahoe's west shore, near today's Sugar Pine Point (about 2-miles of Tahoe lakeshore). On this ground he had constructed a summer residence with the amenities and features he needed to keep him and his family comfortable while "summering" at the lake. Completed in 1903, for Hellman, this was to mean a majestic three-story home, complete with the essentials of a tennis court, a boathouse and of course, servants quarters. He also filled his summer home with ornate furniture and artistic handmade fixtures. One did need to be comfortable, and Hellman could afford it all, thanks to his banking interests.

The other man, the other president of Wells Fargo to enjoy the lake, so much so, that he also bought some shoreline, was Lloyd Tevis. Tevis had come to California during the great gold rush. But like so many ex-49ers, was to make his money not in the gold fields, but in business. A lawyer, he opened up a practice in San Francisco where he was soon involved in land speculation and banking and was eventually involved in scores of business deals, and always, it seemed, he was making money. Tevis in 1899 purchased lakeshore property, but was to pass away before moving here. His son Will, however, was to build a summer retreat there (now a part of the Tallac Historic Estates). The Tevis family had to sell out to the Pope Family in the 1920's, but their name lives on today, through the annual Tevis Cup 100-mile horse-rider endurance ride. Hellman and Tevis, two bankers with a love for our lake.

JOHN HAINES
A PIONEER

His life wasn't filled with glamour and glory, nor did he become wealthy, and his name has quietly disappeared into the pages of history. But John Haines was an honest and capable man, and a trusted man, and for that he should be remembered. John Haines was also a pioneer of our region, and was one of those unheralded people that helped to build our nation, the west and the Comstock Country. He was born in Canada in 1826, the son of a farmer who'd recently moved there from Vermont. His family moved again, when he was barely six-years of age, to the backcountry of Ohio. There, he worked on the family farm until, at age 17, the call of adventure compelled him to leave the plow behind and head for the Great Lakes, where he found a job as a sailor, spending six years learning how to stand up to howling gales and frigid waters. He might of found a lifelong home on the lakes, but in 1849, when the rumors of a gold strike in a far away place called California reached his ears, he didn't hesitate. Haines went searching and soon joined a wagon train headed west, even managing to get himself appointed as a "captain" on it. The group struck out across the continent, filled with dreams of new wealth and new beginnings, finally arriving in Placerville on the 31st of July in 1849. He was now in the so-called Promised Land, the land of El Dorado.

But for Haines, like so many others, his future wasn't to strike a gold vein. He soon realized that the true wealth of the region was in establishing a successful business. Anything that might make money would do, and so he partnered up with a man named Lyons and opened up a mercantile business in a place that was then called Sacramento City (today's Sacramento). Not content with that, John Haines decided he'd take a run at being the marshal. And even though he had no special training or background in law enforcement, he got himself elected, for people just trusted him to do a good job; and he did. After a few years of this, Haines was getting the itch again to try something new and in 1859 bought a flock of sheep and headed off towards the Comstock Country. Like everyone else, he'd heard of the silver strike, of the Comstock Lode, but had learned to avoid the temptations of becoming a prospector (he'd done that once). He knew the new residents of Virginia City would be hungry for mutton and needful of wool, and he would have made a bundle, but fate and Tahoe's weather stopped him. He'd just gotten over Echo Summit when a blizzard hit, and for 11-days, he was trapped in the Basin. He couldn't make it past Lake Valley. Haines did what he could to protect his herd, but they had nothing to eat for all of that time, and could only lick at the snow for water. By the time the snowstorm was over and he could escape, his sheep were in sad shape, and Haines was barely able to drive them over the eastern grade into the Carson Valley. There he was to spend the winter, while his flock ate and regained their strength.

He came to realize that the sheep business wasn't for him and he sold them to another herder. But he also decided that he loved the area too much to leave, and decided to stay, and so moved into the area to live, becoming one day, a state senator and respected member of the community; John Haines, a forgotten pioneer.

BELLEVUE
AT TAHOE

Visitors from New York used to find themselves ribbed by their friends at home. Friends would ask: "So you went to stay in the nut house?" Or, "I always thought you were a bit crazy." Good natured humor because their friends were visiting Bellevue. The one in New York was a famous, and perhaps infamous institution. But the one in Tahoe wasn't, and actually never would be. But in the late 1880's it was a small resort that had a grand name and a beautiful setting near Sugar Pine Point. It was constructed at what had been a popular camping ground where majestic sugar pines with their long pine cones graced the shoreline and caught the eye of Tahoe resident Billy Lapham. He saw the opportunity to repeat his earlier hotel successes around stateline, where he'd built and operated a thriving hotel. At Sugar Pine Point, he developed an attractive facility for the eastern tourists, a nearly 3-story high luxury hotel, with large spacious rooms and handmade panels, detailed tapestry's, and manicured lawns. Of course that was only a part of the attraction of this new resort he called "Bellevue." He added other amenities like an ornate parlor, a well stocked bar and a billiard salon. At the end of a 100-foot long pier Lapham constructed a combination boathouse-saloon & cottage dormitory. Painted in the standard white, the hotels name was visible halfway across the lake.

The future of the resort looked promising, and Lapham was joined by a new partner: David Kaiser of Carson City. It was he who decided to add some additional amenities to attract the desired crowds, with a fleet of row and sailboats were added. And to make sure the mail steamships docked regularly at the resort pier, Kaiser got himself appointed as the local postmaster, and converted a part of the resort into a post office, to which he gave yet another unusual though refreshing name: "Sunbeam." Together, the partners added a livery service to the north end of the lake, and a score of small individual cottages; each one painted a glistening white. An 1888 article in the "Truckee Republican" was to declare that "Bellevue was the most attractive looking hotel on the west side of Lake Tahoe." It seemed to be the perfect little get-a-way at the perfect location, and despite its funny name managed to do well for several seasons. But fate was against this small resort as a fire in 1893 all but burned it to the ground and it was never rebuilt. The resort's name however was to live on. But sadly, it's the one in New York that comes to mind when we say the name "Bellevue."

BUSTER KEATON
MOVIES

The scenic beauty of the Lake Tahoe area hasn't just attracted millions of visitors each year, it has also attracted the attention of Hollywood producers. Since 1915, over four hundred films have been created in the Central Sierras; a few classics and a few bombs. Movies that ran the gauntlet of themes from high adventure, psycho-thrillers, to contemporary lovestories and comedies. All with Lake Tahoe, or the Truckee River, or the majestic scenery of the Sierras in the background. The classic Tahoe movie is generally considered to be the 1935 adventure-lovestory "Rose Marie." The tale supposedly taking place in the Canadian Rockies, but actually around Cascade Lake and along the shores of Emerald Bay. The movie plot had star Jeanette MacDonald searching for her brother, a fugitive from the law, played by a young Jimmy Stewart, and he's trying to avoid capture by the movie hero, Royal Canadian Mountie Nelson Eddy. In the movie, Eddy of course, couldn't help but to fall in love with the lovely Jeanette, and that set the scene for a musical number and a love-song "Indian Love Call," a song that was to become the centerpiece of the movie. Over 300 extras were used for the film, including 90 Hollywood dancers who were featured in a scene called the "Corn Dance." A mythical Hollywood version of a Native American ritual. Despite the usual screen-writers liberty with the truth, and the predicable ending, thanks to the lovesongs and beautiful scenery, it was to become a successful movie and over time, a classic.

Another film that was made here, was also to reach the status of a classic. Highly praised by today's movie reviewers, but when it came out in 1923 it was a commercial failure. The movie's star and producer was Joseph Frank Keaton, more familiarly known as "Buster Keaton." Partnering with producer Joseph Schenck, Keaton in the early 1920's bought out the old Chaplin Studio and had his own production company. This was the day of silent films, and Keaton was a master at developing plots that mixed action, slapstick humor and drama into a movie short. For a movie he called "Our Hospitality," Keaton selected Tahoe and the Truckee River as his backdrop for a plot that was loosely based on the well-known southern feud between the Hatfield's and the McCoy's. Set in 1831, Keaton played a member of one clan who fell in love with a young lady who belonged to the other family, and he found himself being chased down the Truckee River Canyon by them; mixing in some risky and amazing stunts that he did himself. So risky that when filming them, he nearly drowned in the rapids of the river! During the final scene, Keaton of course had managed to win his lady's hand, and was reluctantly accepted into the rivaling clan, a truce had been called. Unfortunately, audiences weren't especially enthused by the movie plot, but they were thrilled with the exciting action scenes and the beauty of the lake. And that is what, over 80-years later, has made this movie a classic.

DUANE BLISS—
TAHOE PIONEER

His name was Duane LeRoy Bliss, and he put together an empire at Lake Tahoe. Later building a family business that was to dominate much of the lakes early years, he began as an obscure partner and manager of a small bank over at Gold Hill, Nevada. Though he was also to become known as a timber baron, in relentless pursuit of Tahoe's forests, to cut down to fuel his woodmills, he was also known as a man of his word. He might of spent his whole career as a small-town banker, but fate stepped-in when, one day, the bank that Bliss worked in was acquired by the powerful Bank of California. They fired everyone else but kept Bliss on, because he was a first-rate cashier. Soon Bliss was to win the attention and the support of some of the banking officials; influential friends who were later to help him acquire over 50,000 acres of land around Lake Tahoe. For Bliss didn't stay very long as just a cashier. As first, with the considerable help of the Bank of California, he got involved with logging, then with railroads and steamships, all of it in the Basin.

When the logging era was over, and two-thirds of the Basins trees were gone, Bliss just knew that another era was on the horizon. And so to jumpstart a fledgling tourist industry, he moved his logging trains from Glenbrook over to Tahoe City; there to be converted to passenger trains. And from there, Bliss was to initiate rail service between the lake and Truckee (a depot on the transcontinental railway line). The tourists began to flow into the Basin and Bliss was there to serve their needs by developing a steamship service and a major resort on the North Shore. He had quite an enterprise going and a family empire here at the lake; like the mythical Cartwrights of Bonanza fame.

But there's also a small tale to tell about Duane Bliss that showed he was a man of integrity. The year was 1878 when the Murphy bothers (George and James), settled on lands near today's Meeks Bay. They'd worked hard and had been saving their money and had hoped to purchase these lands for a dairy ranch from their landlord, the Central Pacific Railroad. They finally had the $250 purchase price and were just about to make their offer, but then they discovered that Duane Bliss had beaten them to it, having snatched the land away from the railroad just a few days earlier. Soon, loggers working for Bliss's timber company were scurrying around, dropping every large tree they could find, some almost landing on the brothers dairy cows that were pastured near the lakeshore. James Murphy resolved that he needed to talk to Bliss, now! And so he jumped on his horse and raced towards Bliss's home at Glenbrook. As there was no road around Emerald Bay in those days, Murphy made his horse swim across the Bay to the far side and from there on to Nevada and a meeting with Bliss. He had his meeting, and Bliss agreed to sell the land back to the brothers (after he'd harvested its timber). And after that was done, that's exactly what he did, for exactly $250. The Murphy's, minus their trees, had their lands, and Duane Bliss had shown he was indeed, a man of his word.

MULEJUSTICE

Mules usually don't come to mind when you're talking about pioneer day justice. But here and there, in the annals of western history you do encounter the odd tale where a mule played a central role. One tale told of a mule that was to administer justice. Another told of a mule that was to provide an excuse for it. The tale of the first mule took place in frontier California, near Sonora. The year was 1850 and a miner by the name of John P. Jones happened to witness a strange event on a day when he'd come to this Sierra mining town to buy some supplies to take back to his mining camp. Another miner, who'd also come into town for supplies, had been in a hurry and carelessly failed to correctly tie up his mule, and so it easily managed to pull loose from its tie-rope and had wandered into a nearby corral, full of horses who were eating their fill of some fresh hay. Hungry, the mule charged straight for the feed trough and in no time had kicked and bitten its way to the hay pile. The horses of course did their best to fight back, but this little mule was tougher than any of them and they all ran out of the corral and down the street, all of which John Jones observed. He immediately tracked down the owner of that mule and bought it, for he had a use for it.

A man by the name of Joggles happened to live in the same camp as Jones, and he owned one mean, nasty tempered stallion that kicked and bullied all the other horses and pack-stock in the camp. Joggles got a kick out of it, but the other miners were getting frustrated with his cocky attitude and his indifference to their complaints. A little justice was needed, and it arrived when Jones arrived back in camp with his newly purchased mule. Jones placed his mule in the same pasture as the stallion and sat back to see what happened. It didn't take long as the two animals soon went after each other, and despite its best efforts, that stallion was outmatched and soundly whipped by that mule, and the horse took off running. And it kept on running, to Joggles extreme displeasure! And it took all the diplomacy that Jones could muster to keep Joggles from exploding in anger, but justice was served. Then too, there was the tale of that mule that was to provide an excuse for justice. A traveling parson had his one-eyed mule stolen by a man named Bowles. He'd done the deed all right, but Bowles was also a good friend of the judge, who felt bad when he sentenced Bowles to a mandated year in the Territorial Prison. In fact, one-time Bowles had even saved the judges life, and partially because of that the judge was wishing there was some way, he could assist his old friend, but couldn't just let him go free. So the judge sent the prison warden a note. A note that stated that since it had poor eyesight, it really wasn't much of a mule, and that a year was simply too much for this crime, so he asked the warden to let Bowles out after only six months. And too, in the meantime, if the judge could get that traveling parson to forgive the theft, he'd pardon Bowles even sooner. It "was" a justice of sorts, with the help of a mule.

DANCING

If there was anything during the frontier days that every primitive settlement or civilized community held in common, it was a town dance. For someone, some resident, or passing miner or logger or rancher or whatnot, had a fiddle or violin and that was most of what was required. Dances didn't take a lot of pre-planning, nor extensive equipment, nor even a special occasion. They took place nearly everywhere, on wagon trains, in mining camps and logging camps. They were part of the social rituals of barn-raising, weddings, birthdays, and holidays. Especially on days like the 4th of July. They'd start up when the candles were lit, and oft-times last until the rooster welcomed the morning sun. Mark Twain described his joy at a local dance that he'd attended one-time. Describing himself as longing to be a butterfly, high-stepping through the air. He did though have to admit that his waltz and two-step were a bit awkward, and that his dancing skills were unique. Something that was peculiar to him and to kangaroos.

Even in remote communities people would come from miles around to attend a local dance. If the way was far, the ladies would carefully pack their finest dresses in a protective bag and then head off to the celebration. There to transform into a vision of elegance and charm. Sometimes even packing several changes of clothing . . . just to make sure they always looked their best. It was always a surprise to the men, how a lady could manage to create a fashionable dress out of simple calico and lace, but they somehow did, and never failed to wow the men and perhaps, impress the other ladies attending the dance. For a dance was always an opportunity to show off a bit, catch up on the latest news and gossip, and to discuss and solve the nations political and social problems. But sometimes, particularly in our nation's early days, there weren't many ladies living in the western mining regions, but that didn't stop dancing! One 1850's visitor to the California gold camps recounted how he'd attended a dance one evening and there wasn't a lady in sight, but that hadn't dampened the excitement, the enthusiasm and the energy of the evening. It was a strange sight to see however: long-bearded men, in heavy boots and flannel shirts, their faces sun-burned, their belts stuffed with pistols or Bowie knives, smiling and laughing, and jumping around on a make-do dance floor, having a great time. A fiddler was giving his best, and the air was filled with a mixture of music and shouting and the sounds of stomping feet. Despite the lack of female partners, the men were giving the dance all their heart with all of their might. For the dance, some of the men did have to assume the role of a lady, tying a bandana on their sleeve to mark their new identity. And in fact, some mining camps even adopted a rule that declared that any miner with a patch sewed on to the seat of his pants, would automatically "have" to assume the role of a lady during any town dance. But this was usually done without protest for dances were a lot of fun and were always looked forward to. Especially when there were ladies there too!

FATHER PATRICK MANOGUE

Mark Twain puckishly was to comment that "To lead a life of undiscovered sin, that was true joy." No one around to point out your frailties, your shortcomings, your lack of moral character. He also was to proclaim that he had absolutely no confidence in a man that didn't have at least some petty vices. But, in truth, Mark was both a man of solid moral character and integrity. Well, he was anyways when he was around a strapping young priest in Virginia City in the early 1860's. An Irishman, 6 feet 3 inches tall, and weighing in around 250 solid pounds, Patrick Manogue ("Father" Patrick Manogue) was a man of passion, and a man of legend. Not one to overlook the follies of a former river-boat pilot. A most unusual man, Patrick Manogue was born in Kilkinny County, Ireland in 1832. Orphaned at an early age, he migrated to this country the year before the great California gold rush began in 1849. He found work back east, and managed to gain entrance to a college there. But Patrick also wanted to bring his brothers and sisters to this country, and so immigrated west to Nevada City. There, in 1853 he began working inside one of the areas many gold mines, as a miner. Day after day he worked in the semi-darkness, digging and blasting, but he also saved his money. Four years went by, and he finally had enough money to send back home to his siblings, and to follow his dream of becoming a priest. He'd managed to make and save enough money to journey to Paris, there to enroll in a seminary. After several years of studying he was ordained a priest, and found himself in 1862, being assigned to one of the most challenging locations a young priest could ever be sent to. A wild boomtown in Nevada by the name of Virginia City. The church leadership had recognized that only a strong man, a man with conviction and a man who could relate to the rough and rowdy miners could succeed in this new parish. And they chose the right man for the job. Father Manogue was a fighter as well as a man of passion and above all, a man of faith.

The stories of his life in the Comstock grew with the years. Stories how he faced down angry miners to keep them from hurting a mine manager who had threatened to reduce their wages during a market slowdown. Stories how he rushed to the bedside of a sick woman to tend to her needs, after first decking her (church intolerant) pistol brandishing husband who'd tried to prevent him from entering their cabin. And stories about how Father Manogue had ridden 350-miles in snowstorms to obtain a pardon for a man he'd believed was innocent and was about to be taken to the gallows. And stories about how he would literally walk into a saloon and pick up and carry an errant husband away from the gambling tables and back home to his wife. Whatever it took to care for his sinful flock, that's what Father Patrick Manogue did.

PEAK NAMES

Surrounding our big blue lake is a multitude of mountain peaks. Many with well-known names, like "Tallac, Freel, Rose," and "Pyramid." But there are many more peaks surrounding the Basin with names that are less well known to visitors and residents alike, unless you've taken a hike into the Tahoe backcountry or have spent some time pouring over a Basin area quad map. Somewhat surprisingly, not every peak around the Basin has a name, and many still are identified only by a United States Geological Survey number or simply by their elevation. Nowadays, by the way, the process to name a peak can be time consuming and complicated, requiring the involvement of the US Geological Survey, or an appropriate state agency. Anyone proposing to name a peak in this country on federally administered lands must submit that name and the justification for the re-naming to a Board of Geographic Names. And of course, no living person can have their name adopted for a geographic feature in this country. But in the old days, naming a peak was far simpler, and most of the Tahoe area peaks were named after pioneer residents, or in some cases, after notable people of their times. And too, people that didn't even come to Lake Tahoe.

In the Desolation Wilderness, we have "Mt. Price" and "Dicks Peak." Price was named after William Whitman Price. A naturalist from Stanford University, Price was a Tahoe pioneer, visiting the Fallen Leaf Lake area in the late 1890's, he was to make that area his summer home for years. Establishing a boys summer camp in the Glen Alpine Springs area, and later, a resort near the lakeshore, Price was to spend many a summer day hiking the rugged canyons and peaks of the Desolation Valley, and was to leave his name on one of those Sierra peaks. Dicks Peak was named after the old salt of Emerald Bay fame, Captain Dick Barter, even though he seemed to prefer the comforts of a Tahoe tavern than a hike up the sides of a mountain. "Phipps Peak" is another backcountry promontory that was named after a local pioneer, William Phipps. An old Indian fighter who, in the mid 1800's spent 23-years living in the area we now call "General Creek." Another man who was remembered with a local Sierra peak named after him, "LeConte Peak," (located near Pyramid Peak) was never to step foot here, but Joseph LeConte was so honored because he was considered to be the greatest naturalist in the country, and he was heralded as the father of glaciology. A tireless advocate of the theory (radical thinking in his day), that a great ice age had once gripped the world. But finally, there's one Tahoe peak with an unusual basis for its name (Rubicon). It's not named after a person, but a historical event: the 49 B.C. crossing by Julius Caesar of the Rubicon River to fight a battle with a Roman General (Pompe). When the peak was named in the 1870's, the phrase "to cross the Rubicon" was a popular figure-of-speech, indicating that, at that point, there's no going back. An interesting name for a Tahoe peak.

MINERS

OCCUPATIONAL

HAZARDS

When author, lecturer Mark Twain got sick, he had a simple way of treating himself. He'd just (temporarily) give up some of his vices, mostly smoking and drinking. That was, until he felt better, and then he'd go back to his old habits. It worked for him anyways! But the Twain method would not have worked for those ailments and miseries that plagued other pioneer professions. For many of those 19th century pioneer jobs had their share of afflictions. Blacksmiths had their singed hands, and their sore backs. Woodcutters had their blisters, and their constant exposure to a logging or milling accident. Farmers had to face summer heat, winter cold and had their own battles with aching backs and long workdays.

But of all the pioneer professions, none was more dangerous and generated more health problems for its workers than the profession of hard-rock mining. Not only did these hardy individuals have to contend with temperatures that usually exceeded 100 degrees, they commonly had to work in dim light, around scalding water, often having to breathe foul air with suffocating vapors. For especially in our regions Comstock mines, there was rarely decent ventilation, and never any facilities for sanitation. Miners would come out of those thousand foot plus deep tunnels half-blinded and mumbling incoherently. Some men would remain in a daze for weeks before they'd recover enough to go back to work. To add to those conditions, the air pressure variations between the surface and the lower tunnel levels would be enough to trigger a case of the "bends," just like divers might experience should they rush to the surface without properly first decompressing. Miners would also experience what was known as "cage blindness." The cages were essentially elevators that lowered the miners down into the tunnels, and would later lift them back to the surface at the end of their shifts. But sometimes, because of the heat, the bad air, and the darkness, from time-to-time a few miners would imagine they saw a cage waiting for them to step on board, when there was none. It was only an illusion, but a deadly one, as some miners would step into thin air, and fall down a mineshaft. Veterans would keep an eye out for each other, to try to prevent this from happening. And miners took all those risks and miserable working conditions in stride.

But there was one affliction that no one it seemed ever figured out how to deal with. It took place in a Nevada mine. It seems that for some reason, all of the miners who worked there found their hair, their eyebrows, and their beards turning green. From the brightest green to the darkest shades, every man who worked in the tunnels found themselves changing color. They guessed it had something to do with some unusual underground vapors, perhaps something in the ore, but no one knew for sure. But no one quit or complained, for they had to endure far worse things and this was just another part of the job; one of those occupational hazards.

SINGLE MENS PROTECTIVE SOCIETY?

While most clubs such as the Rotary Club, the Kiwanis, and the Lions were established to provide community services and opportunities to socialize, you've probably never heard of the club known as the "Single Men's Protective Society." This was formed by a group of men that banded together to protect themselves from marriage! It was back in the 1870's, in a small but wild town in Nevada. This rip-roaring town of 6,000 inhabitants was made up almost entirely of men, and the towns seventy-two saloons were constantly breaking out with miners fistfights or gunfights. That was, until women started to move into the town, brought in to join their lonely husbands, or single ladies attracted by the prospects of finding a mate among the thousands of eligible bachelors. But this influx of single women was a bit scary for some of these men.

A July 1876 edition of their local newspaper, the "Daily Record" announced that a new association was being formed among the "unprotected male sex," the purpose of the group was for single men to band together so they could protect themselves from the encroachments of the aggressive female sex. The paper went on to state that it was becoming frightful for men in the town as females were arriving from all directions daily, hunting for a husband, and men were becoming afraid to walk on the streets anymore for fear of being snared. The new society had five-dollar dues, and all its members took a pledge to "withstand the wiles of all females who should propose marriage throughout the coming year." But when they were in the middle of their first meeting, behind locked doors there was a sudden banging at the door, and then a loud crash! The door had been battered in and a crowd of angry women stampeded into the room. There was a lot of yelling and screaming as the female intruders chanted their demands to be heard. They weren't going to let a bunch of faint-hearted men form this society if they could help it! And they succeeded, as the Single Men's Protective Society was never heard from again, at least publicly. And judging by the increased number of marriages that took place in town over the next few years, it was clear that the men didn't stand a chance of resisting the ladies anyway. No matter what kind of club they formed.

THOMAS STARR KING.... HE WAS ELOQUENT

He was known for his eloquence, and has been credited by some historians as being the individual that first suggested "Tahoe," as the proper name for our lake, for he preferred that name instead of "Lake Bigler." For a time, Tahoe was officially named after John Bigler, an early-day California governor, who also was a supporter of the Confederate cause. Thomas Starr King also fell in love with our lake, and spent hours sitting on an overlook, admiring the patterns left by the winds, the ever-changing colors, the moods of the waters. But while he held a poetic spirit, he first came here because he was involved in a crusade. Which made some sense because he happened to be a Unitarian and Universalist minister from San Francisco.

Thomas Starr King was a frail man, not especially tall and unusually thin, but he held the heart of a small lion, and his passions were as strong as his unshakeable conviction that he needed to do something, or California might leave the Union and join the south. For Lincoln had just been elected President, and he was well aware that many of the California newspapers had opposed Honest Abe. A war was about to begin, a civil war, and King knew he must throw all of his efforts into a crusade to stir up a patriotic fervor, crying out for loyalty to the north.

He began arguing his cause from his pulpit in San Francisco, then ventured out into the Sierras. A journey that took him into Nevada, to the Comstock to stir up support for the Union, and to blast away at the secessionists that wanted the riches of the Comstock Lode for the south. Virginia City was a frightening place for King for the miners were armed to the teeth. Every man it seemed carried a handgun and a knife stuck in his belt. But King persisted, giving his sermon with a passion that had people mesmerized, even many southerners. And when he was finished, they would stand up and cheer and even throw silver dollars at his feet. King's eloquence made him a legend during his time, and he was credited with helping to convince both California and Nevada to stay with Abe Lincoln; so much so that there is a statue of him in the National Statuary Hall in the Capitol Building in Washington. Thomas Starr King was a man who loved Abe Lincoln and our lake.

BAD SNOW YEAR?

Often we're still enjoying summer, when people around the Tahoe Basin start wondering about what the upcoming winter weather is expected to be. Well over a century ago, while having a meal in Carson City, legendary humorist Mark Twain was to remark that "Sometimes we have the seasons in their regular order, and then again we have winter all summer and summer all winter (in Nevada). It is mighty regular about not raining though. But as a general thing, the climate is good, what there is of it."

But any talk about an upcoming Tahoe winter always brings a few stories to mind about the winter. Certainly Tahoe over the last century has seen its share of nasty storms, and winters that not only left homes buried to the rafters, roads closed and those hardy year-round residents here would end up spending hours of shoveling to keep the doorways clear and roofs from collapsing. Those that were around in the 1930's can remember some doozy Tahoe winters.

And there were certainly other heavy snow years; in the early 1950's, the late 1960's and again in the early 80's. When you live high up in mountain country like we do here, those kinds of winters at least can be expected from time-to-time, but in the high desert lands to our east, while snow is no stranger, blizzard years are rare. The snow-year of 1889-90 was one of those kinds of winters. Only a few days after Christmas, the winds picked up; frigid winds that began howling across the region, and ice began to form around sheltered coves and giant waves slammed against the shore. No boat dared venture across Tahoe. It wasn't long before the snows began to fall. Lightly at first, but as the days slipped by, they grew heavy and inches became feet. The winds piled the snow into heaps that reached 30-feet deep, and 20-foot drifts blanketed much of the region from Tahoe to Virginia City. Trains were stopped, all roads in the area were closed, and even the telegraph lines had been buried. In communities around the eastern foothills people began to run short of food and supplies. It was also a wet and consequently a heavy snow, about 60 pounds per square foot, and soon roofs weighed down by a mountain of snow were collapsing. A two-story building in Virginia City was to collapse, as were a score of smaller structures. After three-weeks of this, food had to be rationed and there wasn't much coal or firewood left anywhere. But characteristically, especially in those pioneer days, people pulled together, and communities not snow-bound rallied to help, even carrying in sacks of flour and potatoes through old Comstock mine tunnels to avoid the snow-drifts and freezing winds. By early February, the skies had cleared and the trains and roads could be re-opened. Truly that was a winter to remember.

JOHN BIGLER AND TAHOE

The year was 1945 when the California legislature finally got around to correcting what had been an outdated and ignored piece of legislation: the 1870 Act that had declared that what everyone today calls "Lake Tahoe," was to be known as "Lake Bigler." The truth was, that people in general simply preferred the Native American name for the lake than the name of some politician.

But despite the controversy over the lake's name, and the debates over what the word "Tahoe," even meant (and even today it's unclear whether "Tahoe" translates into the term "big water," or perhaps its "water in a high place") the man who's name once legally graced our lake was in truth, a man of some integrity and over the years, had earned the respect of the residents of the state.

John Bigler was born in Pennsylvania in 1805. His earliest job was as an apprentice to a printer, and from there he progressed to become a printer, a writer and eventually an editor for a newspaper. John Bigler also came to love the law, attending law school and beginning a small practice back east before packing up all he owned, and heading west, drawn by the lure of gold in California; Bigler, like thousands of others, became a "49er." He drove a wagon of oxen cross country, and after a short time in the gold fields, he settled in Sacramento, where he became a local legend, and was soon to become known as a man of compassion. For while he was living there, Sacramento was to be stricken by a devastating epidemic of cholera. It swept through this young city and in only a few weeks, hundreds of people were sick or dying, and the numbers were growing. Instead of fleeing like so many others did, Bigler not only stayed to help, he tirelessly worked to nurse and care for the sick, and to bury the dead, even though he himself was soon exhausted, and contracted the disease . . . nearly dying from it. But he survived, and gained such a strong reputation that he successfully ran for the office of Governor . . . and he won. Becoming in 1852, the 3rd Governor of the State of California. And later that same year for a time, he was elevated to hero status, when he personally led a rescue party into a snowbound Tahoe Basin, to rescue a group of stranded emigrants. Not only did the grateful citizens of the state name the lake in his honor, a few years later, they re-elected John Bigler to the governor's office.

His vision for the state was bright, his confidence high, and his support for free enterprise and economic expansion was unbridled. Bigler believed that Californians were blessed with a providence that had no parallel anywhere else in the country. That the gold and more importantly rich agriculture and potential for commerce had no limits, and his policies while in office reflected that boosterism, and during his two terms, California's growth and development was explosive. But John Bigler was also a champion of other states rights, even if those states embraced a volatile and morally deplorable practice of slavery. For that reason, as the nation moved towards a Civil War, John Bigler lost the support of many that had once called him a hero, and his name became a synonym for the Southern cause, and throughout California, a slave-free state, the name of John Bigler was no longer held in respect. And so it was that years later, one-day his name was removed from our lake.

BLACK BART
AND JAMES

One of Tahoe's streets is named after a legendary bandit. The street is called "Black Bart Avenue," and is acknowledgment of this man's fame and his bad poetry. For Black Bart (his real name was Charles Boles), was more known for his verse than his success as a stagecoach robber, though before he was caught, he successfully managed to rob twenty-seven Wells Fargo stages. Originally a schoolteacher from New York, Black Bart came to California seeking a new life after the Civil War and drifted into the road agent business. An amateur poet, Black Bart was to establish himself as a unique bandit, when he started leaving some of his verses inside the strong boxes that he'd emptied out. Typical of his verse was: "Here I lay me down to sleep; To wait the coming morrow; Perhaps success, perhaps defeat; And everlasting sorrow; Let come what will, I'll try it on; My condition can't be worse; And if there's money in that box; 'Tis money in my purse." For seven years Black Bart got away with his robberies and his modest poetry, never shooting anyone and never robbing passengers, just stealing the strongbox. He was to become a thorn in the side of the giant banking and shipping company. But all good things do come to an end, for in 1883, Black Bart was caught after he carelessly dropped his hat and freshly laundered handkerchief during a failed holdup. These items were turned over to Wells Fargo detectives, and they were able to identify and track him down from a laundry-mark on the handkerchief. After serving four years of a six-year sentence, Black Bart was to leave prison and then to disappear from public view, perhaps to write a book of poetry.

The man who was largely responsible for capturing Black Bart was the chief of its famed detective division; a man who was also in his time, quite well known around our part of the region, James Bunyan Hume. For long before he became the head sleuth for Wells Fargo, he had built himself a solid reputation as a capable lawman. Hume was elected marshal for the town of Placerville. After that, he was to become the sheriff for all of Eldorado County. Hume was so good as a lawman, that when trouble broke out in the Carson City prison in the early 1870's, the Governor of Nevada personally pleaded for James Hume to come to Carson to take charge of the prison. In 1873, he was recruited to head the law enforcement division of Wells Fargo. He took the job, and was to spend the next 32-years of his life chasing after, and usually capturing the bandits, thieves and robbers that dared prey on Wells Fargo and its customers. When he passed away in 1904, James Hume had established himself as a legendary lawman and he was nearly a saint within Wells Fargo.

But interestingly, if you look around Lake Tahoe, while you do find one named after Black Bart, you won't find a street named after James Hume. Perhaps, he should have learned to write poetry.

HENRY KAISER

He helped to win a war and created one of the most comprehensive health maintenance organizations in the world. And for a time, he made Lake Tahoe his home. His name was Henry John Kaiser, but many knew him as "Henry J." Born in New York in 1882, Henry J. Kaiser was to make a score of lists as one of the last century's most influential movers and shakers. He belonged on that list as he helped to reshape the economy of his time. As a young man, he worked for a gravel and cement dealer in the Pacific Northwest, learning the business inside and out, and learning how to make a profit. Kaiser was to secure a loan and start up his own business, and for the next 30-years, his small but expanding company tackled projects all over the country. He constructed dams and levees, and roadways, and even helped with the construction of the Bay Bridge. Kaiser built highways in Cuba, and supplied concrete for massive projects in Canada.

It was in 1938 that Henry J. in partnership with Dr. Sidney Garfield, established a group-practice, pre-payment health plan for his employees. This was the beginning of what is now called "Kaiser-Permanente." During the war years of the 1940's, Kaiser was to put his enormous resources to work to help this country to victory. He opened shipyards and began to build freighters, that were soon to be called "Liberty Ships." Just to staff his shipyard in Richmond, California, during the war years, Kaiser hired 100,000 employees; many women and African-Americans, and the legend of "Rosie the Riveter" was born. Day and night they worked, and soon his shipyards were launching these ships faster than the enemy could sink them. These ships were to prove critical to our winning the Second World War.

It was in 1939 that Henry J. Kaiser decided to build himself an estate on Lake Tahoe. He'd recently finished working on the Hoover Dam, and was looking for a secluded spot where he could relax and entertain, and he was in a hurry! In characteristic fashion, Kaiser threw himself into this project, and with his fortune and experience he managed to construct that Tahoe Estate in about a month! To accomplish this seemingly impossible task, he used three hundred carpenters, who working 24-hours a day, in three 8-hour shifts, built a score of assorted cottages and homes, an enormous boathouse and yacht club. He even had a guard house placed at the end of a long pier. It was called the "Fleur du Lac," the Flower of the Lake. Though it wasn't owned by Kaiser then, this private estate was to become nationally famous in the early 1970's when the Francis Ford Coppola movie "The Godfather II" was filmed there. Kaiser was to pass away in 1967, and most of his original estate has since been remodeled or removed to make room for exclusive condominiums. But he left a successful business and philanthropic legacy behind, including an estate right here at Lake Tahoe.

A PIECE OF STRING

What's the value of a piece of string? Probably not much, that is, unless your life depended on it. And that happened to two young men nearly 150-years ago in the Carson Valley, just east of the Lake. It was during the early 1860's, and that was a troubled time as miners and immigrants were flooding into the eastern foothills of the Sierras, and a war was stirring between them and the native Paiute Indians.

Into this smoldering country wandered two ignorant, and perhaps foolhardy German adventurers who wanted to do some prospecting. Their search took them through the heart of the foothills and right in to the camp of 500 Paiute warriors; the camp of the great Paiute Indian Chief, Chief Winnemucca. They were quickly grabbed and held hostage, while the chief pondered what to do about them. All the while angry tribe members walked back and forth venting their anger about the white intruders and brandishing their knifes, threatening to do away with them. But the two Germans had a friend in camp they didn't know. A member of the tribe who had once been befriended by some other German explorers, and he talked the Chief into letting them go. So the old Chief told them to leave this country, immediately and go directly to Genoa, where they'd be safe. And to make sure they had a safe passage through the Paiute and Washoe lands, they were given a string of tendon that was tied in a series of knots. And he gave them careful instructions on how to use it, and how to follow the trail to the white settlement. If they strayed, they'd be attacked. So thankful, the two Germans rode off, and several times along the way that day, they were stopped by a band of Indians. And each time they quickly held up the sting with the knots in it. And each time, an Indian brave would take the string and untie one of the knots, and then let them go in peace.

And so they continued their perilous journey, and were only a few miles away from their destination when they heard the thunder of hooves behind them, and turned to see a band of painted warriors. Fearfully, they held up the piece of string with only one knot left in it. A warrior grabbed it, untied that last knot, and laughing, rode off waving it in the air. The two young prospectors looked at each other, took a deep breath and rode off towards Genoa. Grateful for their passport to safety, a piece of string.

BAD STAGE DRIVER

During those days when the stagecoach was the primary mover of people and freight through the Sierras east to the Missouri, there were all kinds of drivers, good ones and bad ones, a few that were great and others that weren't so great. There were those legendary drivers; the Hank Monk's, the Curly Bill's, the Ben Wing's and Pop McCray's, who were heralded as the best in their profession. Then there was a driver by the name of Bill Colby. A young stage driver out of Nevada County, Colby is someone that should of had a different job.

At first he did have a few minor accidents, but his employer chalked that up to being inexperienced. But those accidents continued and the stage company owners became concerned. One day, just as he was about to step down on the brake to slow the stage down, the stage hit a big pothole, and he bounced hard in his seat, and ended up falling off the stagecoach. And the horses kept on going down the road. Fortunately none of his passengers were hurt. Another time, while he was stopped alongside the road doing a quick repair of a harness, and his passengers were standing around stretching their legs, a big grizzly popped up in the middle of the road, and the horses spooked and took off in a fright. They went one way down the road, away from the bear and Colby and his passengers ran the opposite direction; also in a hurry to avoid the grizzly. But then you couldn't really blame Colby for that mishap. After all, those things in the late 1800's around our region weren't that unusual.

But then there was that day when Colby returned to the company office with only the stage horses and no stagecoach or passengers. It seems that on a routine stage run towards Nevada City, that Colby had reached one of those nasty, narrow stretches of road that were constructed out of the side of a mountain. He was heading down that stretch of road when he ran smack into a stagecoach that was headed up that same road! So, being cautious, Colby asked the passengers what they wanted to do. And they all decided to get out and walk around both stagecoaches while Colby tried to steer his team around the outside of the road edge to get past the upward bound coach. Unfortunately he didn't get very far, for the road edge crumbled, and the stage, and the horses all dropped over the edge! The passengers stood by the road, wide-eyed, listening for the crash of the stagecoach on the rocks 300 feet below. But there was no crash, and moments later they were shocked to see the stage horses clamor back up onto the road though minus the stagecoach. For providentially, just below the road, a large tree had caught the stage, and broke the hitch, releasing the team to escape the cliff. Colby survived too, having jumped off his seat to safety, though his unhappy passengers had to walk to the nearest town. However, Colby didn't survive the chewing out he got from his bosses, and he was fired. He just wasn't cut out to drive stagecoaches!

MAN'S BEST FRIEND

We've all heard that a dog is mans best friend. And for some miners that was especially true, for they discovered that faithful old rover could be useful to sneak gold out of a mine. The practice was called "high-grading," and it revolved around the practice of opportunistic mine workers, paid by the shift, of pirating gold (sometimes flakes, sometimes small ore nuggets) out of the mines and under the noses of the mine operators. It was a kind of "do-it-yourself" bonus system; if you didn't get caught. Mine owners went to great lengths to discourage this practice, but miners were too creative for them. So it was that one high-grader struck upon the successful idea to use his big and friendly dog to help him steal a few extra gold flakes each day. During lunchtime, the man was allowed to bring his dog into the mine, where he fed him . . . but what the mine owners didn't know was that the dogs lunch; bacon and gravy-covered biscuits, was spiked with a sprinkling of gold flakes. Flakes that had been stolen during the morning shift. The miner had only to wait until nature took its course that evening and he could recover his stolen gold. The dog, it seemed was never harmed by this.

But other miners had more concern about their dogs health, and also had more pride in their canine friends intellectual prowess. One man sadly lost his dog, after it was struck by a train. He took the case to court, claiming that it was the railroads fault, because they had changed the train schedule, the trains would now arrive a few minutes earlier each day, and they had neglected to inform the dogs owner, who would have immediately relayed that information to his dog. Arguing that his dog wouldn't have been on the tracks if he'd only known the train was due. Unfortunately, he lost his case. There was also JJ McEwen's dog. For years, he'd greeted the local train, where the mail-handler would toss the dog the daily newspaper, and the dog would trot home with it. That was until McEwen changed papers, subscribing to a different paper. From that moment on, the faithful dog refused to carry the newspaper back home. Only when McEwen re-subscribed to the original paper, did the dog resume his paper route. McEwen had only one explanation: his dog obviously believed the original newspaper was the better one; with better editorials and better news coverage. This "man's best friend" was obviously a discriminating canine.

NEW WEALTH

Sometimes, it is possible for someone to actually have too much money! It was clearly the case during the heyday of the Comstock Lode when millionaires were made overnight. Though over time, they were just as quickly to see their fortunes disappear. But for a time, especially in the early 1860's the Comstock mines were pumping out money into the hands of investors, dreamers and plain folk who for the first time in their lives had an opportunity to live the good life. And they didn't hesitate. One of the first highly visible examples of the spending of the new rich was the proliferation of massive brick and stone homes around Virginia City. The simple board structures that were the homes of the soon-to-be wealthy were no longer good enough; for they were no longer impressive enough.

But this was only the beginning of exhibition spending, as new and more unusual ways of displaying extreme wealth began to be seen along the Comstock. One Jerry Lynch decided he needed a new set of shoes for his new prized thoroughbred horse. But plain old iron shoes weren't good enough for Jerry's horse, so he had a custom made set of silver shoes made. And he liked the looks of them so much, that he had a dozen additional sets made for the other twelve horses he also owned. But he was just warming up to the pleasures of having lots of money, for in his new brick mansion, he had a fourteen-foot high walnut headboard carved to cover his bedroom wall from floor to ceiling. Another instant millionaire, Johnathon Parks, paid to have a fresco painter come in from Europe to paint the dark stair landings of "his" new half a million dollar mansion, so that the surfaces looked like sunlit gardens filled with lilacs and aspens. Other new rich, after filling their homes with expensive custom-made furniture, drapes and bric-a-brac also turned to the stables, purchasing silver harnesses on their coaches and teams. And when that seemed to be too mundane, some decided to out-compete the neighbors silver-plated carriage, by plating their harness with gold. One fellow on his wedding night filled his thousand-gallon water tank with champagne. His guests helped themselves to the bubbly by simply turning on a faucet.

Two legendary Comstock millionaires that would taste extreme wealth, and be swept away by it before they lost it all, were Sandy and Eilley Bowers. Just in 1863 they took out a million dollars from Sandy's Comstock mine. On a trip to Europe they spent as much as $20,000 a day in London and Paris buying diamond jewelry, bedroom furniture, glass windows and whatnot to take back to their mansion in Washoe Valley! And to make sure that they maintained themselves at the top of the local social ladder, they brought with them a brass band all the way from Scotland, as entertainers for their next party. They lived to the hilt and seemed to believe they'd be wealthy forever. They weren't, but for a while anyway, they sure enjoyed being rich!

A CHANCE TO
BE A HERO

They were among this regions earliest heroes. Every town of any size had them, including places like Glenbrook, Tahoe City and Truckee. Men who volunteered to drop what they were doing, day or night, and race off to save their town from burning down. To young boys everywhere, other than a circus coming to town, there was nothing more exciting than to watch these red-shirt, leather helmeted firemen race down a street, bells clanging, headed towards a smoking home or a flaming store. These volunteers were critical to the community, as from 1860 to the 1880s nearly every town in and around the Sierras experienced catastrophic fires. For in those early days of clapboard construction, it only took a tipped over lantern or coal oil lamp and the dry wood would catch fire . . . and if not quickly put out, the fire too often got out of hand, spread to its neighboring homes or stores, and a whole city block could be in flames within a few hours. Glenbrook and Truckee had several such destructive fires.

While there was a certain amount of glory to these jobs, and a full measure of prestige, for it was an honor to be in one of these volunteer fire companies; members had to be elected. They came from the ranks of the loggers and the miners, but they were also saloonkeepers, merchants and bank officials. But it was hard and often dangerous work. The flames were hot, the water pressure low, and the volume limited, but they had to get as close as they could to the infernos to drench the burning wood, exposed to blistering heat, hot ashes, choking thick smoke, falling storefronts and smoldering timbers. Many were bruised, cut and battered before the fires were put out. And since this IS snow country, fires in our area would occasionally take place during a freezing snowstorm, and there were stories aplenty of firemen, drenched by their own water hoses, who'd turn into white ghosts as the water froze, coating them in ice. And too, during the heyday of mining, the probability was high the building that caught on fire, the one they were trying to put out . . . held at least a few cases of black powder explosives. But, in spite of these dangers, the risks, the hard work, there was always a waiting list to join one of the volunteer fire companies. After all, it was a chance to be a hero.

KEEPING A
TIGHT LOAD

Those early day roads around the Tahoe area were tough to drive over. Unpaved and unsurfaced, uneven and unfriendly, they demanded a driver use patience, caution and common sense when driving around the lakeshore, especially around the stream crossings. While eventually they all either had bridges or culverts, this regions earliest days saw some "Oh my gosh, hold on to your hats," stream crossings. Like the infamous and deservedly notorious Slippery Ford, which was an especially frisky river crossing that made even hardened teamsters nervous, and frightened less seasoned travelers in and out of the Tahoe Basin. There were accidents and incidents, a few serious. But most often, it'd be a wagon or stagecoach that rolled in the swift current, spilling passengers into the cold waters. Appropriately wary of these early day roads, veteran area merchants learned to carefully prepare for their daily summer trips around the area. Their wagons loaded down with anything from dairy supplies and flour, to garden vegetables; all fresh from

Glenbrook. They knew well that if they didn't take care to tie everything down good and tight, they'd risk some valuable cargo bouncing out.

Though, there was the time in 1890, when Stateline area resident John Averill decided to give his regular, and experienced driver Bill Hanlon the day off. Averill made a mistake, when he rushed off without securing his freight, as Hanlon would have done. And a 250-pound side of beef slipped unnoticed out of the back of his wagon when he bounced across a water crossing. By the time he realized what happened, it had floated away. He eventually found it . . . downstream, miles away. That same thing also happened one time to another new freight driver, whose shipment of whiskey barrels was carelessly loaded and so when he hit a stream crossing near the Carson River, his barrels did what barrels do, they rolled, and he suddenly overturned into the surging waters. The barrels of course did the next natural thing, they floated away. And it took days before the hapless driver could recover his lost load. But not before one barrel developed a leak and emptied out some high proof alcohol into the river, leaving a few tipsy fish and a freshly educated driver about the importance of always keeping your load tight. Which even today is still good advice.

HARVEY WEST ...
A MAN WHO GAVE
SOMETHING BACK

He may have started out making all of $1.75 an hour in a lumber camp, cutting down trees for a living, but he ended up owning most of Emerald Bay. Harvey Edward West was an unusual man, but he was a talented man, and a generous one. He donated the lumber for the American Legion Hall on the south shore, the public library in Pollock Pines and the Seventh Day Adventist Church in Camino. He also donated money, lots of it: $18,000 for lights for a ball field in Placerville, $65,000 for a chapel in Pollock Pines, $12,000 for St. Theresa's, $45,000 for a boy scout camp at Echo Lake and $175,000 for a park stadium in Santa Cruz. A half a million dollars for charity just in a few years. Harvey West was a successful and enterprising lumberman in our area during the war years of the 1940's, operating logging mills in places like Tahoe Valley, Sly Park, China Flat, Pacific House,

Diamond Springs and Placerville. He once owned 30,000 acres of land around Silver Fork and Pollock Pines in the 1940's. West's mills worked overtime to quench the nations thirst for timber products.

But while Harvey West ran a local logging empire, he also had a fine eye for beautiful scenery, and appreciated that a stately pine tree could also be valued for its beauty instead of just for its board feet. West owned nearly 3,000 acres of timberland near Kingsbury Grade, but had long admired the natural beauty of Emerald Bay, and had longed to own a piece of it. A place for his family; but it had never been available. Lora Knight, the builder of Vikingsholm wasn't going to sell at any price. But a few years after her passing, in 1945, much of the Bay was now owned by a Nevada cattleman, Lawrence Holland. And Holland was interested in a land trade with West, and a swap was made. The next several years Harvey West spent his summers living at the lake with his family. The family moving into the spacious Vikingsholm, where West would while away the warm Tahoe days sipping brandy on the front veranda. By the early 1950's, the heyday of West's logging empire was gone, and it was time to move on. He at first tried to sell his beautiful Emerald Bay estate through the Wall Street Journal, but soon had second thoughts and negotiated a deal with the State, once again generously giving away half the value of the land so that a park could be created there. Harvey West, a man who loved to give.

GIANT POWDER

The miners hated to use the stuff, for it was dangerous and far too often would explode unexpectedly; a single spark would set it off. Who could forget the thunderous explosion that rocked Virginia City in June 1873, when a building seemed to vaporize! Small wonder, because inside was stored a veritable warehouse of black powder, and too, there were six cases of nitroglycerine. It was an accident, as some believed that a lamp got knocked over onto a can of black powder by the warehouse owners pet; a monkey. A bit of monkey business that cost this simian his home; and his tail. When a Swedish chemist and engineer by the name of Alfred Nobel invented dynamite, then called "Giant Powder," life in the mines became a bit safer. And after some testing, it became "the" standard explosive in the Comstock. And of course, this spawned a new industry, as several manufacturing centers opened up. A powder-works in San Francisco and the Santa Cruz area supplied the region with the explosive.

It was also a popular tool here at the lake. For during the heyday of logging, both black powder (in spite of its bad reputation) and dynamite were used to do a variety of tasks.

They were used to clear away a grade for roadways, flumes, and railroad tracks. This was the easiest way to remove boulders, and it was invaluable for creating drainage channels for the streams that fed the miles of v-flumes that criss-crossed around the Basin slopes. And the explosives also had another use here. Besides logging activities that focused on cutting the massive Tahoe trees into various sizes of lumber, there was a thriving cordwood industry. It was such a big part of the areas economy, that several of the flumes here were constructed specifically to carry cordwood. Wood that would be used to fuel steam engines and warm homes. Several hundred thousand cords of wood were shipped from here each year. While much of that wood was split by hand; most often by local Chinese crews, a lot of cordwood was created directly by inserting powder charges into holes drilled into the trees. Called "powder wedges," they would split logs, uproot stumps, and were even used to fell large trees, however wastefully. So the Tahoe quiet was often shattered by the sounds of explosions. The miners hated to use black powder, but it was popular here, as long as there were no pet monkeys around!

HE MADE AN OMELETTE OUT OF AN EGG

Before the discovery of gold, the ranches and farms of central California easily provided enough meat and vegetables to meet the needs of every resident. After the discovery, with thousands of people arriving every month, things changed, and for a time there wasn't enough of most things that a growing state-to-be needed. Not enough cattle and corn, or sugar or cloth or leather or steel, or even tobacco. There was a market of scarcity, where demand far exceeded supply. And soon, besides gold seekers, enterprising merchants also began to flood into California. A few brought with them the seeds of a new industry: tanneries, textile mills, sugar refineries and iron works. Though most others brought short-lived dreams and a few scams. For not one man in ten who had his own business in 1849 was still in business just 5-years later. But, especially during the early days of the gold rush, there were opportunities, and some were quite unusual.

In addition to those that freighted pots and pans, shovels and pickaxes cross-country was a man who in 1851, gathered up a cargo of cats, and had them shipped from Mexico into the gold camps, betting there would be a demand for them to help keep rats and mice at bay and provide company to lonely miners. He was right, and other merchants and miners flocked to him, and he sold out, selling the mousers for $8 to $10 each.

Another unique business opportunity involved chickens, or actually one of their byproducts, fresh eggs. There couldn't be enough fresh eggs to satisfy the demand, or so an eastern farmer surmised. So he decided to take a chance, and borrowed all the money he could and gathered or bought up fifteen hundred dozen eggs and had them packed in sawdust and ice and shipped all the way to San Francisco by way of a clipper ship. Every day as the tall masted ship plowed its way through the waves to the west the farmer worried. He might not sell all of his eggs. He might have misjudged the demand. After nearly three-months on the oceans his ship docked in the Bay, where the still-worried farmer found a broker and quickly unloaded, selling all of his eggs, for thirty-eight cents-a-dozen. But after he'd done that, he was shocked to see that around town, fresh eggs were selling for ten times that! And he ran back and repurchased what was left of his shipment, and took them to Sacramento, where he sold every last egg for a handsome profit. This was one early-day businessman who made an omelette out of an egg.

DONNER TRAIN MEMORIES

The Central Pacific Railroad was completed in May 1869, joining with the Union Pacific at Promontory Summit, Utah. A major improvement in this nations transportation system, the railroad transformed the way people moved through the mountains and deserts and they made the trip safe. Gone was the enormous difficulty, the risks, the strain of cross-country travel. And no-other group in the history of the west could appreciate the construction of the Central Pacific more than the members of the Donner Party.

It was barely twenty-three years earlier, that eighty-seven people set out for California. It was early summer, and they were full of hopes and dreams, but they in fact were headed for tragedy. For only forty-seven survived. George Donner was elected their party leader, a sixty-two year old farmer from Illinois who was selected not because he had any experience with leading wagon trains, but simply because he was respected and he was a well-liked man.

George's wife was Tamsen, a former schoolmistress. Tamsen was a petite woman, barely five feet tall and not even a hundred pounds, she had the courage of a lion and the soul of a saint. Both George and Tamsen had previously been married, and between them had five children. The youngest, not quite four, was Eliza. They were just ordinary people. Farmers and merchants, no different than all the others that had preceded them on that long perilous journey across the country. But they had the misfortune, largely due to some poor decisions, and just plain bad luck, to end up at the foot of Donner Summit just as the first heavy snows of that winter dumped snow on the pass; one of the heaviest snowfalls as it turned out, in memory. Several men did manage to slog their way over the pass to Sutter's Fort in Sacramento, to find help, but that wouldn't come until the following spring of 1847. Fifteen desperate people from the lake, who didn't want to wait any longer, struck out towards the Sacramento Valley, but only seven made it, two men and five women. One man, Charles Stanton, who did make it safely to California, turned back to the aid of the snowbound women and children still camped at Donner Lake and Alder Creek, and was to die a little-known hero, of exhaustion and starvation in the mountains. Back at the lake waited George and Tamsen, and their children. But George was dying, and Tamsen had refused to leave him despite several opportunities. Slowly, rescue parties were beginning to arrive, and Tamsen made certain her children would be cared for, arranging to have them taken to safety. First lovingly combing their hair, and then dressing them in their finest clothes. Eliza in her quilted petticoat, woolen stockings and woolen coat with its red hood. And Tamsen, seeing them off, then said good-by to her children, returning to George's bedside. There she would perish along with her beloved husband.

Years later, little Eliza, now grown up with children of her own, was to ride the Central Pacific as it traveled so effortlessly past Donner Lake. She had a window seat, and as the train passed the lake, she stared intensely at it. Lost in her thoughts and memories, of her mother and father.

ALEXIS VON SCHMIDT

He was a good engineer, well respected and a man of some influence in his day, the 1860s and 70's. But he was also a man destined to generate controversy, especially when it came to Lake Tahoe. Born in Prussia in the 1820s, Alexis Waldemar Von Schmidt was lured to California in 1849 by the discovery of gold. Although Von Schmidt was a skilled surveyor, his first job in the golden state, was (like so many others), as a gold miner. And like most, he failed to strike it rich and ended up having to look for a paying job. And he found one as a surveyor, working for the US Surveyor General in San Francisco. Over the next few years, as he watched new communities spring up and grow around the region, he became aware of the importance of finding and supplying fresh drinking water for these communities . . . and so it was than Von Schmidt became involved in several water companies. He even engineered the first water system for the City by the Bay.

His water interests were to bring him to Lake Tahoe,

which he saw as a natural source of drinking water for San Francisco. With five others, he formed the Lake Tahoe & San Francisco Water Works Company, and announced plans to pipe Tahoe's waters through a 163-mile long aqueduct he hoped to build to the Bay Area. While he was working on the necessary financing and political support for the project, Von Schmidt forged ahead with his plans, beginning construction on a dam at Tahoe City, and initiating a survey along the Truckee River for a planned diversion canal. His proposal however stirred up a storm of protest over who owned Tahoe's waters; the two states, or the federal government? And who controlled its uses? And so, as it turned out, Von Schmidt's plan failed. He never got the financing or the support he needed and the lakes waters went untouched.

But a few years later, Colonel Von Schmidt (as he was known by now), was to stir up yet another Tahoe related controversy. For years, the state line boundary between California and Nevada was in dispute. The original eastern boundary of California was loosely based on the Sierra Nevada Range, though not on the highest peaks, and several early day surveys hadn't cleared up the confusion. So it was that in the early 1870's, the California legislature resolved to conduct a final survey to determine the boundary between California and Nevada and they hired none other than Von Schmidt to do that survey. Von Schmidt surveyed his way through the area, re-mapping the boundary line. But in doing so, he moved the boundary (some say it was a mistake, and others say it was intentionally unfair) several hundred yards to the east, in effect, giving California a million or so more acres of land that been considered to be a part of Nevada! That set off another uproar that wasn't settled until 1899, when another survey was completed. Eventually in 1980, the U.S. Supreme Court supported his survey. Alexis Von Schmidt may have been a good surveyor . . . but somehow, when it came to Lake Tahoe, he had a knack for generating controversy.

HORSE RACING AT TAHOE!

Horses have long been a part of the Tahoe and regional history, both as beasts of transport, and for pure sport. They've pulled the countless stages and wagons and carts of the Basin pioneers. They've also been the subject of countless wagers around the lake. In fact, horse racing was one of the Basins earliest spectator events. Back in the 1880's, near Meyers, there used to be a dirt and gravel racetrack. A half-mile long oval was home to weekend races that used to bring fun-seeking residents from all around the area. Over near stateline, at a place then called "Rowlands Station," a one-mile long race course was laid out near the sandy beach of Tahoe, and on holidays such as the 4th, people would pack into their wagons and line up along the route and cheer on their favorite jockey. Usually a local logger or rancher; riding his horse named "Lightnin," or possibly "Old Abe." Around these parts, a formal racetrack wasn't always necessary, as many an impromptu horse-race would start after a few rounds in the local way station saloon, and after a quick wager, and details of the race agreed-upon, the semi-sober contestants would grab their ponies and race down the lakeshore, for glory, a few dollars, and best of all, perhaps a prize of a free drink; courtesy of the loser.

There was also once that strange contest between two soon-to-be Comstock millionaires, William Sharon and William Ralston, who bet a bundle on a horse-race between Carson City up to Glenbrook. One rider was to go by way of the Kings Canyon route. And the other via a road near Clear Creek. The race was run, but the hard-driving Sharon, a passionately competitive man, whipped and drove his horse so hard that he injured it, and couldn't finish the race, giving Ralston the default victory. As the years went by, all of the Basin's racetracks disappeared. But here and there, they were replaced with horse arenas. Especially noteworthy was the one over at Glenbrook. Built in the 1930's by the Bliss family, during the 30's and 40's, it was to become the site of a popular Sunday event: the Glenbrook Rodeo. With its bronco busting, calf roping, barrel racing and wild cow milking contests, it used to be a mainstay summer event of the east shore. And from time-to-time, there would be a cheer, as a starting pistol would fire and a horse race down the lakeshore would be on, just like in the old days.

HOLE IN THE BOTTOM?

On a calm clear day on Lake Tahoe it's fun to look down into the blue depths to search for a fish, or try to make out the details of the rocks on the bottom. But according to a story first printed in an 1883 edition of the "Carson City Morning Appeal," there may be something else on the bottom to look for: a hole.

The story, written by Comstock editor Sam Davis, told a tale that has become a Tahoe classic. It all began when a San Francisco stockbroker, nearly broke from his misadventures in the wild Virginia City stock-market, decided he needed a vacation, and went on a fishing trip to Lake Tahoe. Here, he rowed out about a mile from shore near Carnelian Bay, and while sitting there waiting for a fish to bite, noticed that his rowboat was slowly spinning around. So the broker, a man named William Meeker, looked down into the lake's waters and discovered he was floating over a hole in the lake! Water was flowing down a 4-foot hole about a hundred feet down, towards somewhere, and Meeker thought he knew where.

So he rowed back to shore then ran off to contact another broker friend of his, one Colonel Clair; a rather ruthless but successful Bay Area stock speculator. For when Clair & Meeker decided that Tahoe's waters just had to be flowing into the mines over in Virginia City, they knew they were on the verge of a major hustle. You see, at the time, most of the deep Comstock mines were plagued by flowing subterranean waters that required massive and expensive pumps to keep them dry so the silver ores could be mined. After Meeker confirmed their theory by tossing a piece of wood with his initials on it into the hole in the lake and having it turn up in a Virginia City mine a few days later, they were on their way. After first constructing a giant plug for that hole in the bottom of Tahoe, which they could raise or lower at will, they went about buying up thousands of shares of inexpensive mining stock. Then they dropped the plug into the lake. The waters stopped flowing into the mines, making it far easier & cheaper to extract the silver and boosting mine stock prices and making millions for Clair & Meeker. But unfortunately for Meeker, his partner turned out to be a bit of a skunk as he ended up being done in by a greedy Colonel Clair & was lowered into that hole in the bottom of Tahoe. When after a few days, his body mysteriously turned up deep inside a Virginia City mine, no one back then ever knew how he got there.

A tall tale . . . certainly, but just perhaps there really is a hole in the bottom of our lake; you never know.

HOWARD
AND JAMES

Nevada once had a legendary recluse, a millionaire if not billionaire named Howard Hughes, a mysterious figure who'd once been in the limelight, but in his later years preferred to live in the shadows. But as unique as Hughes was, he wasn't the first or the only person in history who chose to live as a recluse after living a normal life. For long before Howard, there was Stewart McKay. A native of Nova Scotia, McKay came to live in Truckee in 1873. He opened up a hotel; a very successful one, and went on to invest his earnings in other area businesses. Purchasing a sawmill, and several mines and a score of investment properties in Nevada, McKay was to become one of the wealthiest people in the region. But in his later years, Stewart McKay was to turn his back on his money. He sold everything and moved into a small cabin in the forest, where he reportedly wore rags and lived on a diet of baked potatoes, stale bread and water.

There was also James "Matthew" Harbin. He was one of the first people to strike it rich in the California gold rush; a true pioneer, adventurer, soldier, and explorer. He was also a hermit, a recluse who had millions of dollars in his bank account! Harbin was all of 21-years old when he first reached Sacramento. He didn't stop there, joining frontier expeditions to southern California, where he enlisted in the upstart Yankee militia in a war with Mexico. Wounded and taken prisoner, Harbin sat in a cell for nearly a year before the war ended and he was released. But his fortunes really took off after that, for he borrowed some money and bought himself a land grant near Sacramento and stocked it with cattle and horses, and for the next ten years, he ran a ranch, selling beef to the flood of 49ers that streamed into the state. He made a killing, figuring his net worth was three million dollars by 1858. Harbin was one of the states first millionaires when a million dollars was really worth something. He left ranching and went to Nevada, the Comstock Lode and there, he made yet another fortune! Striking it rich with mining, lumber and even oil ventures. Harbin went on to win and lose more fortunes. One day though, he up and decided he'd had enough of the demands and hassles of running a business empire. Perhaps he was worn out, tired, and perhaps he just needed a change . . . but one day Harbin simply departed for the solitude of the Mexican desert. He left everything behind him, and for the next twenty years, until his passing, Harbin, a rich man, lived the way he wanted, the life of a hermit. Just as Howard Hughes did a century later.

A HAIR-RAISING
RIDE

Stagecoaches were normally used for basic transportation; getting from here to there. But surprisingly often they were also used to have fun. Though there were occasional mishaps and serious accidents! Often a race would start because of competition, or because of pride or just on impulse. But a steady gallop down a mountain road would be transformed into a running, all-out, white-knuckled, hair-raising ride!

A race started when a stage came within sight of another coach, owned by a rival company. The drivers would crack the whip, and away they'd go! The passengers variously screaming in delight and fright; often placing wagers on the spot as to their chances of overtaking the leader and being the first to reach the nearest way station. Most often the race would only last a mile or two, and then the drivers would settle back down to a steady pace.

But sometimes the unexpected happened, as was shown in an 1876 story recounted about Tahoe-to-Truckee stage driver John (Jack) Hanscomb. The coach was loaded down, with huge Saratoga trunks lashed to the top and rear compartment, along with scores of smaller suitcases, handbags, valises and hatbags. All belonging to the sixteen passengers who'd been staying at the elegant Tahoe City Grand Central Hotel, but were now heading to the Truckee train station, heading home. But first, they were taking Hanscomb's stage. The first few miles went by without incident. The road was dry although dusty and Hanscomb whipped his six-horse team into a leisurely pace. Until up ahead, he spotted another coach, driven by competitor Henry Burke. As he drew closer, the dust kicked up by Burke got thicker and more annoying, and Hanscomb began to grow impatient for he was also running a bit late. Soon he'd had enough following, and resolved he'd try to pass Burkes stage and let Burkes passengers eat dust! And a race began. Hanscomb cracked his whip and his horses lunged forward, and the gallop became a run. Burke instantly aware of what was happening, did the same thing, whipping his horses into a full run, and on they raced down the Truckee River Canyon, with passengers hanging on for dear life they went! It was then, it happened! A brake rod snapped on Hanscomb's stage, and he lost control. The stagecoach skidded and, loaded down, fell over a thirty-foot embankment and slid to a halt. The stage was destroyed, and clothes were all over the ground and floating down the river. The passengers were thoroughly shaken up, but otherwise ok. Impromptu participants in an exciting stagecoach race that was now over.

A KNIGHT OF THE LASH

He was a traveling actor, a man whose stagecoach was literally a stage. Rolling along thru the Sierras, bouncing on rocks and potholes, swaying in the wind and smothered in dust, usually too hot or too cold, but still a perfect place for a master entertainer, if he also happened to be a stagecoach driver like the legendary Hank Monk.

A melancholy man, subdued yet intense, he also possessed a wry and creative mind that was full of humorous observations about human nature, honed by years of watching his passengers. Hank Monk was a youth of twenty-three when the excitement of the gold rush swept across the country. And he was swept up in it. Though it took a few years to save enough money to get here from New York, Hank managed to book passage on a ship and landed in San Francisco, looking for adventure, and a job. Within a week, he had the job, driving a stagecoach from Carson City to Placerville. And he was a natural! Driving a team of six grain-fed horses navigating through Sierra passes, skillfully cracking the whip, pulling the reins, yelling out encouragement to his steeds, Hank quickly became an expert "Knight of the Lash," and his fame began to spread.

Passengers would pile aboard his stagecoach, his stage, and the curtain would begin to rise. For a stage driver was also a major part of the journey. They didn't just drive the team, they regaled the passengers, and that was part of the fun! As soon as everyone was loaded aboard, passengers when they could, squeezed in on top of the stage, close to Hank, and the stories would begin. Hank dead-panned, spinning fantastic and totally untrue yarns about Indian attacks, and tales of grizzly bears jumping out of the woods and eating the horses. Or tales about bandits waving shotguns waylaying his stage and fleecing his hapless passengers. The stage rolled on, with Hank continuing his all-serious monolog, his passengers thoroughly engrossed with his fanciful tales, dismissing them as only that, yet they hung on to every word. He especially, loved to poke fun at the timid or inexperienced traveler, taunting them with vivid warnings about possible rock-slides, and the likelihood of losing control and the stage rolling over, or off a cliff. But it was all in fun, and most knew it. And while he may not have found the adventure that he'd once sought the day he arrived in California in 1852, he'd become a master at "inventing" adventure, for he'd become an actor on wheels.

THE METEOR

In 1939, she was slowly towed out into the lake by a small steamer out of Camp Richardson, to a spot five or six miles north, where the charts showed a submerged peak under Tahoe's blue waters. A cold wind was blowing that morning and waves were lapping against her hull. Then, her valves opened wide, she was let loose and allowed to slip beneath the surface; dropping 900-feet to the bottom to darkness and into history. Her name was "Meteor," and now she was gone. She'd been on the lake since 1876. An eighty foot-long workhorse, originally built to tow huge rafts of logs to the nearest mills, for over twenty years she battled storms and strained against thousands of massive sawlogs, without missing a day. Later, she was converted to carrying passengers, and here too, for years more, the Meteor served the lakers faithfully.

But her proudest moments were to take place during an 11-month period. It was in October 1879, that her Captain, Ernest J. Pomin told his crew to polish the brass extra bright, and swab the decks extra clean, for they were expecting an important passenger! A recent President and Civil War hero: Ulysses Simpson Grant. They picked him up in Tahoe City took him and his companions over to Glenbrook, where he then headed off to a visit of the Comstock. Eleven months later, the Captain told the crew to polish the brass again, for the Meteor was hosting another special passenger. This time it was President Rutherford B. Hayes and his group, also on a whirlwind trip of the Comstock. The sturdy steamship proved she could proudly host touring VIPs as well as tow log-booms across the lake.

But strangely, years earlier, on her launching day in 1876 there were grave doubts she would float, even by some of the men who put her together. For the Meteor was Tahoe's first iron-hulled steamship. One man in particular, was absolutely convinced the heavy hulled vessel wouldn't last long once she was let down the boat-way of Glenbrook, that she'd sink within seconds of hitting the water. He was the editor of the Carson City Appeal. On this momentous occasion he'd been invited by the ships builders and owners to celebrate the event and capture the moment in a news story. But after walking around and on the steamer, he became so skeptical it'd float, he wrote his story detailing the launching and the immediate sinking of the Meteor even BEFORE she was christened and launched! The editor confidently even bet a bottle of red eye that she'd go down. But to his surprise and chagrin, the new steamer hit the lake with a splash and then bounced up again, rising high in the water. And so she did float. For over sixty years! Towing logs, carrying passengers, and on two occasions, men who had been or were President of the United States. Not a bad record for Tahoe's first iron-hulled steamer, the Meteor.

THEY CALLED
IT JUSTICE

Anyone who has done research into our area's colorful history comes to recognize, when the wave of European-based civilization washed over this region in the mid-1800's, it also brought with it a revolution of new cultures, increased populations, major changes in land uses, and enormous societal changes. New citizens to our region brought with them the desires to establish their own framework for a government, with appropriate civil laws and a system for justice. Sweeping away what had been there before, established by the early Spanish settlers and the Native Americans. Something more "organized and formal," but in comparison to today's norms, still relatively primitive.

Most notable, were the commonly accepted punishments that were meted out to the lawless during the mid to late 1800's in our region. Punishments that have long since been replaced with more humane methods of treatment. One of the least harmful, but common early day rules was to "banish" a lawbreaker from the area for crimes such as rowdy behavior or even robbery. Lawbreakers who received this sentence from a court of miners or loggers could consider themselves quite lucky. Others were somewhat less fortunate for their stealing. George Ruspas and David Reise, both lost an ear as penance for what they'd done in Washoe Valley in 1860. They stole a yoke of oxen from an unguarded freight wagon. An impromptu jury of locals took a vote and decided that the two men should suffer this penalty for their actions. After the sentence was carried out, both Ruspas and Reise were released, and told to go on their way, which of course they did, quickly.

Then, too there was that well-used punishment of tarring and feathering. This was the sentence of choice when the crime was notably unsavory, like insulting a lady, or being obnoxiously objectionable to a town's citizenry. One fellow (a W. J. Jones) found himself bound and gagged by a party of men, a local vigilance group, and taken to a bubbling kettle of hot tar. And there, he was deprived of his clothes, thoroughly coated with the hot goo, and then plastered with a basket of feathers. His clothes were then returned to him, and he was guided to Truckee, there to take the train to somewhere else, which he did.

Then there was the 1879 case of James McCarthy. He had a nasty temper, and nor was he a good husband either, for he tended to take his anger out on his poor suffering wife. But one day, the good citizens of Carson had enough of this brute, and decided enough was enough, and resolved to teach McCarthy a lesson. After a short trial, they convicted him of being a bullying husband, and for his sentence, he was tied to a fence post in front of the Capital building for all to see, a sign placed over his chest: "wife-beater." This justice apparently worked, for never again did McCarthy take his anger out on his wife.

I HAVE COME
TO SEE THE
ELEPHANT...HUH?

Nowadays, we usually only see or talk about them after a visit to the circus, or to the zoo. But during the mid-years of the 19th century, the elephant, although still an exotic animal on this continent, was something of an icon, a widely known symbol of adversity and hardship and challenge. For the term "I Have Seen the Elephant," was used throughout the country; especially by the 49ers and immigrants who'd faced Indian attacks, floods, fever, starvation and storms on their way to, or in, the goldfields, and not always successfully.

Why the majestic elephant was chosen to represent hardship was derived from a story that made its rounds in the east and mid-west, early in that century. A farmer, who'd grown up in the remote backsides of the country had wanted to see a real life elephant his entire life. He'd heard about them and had even seen a picture once, but he couldn't believe such an animal really existed. But one day, that farmer heard about a circus coming to town, and they had an elephant with them! A real elephant! The day they arrived, he loaded up his wagon, dressed up in his best suit of clothes and headed off down the road to find them. At a turn in the road, just outside of the big-top, he spotted the elephant. He was enthralled, but his horse, who hadn't seen an elephant either, wasn't, and reared up in a panic, tipping the wagon and spilling out the farmer and all of his belongings. Then the frightened animal raced off back home, leaving the farmer dazed and afoot. Some people ran over to help out the hapless farmer; his suit ruined and head bruised. They offered their sympathy for what had happened, but the farmer just smiled and said "I don't care, because at least, I got to see the elephant!" So it was that the elephant came to be seen as the embodiment of the unseen and uncontrollable terrors and travails of the west. There was no embarrassment in "seeing the elephant," or having to back off or quit. For the elephant was to represent those things that were just too big to handle; like floods and storms. And many were a pioneer that would say "Well, I sure saw a part of the elephant."

During the mid gold rush years, the meaning of the term was slightly revised as "I've found the elephant," or "I'm off to see the elephant," came to mean a miner struck it rich or was trying to. And so it was that an animal more common to Africa and India came to become a unique part of OUR history.

LINCOLN HIGHWAY

Part of the Tahoe story, is its roads. This nation's first transcontinental highway came right through the Lake Tahoe Basin. Called the "Lincoln Highway," it was a grand experiment, and it provided an opportunity for a national test. The Lincoln Highway connected New York with San Francisco, and while that did improve the nation's interstate road systems a bit, it was still primitive. More of a hodge-podge than a coherent system of roads. Roads would often just dead-end at a county or a state line. And it wasn't just a matter of convenience and comfort as there were national defense concerns too. World War I had clearly shown that this nation's defenses would need to depend upon its armed forces being able to move quickly from one shore to the other with the necessary troops and equipment. The War revealed how horses and mules were just too vulnerable to enemy weaponry, so the US Army decided on a test to see just how much time and trouble it would require to send a convoy of vehicles across the country; using the Lincoln Highway.

The trip was to be operated under assumed wartime conditions, where all bridges, tunnels and facilities were supposed to have been destroyed by secret agents from an Asian country. This was only 1919, but cautious eyes were already looking towards Japan.

The convoy was commanded by Lt. Colonel Charles McClure, but he was joined by a young captain that was bored at the time, looking for something interesting to volunteer for. The young captain was Dwight D. Eisenhower.

There were 60 trucks, staff cars, motorcycles, transports and even a pair of ambulances; about 285 officers and enlisted men: drivers, engineers, mechanics and soldiers. And they had a tough time of it. Vehicles often broke down on the potholed roads, or bridges were either too small or too flimsy to handle the weight of the convoy. One day in the Nevada desert they ran into a raging sandstorm and every vehicle had to be pulled thru a massive sand-dune blown across the road. Eventually, essentially following today's Highway 50 route, they pulled into the Tahoe Basin, where after a short ceremony, they headed off towards Sacramento. From there they headed to their final destination, San Francisco. It took them two months to complete the journey. Thank goodness there was no war going on at the time! The trip was such an experience for Captain Eisenhower, when he later became President, he made sure federal funds were set aside to construct a high quality system of interstate highways across the country.

IF ONLY...

Of all the tales of the people that once lived here at the lake during the 19th century, one poignant incident often comes to mind. A few years after the Civil War, the Carney family established a way station right on the stateline. They had a thriving business, and had reason to believe that Tahoe was a wonderful place to raise their four young children. But, one night in 1876, an old friend, a fruit peddler, happened by for a visit. The Carney's didn't know that the man was recovering from a contagious disease, diphtheria, and all of the children were exposed, and two of their little girls, Ellen and Catherine were to be afflicted; falling to the disease after only a day. Mrs. Carney, in a mix of despair and love, carefully lined their pine coffins with the finest and most cherished fabric she had; her wedding dress. They were buried in a plot near today's Bijou.

This isn't just a tragic tale, it is also an illustration of the sometimes harsh reality of the world barely a century ago, especially the primitive state of health care. But pioneer physicians were not aware of antibiotics, and it would be years before they would become a common medication. Even during the turbulent years of the Civil War, despite all the battles, disease was the greatest killer, causing more soldier casualties (560,000) than from wounds (200,000). Two soldiers succumbed from disease for every soldier hit on the battlefield. This country had largely escaped the typhus epidemics that devastated Europe in the early 19th century because our nation wasn't, at the time, as overcrowded, with the filth and poverty that promoted the transmission of body lice. But typhoid was prevalent here, and so was dysentery, malaria, cholera and . . . diphtheria. During the time of the gold rush, old diaries suggest that anywhere from five to fifteen percent of travelers wouldn't make it to California because of diseases that the medicines of the time couldn't treat nor did the physicians of the time fully understand. Even in the gold fields, the estimate was that as many as one in five of those who came to California fell to malnutrition, accidents and mainly disease. Life insurance companies of the times refused to write new policies for those who came to the gold fields. Thank goodness our knowledge of prevention and cures have come a long way since those days, so the children of today aren't exposed to those health risks that shattered the Carney family here over a century ago. If only they had known about penicillin. But it wasn't to be discovered until 1928.

EARLY TRAIN PASSENGERS

The earliest days of the transcontinental railroad were good ones for tourists and for hunters. Following its completion in 1869, the trip across the country by train was considered to be a great adventure. People who would never have journeyed out west were suddenly lined up to purchase a ticket to the Golden State. The train offered people a view of the heartland of a young nation that was still largely undeveloped in the 19th century . . . a nation filled with scenic wonders and natural beauty. So it was that a train trip to the west was all the talk throughout the east. Atlantic Ocean steamship tours went begging as people sought out this new opportunity for travel. For the wealthy, this meant a small shift in creature comforts . . . trading in a plush steamer stateroom with wall-to-wall carpets, fine furniture and room service for a swaying train car . . . with wall-to-wall carpets, fine furniture and room service. The Pullman Palace cars were luxury on rails and the well to do eagerly paid the premium prices necessary to book a comfortable car for their sightseeing sojourn.

Other passengers, not so lucky as to be riding in one of the Palace cars still had an unforgettable time. As the train chugged along at the heady speed of perhaps forty miles an hour; though more often closer to a slower twenty-five, there was plenty of scenery to fill the eyes. The countryside seemed to go on forever . . . the plains reached as far as the eye could see and still went on. The great high desert country of Utah and western Nevada was everything it was said to be (dry, barren, dusty and yet fascinating for its stark natural beauty). By the time the trains reached the mountains, nearly every passenger was sitting glued to the nearest window . . . watching the rugged canyons and craggy peaks slipping by as the train slowly pulled its way up towards the Sierra summit. Nighttimes, the porters would light the kerosene lamps, and the passengers would gather together around a small organ in a cramped club car to sing western songs, and talk about all those wondrous things they saw that day, and what was ahead, down the tracks.

Of course one of the most fascinating of the sights for train passengers were the massive herds of wild animals that grazed or wandered near the tracks. However, the trains also fostered a cruel sport. A pioneer form of drive-by shooting, as passengers would blast away at most anything that was within range of their pistol or rifles. At the cry of "deer ahead," or buffalo, men took out their weapons and a storm of shots was fired the length of the train at escaping animals. And rarely did the train stop to gather any fresh meat that might have been used, even though the trains didn't carry any food as passengers were only fed at stations, which were sometimes twelve-hours apart. Later on there were special trains put on for private hunting parties that would wreak havoc on the plains wildlife. But for these first passengers of the transcontinental railroad, there were wildlife aplenty, and the experience of a lifetime. This was a trip to remember!

HANNAH CLAPP...
GOOD AS ANY MAN

She was one of the first champions of women's rights in our part of the country. A Nevada pioneer, an educator, a leader, Hannah Keziah Clapp earned a degree in the 1850's at the Michigan Normal College in teaching. She could have stayed in the east and secured a job at any of the multitude of schools that were established there, but Hannah Clapp resolved she wanted to go where there were few schools and there start one of her own. She joined a wagon train headed west towards Nevada. One tale suggested that along the way, the train encountered a band of plains Indians. The chief of which became so enamored of Hannah that he offered to exchange a small herd of ponies he had to the wagon master for Hannah. The trade of course wasn't made, and eventually Hannah made it across the plains to Carson Valley. There she formed a lifelong partnership with another pioneer educator, Eliza Babcock, and together formed a co-educational school; a highly unusual concept in the east, but a soon to be adopted standard in the west.

For over 25-years Hannah taught and administered what was to be known as the "Sierra Seminary." Children from all over the region attended her classes. Hannah was also to be appointed to a prestigious post in the young state, becoming educator and librarian of the University of Nevada in Reno. This at a time when there was only one other teacher, LeRoy Brown (who also doubled as the university's president). Between them, they taught every subject on the UNR campus.

Hannah was always concerned about the status of women. She often led protests against their status as second-class citizens, the lack of a right to vote, and the then practice of polygamy in Utah Territory. One of her proudest accomplishments as a champion of women's rights, was when she proved that a woman contractor can be just as good as any male counterpart. It was perhaps a small event, but at the time, it was highly symbolic, and it proved her point. The State of Nevada wanted a new iron fence about the capital building in Carson City, and had authorized $25,000 for the project. They solicited bids all around the region, receiving one from a contractor by the name of "H.K. Clapp;" the lowest bid as it turned out. So it was that H.K. Clapp was awarded the contract. It was only then the state officials realized the H.K. stood for Hannah Keziah. She got the job but the other bidders were angry that a woman was given the job, a job doubtless she couldn't possibly do. But Hannah proved them wrong! Hiring capable workmen and obtaining materials at competitive prices, she completed the job in two months, and made her point that a woman should never be underestimated. Hannah Clapp . . . a memorable pioneer.

HE WORE HIS TEETH OUT

The early mining towns around the Sierras had their share of what were then, called "Chief's." Rough and cold-hearted gun-totting bullies who ruled the towns and preyed on the weak, like the Sam Browns. A step down the macho ladder were the common ruffians or saloon roughnecks who weren't quite as notorious and were sometimes even kind of offbeat. For instance there was Gordon Ellis, a man who was a deadly shot and a lightning fast draw, and he never missed. But he preferred to only shoot his opponents in the leg! And when he got really mad at the other guy, he'd just shoot him in both legs, and then walk away. There was also a saloon tough by the name of Mike Kennedy. He always walked around with a bunch of six-guns strapped on his belt, and he liked to scare the dickens out of other saloon patrons by screaming and waving around his pistols as he walked around the barroom floor. Unfortunately though, in a case of poor judgment, one day he picked on a quiet, mild mannered miner by the name of James Lund, and the gunfight was on, with no one expecting Lund to have any kind of chance against Kennedy. But moments after the smoke cleared, it was Lund that walked away without a scratch, and it was Kennedy . . . riddled with bullets that went to boothill.

But one of the most unusual early day saloon ruffians was the man known as "Red Mike," or the "man-eater." That was Mike McCowan, and he originally earned his nickname in Virginia City, by biting off the ears and noses of the men he got into saloon fights with. McGowan was a cook by trade, and a fairly good one, but when he spent too much time drinking in the saloon, he became the terror of the town. At one point, he was escorted out of Virginia City, and wandered down to Bodie, but he wasn't there but a few days, and got into trouble there too, and he was thrown into the town jail. But not before he took a bite out of the leg of the Bodie Sheriff, and also threatened to chew the ears off the local Justice of the Peace. So when they finally let him out of the Bodie jail, he was given a choice! Either have all of his teeth pulled, or leave town. And that was what McGowan did! He wandered back into Virginia City, where he continued his old ways for while, but he eventually disappeared from the pages of history. Evidently all that biting must of worn his teeth out.

HER DAY WAS DONE

They finished pounding the last nail in 1901. No one knew how many it had taken, tens of thousands anyway. Her 223-rooms had taken a hundred trainloads of lumber from the Truckee mills. The shingles alone must have required a dozen flat cars to carry. When she opened her doors for business that summer day in 1902, she was instantly dubbed as the queen of the north shore. She was the elegant; the grand Tahoe Tavern. Over the years, a majestic ballroom and casino were added, along with another 50-rooms; bringing the total to 275. During the summers, the rooms were packed with people. Tourists from all over the world came there, individual families and large conventions, to enjoy the scenic beauty of Lake Tahoe, and a touch of elegance. The lavish dining room with the six course meals offering the finest wines, the golf course, the movie theater, the riding stables; even a swimming pool for those too timid to brave the lake's cool embrace. Located just south and east of Fanny Bridge, the Tahoe Tavern was THE place to come to.

Even as the years slipped by, the Tavern still held her magic, for the tourists continued to flock to her each summer through the 1950's. But in her sixty-third year, her day was done. Her roof was beginning to leak in a few places, and her walls here and there, began to sag a bit, the plumbing was now leaking more often. But perhaps more importantly, the Tavern had begun to look too "old fashioned;" too "out-of-date" to be competitive in the 1960's. And also, there was another reality to face, for Tahoe's north & west shore in the early 1960's was having to connect to a new sewer system, and for a resort hotel, that was VERY expensive. And so the Taverns owners knew it was time for her to go. Oh there was a small chorus of protest over the thought of destroying this Tahoe landmark, but in the end, that was to be her fate. They scheduled two days in September of 1964 to hold a public auction; to sell off anything and everything, from the furnishings, the dishwashers, the adding machines and tablecloths, to windows and doors and even the bathtubs.

Nothing was to be left before the wrecking company came in and did its work. But fittingly, a few days before the planned auction, Tahoe residents were given a chance to pay their last respects to the legendary tavern. A last banquet was held at the Tahoe Tavern. Thousands came to eat and to say goodby. A few days later, she was gone.

LOVE AND MARRIAGE

Love and marriage; most of us would agree that the two should always go together. But sometimes, love is less the goal than simple but important companionship. That apparently was on Dorothy Scraggs mind in 1849 when she placed an ad in a Marysville newspaper; an ad for a husband. She started out her quest by stating "her" credentials. Declaring in the paper that she could wash and cook. She could also sew clothes and feed the pigs and raise the chickens. And too, she could chop wood and hoe the garden, and a whole lot more things than there was space to mention. But then Dorothy went on to list those things she expected from her future husband. He couldn't be old, and he did need to have a good education (at least better than hers), but most importantly, he needed to have a lot of money. And in fact, Dorothy demanded that before she would enter into a marriage contract with a man, he would first have to give her a signing bonus: a lump sum of $20,000. Dorothy knew that money alone couldn't buy love, but she obviously was also well aware of the value of a buck.

There was also the similar tale of William Berry. He was to place an ad for a wife in another period newspaper. His ad stated: "wanted, a nice, plump, healthy, good-natured, good-looking, domestic and affectionate lady to correspond with. Object . . . matrimony. She must be between 22 and 35-years of age and must not be a gad-about or given to scandal, but must be one who will be a help-mate and companion and who will endeavor to make home happy." But while putting an ad in a newspaper was one way to seek a mate, there was many an old tale about ladies that selected their husbands-to-be, by having her suitors compete for her hand through contests of pugilistic skill. The winner of a knock-down, no-holds barred boxing match was to win her hand. The loser was banished to find true love elsewhere. But then too there was also that 1874 tale about a young lady in a Nevada pioneer town that had a dilemma. She had been courted by a score of young men, and she just couldn't make up her mind, for they were all sooo charming. So it was that someone came up with an idea of a race! A footrace to determine who would marry her. And so a course was laid out and a race was held. All her suitors ran their hearts out, for she was a prize, but only one lad was to win, and true to her promise, she married him. Although she was to later learn that he had cheated, for during the race he'd slipped away from the pack of runners, and unseen, managed to take a short cut, and so came in first, ahead of everyone else. But then, it really didn't matter to her, for she reasoned that he'd cheated because he truly loved her. Goes to show that sometimes cheaters do win, and that love can be blind.

MEDICINE MEN...
THE DOCTOR IS IN

Theirs was a position of honor, and prestige. And depending upon the tribe, a position of risk. Native American health practioners of the 19th century had to be specialists in everything from birth to death. Having to treat anything from sunburn, broken bones, stomach aches to mental illness and pneumonia. However, if they made a mistake, there was no such thing as malpractice lawsuits. Patients, or their surviving relatives would have a few words with the medicine man ... perhaps helping him to walk off a cliff.

Generally, there were two classes of Native-American health providers: herbalists and medicine man/shaman. Herbalists treated the minor ailments; the upset stomach, the simple fracture, the sprained ankles. He or she used various natural remedies, mixing various amounts and kinds of native plants into a concoction that was applied internally or externally. The Northen Paiute tribe were considered masters of herbal remedies, carefully guarding their knowledge. The Washoe, without this storehouse of herbalistic wisdom nevertheless knew all the basics, trading with other tribes for any medical herbs they might need.

More serious medical conditions normally required the attention of the medicine man/shaman. These individuals didn't just heal the body, they also dealt with the spirits for more serious conditions were often believed to be the handiwork of an angry spirit. Part psycho-therapist, part-medical specialist they often promoted the belief that internal aches and pains were caused by an invasive object. And they went to great pains to exorcise their patients using a mixture of showmanship, dancing, chanting and magic tricks. And generally, it worked, some patients feeling better with all the attention, others benefiting from the herbs and medications. But when the medicine man/shaman failed to improve his patients condition, his usefulness to the tribe was diminished. Too many failures, and the practitioner may find himself in serious trouble, depending upon the tribe. A Shoshone tribe shaman had three patients pass away in a short time, and he was sentenced to be thrown out of the tribe; banished to the desert country. But he was luckier than the Northern Paiute medicine man that had a similar experience after a score of members from his tribe were stricken with a devastating form of pneumonia. His fate was to be taken out into the Nevada desert and they stoned him, permanently retiring their unfortunate doctor. But in spite of their risks, happily there was never a shortage of candidates for this important position.

IT WARNED
THE SAILORS

A lighthouse is not something you'd ever expect to find at a high elevation lake, or in fact at any lake. No, it's far more common to see one of these standing guard along a remote coastal shoreline. Wind swept ocean waves pounding the rocks near its base. A bright light reaching into the fog and darkness to warn sailors away. For to come any closer would bring danger; a collision with hidden shoals or reefs.

But these lighthouses of old also had another purpose, for the beacon also reassured sailors they weren't lost. Before the days of radar, particularly at night, it was a welcome sight to spot that beacon of light streaming out from a land-point, as they were important navigational aids. It was for both reasons, that a lighthouse was constructed along the shores of Lake Tahoe in 1916. The United States Coast Guard had been watching the lake's boating traffic grow. A handful of steamers and sailboats were being joined by an increasing number of privately owned vessels, and there were new concerns about the need for a navigation aid along the westshore. Not only did Sugar Pine Point reach out quite a ways into the Lake, the lack of any homes or development between Sugar Pine and Emerald Bay meant there weren't any lights along the lakeshore for a Tahoe mariner to mark their way after sun-down. So, overlooking Rubicon Point, the Coast Guard constructed a twenty-two foot high lighthouse. A powerful gas powered lamp was installed, and the little beacon was activated. It was operated dawn to dusk, May through December. The light could be seen from all around the lake. A flashing brilliance that made the lake a little safer, a little less confusing for lake travelers to find their way. But over the years, Tahoe's lighthouse had outlived its day, for it was expensive to maintain and operate, and eventually fell into disrepair.

Today, it's just a shell of its former self. Located inside Bliss State Park, it is visited by thousands. Many who skeptically read the weathered wood sign identifying this rustic and sad-looking little structure (nowadays it looks more like a storage shed) as a former lighthouse. But there are plans to restore it. So one-day soon, dignity will return to this forgotten lighthouse, which served Lake Tahoe for so many years.

IT WASN'T EASY TO BE A POSTAL WORKER

It's never been easy to be a postal worker. Back in the early days, mail service was provided locally, by way of the stagecoaches that used to travel to all those towns and settlements that weren't directly served by a railroad. That's how the Tahoe Basin got its mail in the late 1800's. And those early day postal workers, actually employed by Wells Fargo or Pioneer Stage Lines, didn't always have an easy time of it, even back then. For example, delivering the mail over the Sierras has never been an easy task and almost impossible during the winter months. During one severe winter, Wells Fargo messengers had to bring letters over the passes by snowshoes. And sometimes, they replaced the wheels of a stage with skis to make sleighs out of them. But the horses still had to struggle to break through the drifts on the roadway.

William Bennett was one mailman who drove such a sleigh between Virginia City and the lake, and during one storm, his team was overwhelmed by a blizzard, and one-by-one his horses started to lie down on him, freezing to death. He had to unhitch his one remaining live horse and gathering up as many parcels as he could, slinging them on his back, he rode through the storm to safety, satisfied that at least most of the mail had gotten through.

Blasting was another danger that the early day mailmen used to face, when the coaches were traveling through areas that were being cleared for the railroad. For the construction gangs didn't always do a very good job of posting lookouts to warn anyone they were shooting off dynamite near the roadway, and more than a few times, a passing stage would be crushed by falling boulders. The mail would be lost, along with the horses and passengers. But the trip itself wasn't the only the hazard facing the early day mail-coaches. Sometimes it was the mail itself.

The most infamous incident happened outside of the San Francisco office of Wells Fargo, on Friday, April 13th of 1866, when a box that was being shipped to a mine near Carson City, was improperly marked as just "merchandise." But inside, it actually contained nitroglycerine, and unfortunately the box developed a leak, and a freight agent decided to open the box to see what had broken. And, there was an explosion that left a big hole in the side of the office building! But at least it wasn't all for naught, since the mail-service division of Wells Fargo sent out a memo to all of its agents declaring there was to be a new company policy. That henceforth, NO gunpowder, matches, nitroglycerine or loaded firearms were to be shipped marked as third class merchandise. They didn't say anything however, about "first class."

MISSING HUSBANDS

It was a difficult time for many families. But there wasn't much choice, for it had to be done. Someone needed to head west to the California gold fields to try to make some money for the family. Life on the farms was difficult and for many, the stories of easy wealth were so rampant and so prevalent they were not only believable, they were irresistible. In most cases it was a husband, a father that packed up and made the journey while his wife and children waited at home. And most often, after a year or so in the Sierra foothills, those same men returned to their farms. A lucky few made enough money to send for their families. But, for some wives there was to be no homecoming, only uncertainty and apprehension, for their husband's failed to return. At first there had been a few welcome letters from the goldfields, then there was only silence, and so they waited and worried.

Lucinda Mann waited three years for her husband to come back. Finally resolving she was going to go find him, she packed up her children and headed for California. Arriving in Jackson, his last known address, she was shocked to find that he had been in a mining accident and had died several years earlier. But instead of returning to her farm back east, she decided to stay, opening up a store in town. Lucinda not only became a successful businesswoman, but she was also to fall in love with another miner and soon remarried.

Martha Jane Creighton's husband had been in the goldfields a long time; too long. Twelve years had gone by since her husband James had struck out from their family home in Maine. He'd faithfully been writing her and their three children, along with sending them money. But Martha's patience had come to an end, and she was going to try to find him. He was somewhere around a place known as "Eldorado County," and that's where she would head. With her children in tow, Martha first sold their farm, then boarded a boat out of Boston Harbor and sailed south; crossing the malaria ridden Isthmus of Panama, and then up to San Francisco. Months after she'd started, Martha arrived in Placerville, only to discover her husband had gone, to Nevada, looking for silver. And so she continued on. And in Virginia City she found him! The disbelief in James face was soon replaced by tears as he was embraced by his family. After twelve long years, they were together again. From that day on however, Martha made sure she never again, let James wander far from her sight.

KING LEAR ON
THE HIGHWAY

Even back in the frontier days, people loved to be entertained. And so it was that the floods of gold seekers to the west were also joined by a trickle of actors, musicians, minstrels, impresarios and charlatans. Entertainers lured to California and Nevada by the prospects of hitting it big on the stage. And there was never a shortage of theatrical talent. But life for these artists was rarely easy. In some of the mining camps, the actors had to face the peril of being pelted with a garden full of carrots, cabbages, pumpkins, potatoes, sometimes sacks of flour, chimney soot, and occasionally even a dead goose, if the audience didn't like the performance. And if that didn't get their point across, a bag of lit firecrackers tossed onto the stage would usually clear the actors off the stage, and the audience, would file out to the nearest saloon to celebrate what a great evening it was.

And those road trips between camps could also be an adventure all by itself as one troupe found out near Sonora one day, when their company wagon was waylaid by a bunch of cutthroat outlaws, who quickly discovered the actors were broke; which was pretty typical for actors in those days. So the bandits decided they were going to get something out of the troupe one way or another. So they made them put on a show! Right there on the side of the road. And after a few acts of "King Lear," they were allowed to go, unharmed, on their way. And too, there was that group of traveling actors that had their stagecoach tip over, by the American River, and out spilled all of their costumes; wigs, makeup and all. Fortunately no one was hurt, but they had to spread everything out in the sunlight to dry things out. And, as the tale went, it was then that a small band of supposedly renegade Indians came riding down on the actors, whooping and yelling and firing their rifles. But when the Indians saw all of those wigs spread around the ground, drying out, they stopped cold in their tracks, turned around and rode off as fast as they could! For to them the wigs looked like battle trophies; scalps! And they weren't about to harass such an obviously battle hardened group of white warriors. For their part, the so-called "white warriors," frightened out of their wits, quickly picked up the still-damp costumes and took off as fast as *they* could to the nearest town. Back to the stage, where there they only had to worry about a barrage of vegetables. And such was the life of early day entertainers.

LOOKING FOR
HIS DREAM

He was one of the earliest land and logging barons around Lake Tahoe. In the 1880's he controlled over 10,000 acres of forested lands from Sand Harbor to Round Hill. His logging company, the Sierra Nevada Wood and Lumber Company cut down a thousand trees a day, which his mills cut into lumber; over a million-board feet before they were done. His name was Walter Scott Hobart, and he was a major early figure in the history of our Basin.

Hobart was born in Rutland, Vermont in 1840, and was just old enough to witness, but not join in the excitement of the 49'ers rushing west to California, to look for gold. But he didn't miss the next one, the rush to the Comstock, as by this time he was 18-years of age and nothing would hold him back. So Hobart went to California. But try as he might, he had no luck at prospecting. Working hard all day, digging and shoveling, but there was never any gold in his pan; he only had blisters on his hands. So Hobart headed east into Nevada and the silver mines.

But here too, he was destined to days of sweat and toil with only his dream of becoming a millionaire to keep him on his feet. For the only job Hobart could find was the harshest work, pushing heavy ore cars up and down the tracks deep inside of the mines. In hellish heat and foul air, for all of four dollars a day! But with each step he was getting closer to his dream, as he was saving his money. Barely eating enough to keep up his strength, and never wasting his precious pay on saloons or other diversions that would delay his goal. Hobart labored on for long months that turned into years. At times it did seem hopeless. But on one day, as he carefully counted his savings, the pile of banknotes and coins had grown, though ever so slowly into a tidy sum. Hobart realized that finally, it was enough for him to buy a part of a milling business. It wasn't much, but it was a good business. A profitable one and most importantly it meant freedom for Hobart from the mines. And with his persistence, business tact, and intuition, Hobart began to build what became his empire; buying mining stock and land that brought him to Lake Tahoe. Here he created a logging center to supply the needed timber for the same mine where he had labored so long. Walter Hobart did become a millionaire, thanks to Tahoe's forests and his strong back.

PIONEER SOCIALIZING

Whether it was in the Sacramento Valley, the Carson Valley, the Tahoe Basin or even back in Kansas, early day homesteaders lived a demanding and challenging life. Most grew or raised their own food, chopped their own wood, made their own clothes, and tended to their own ills. So it was always a relief to have a little fun, and homesteaders took every opportunity to visit their neighbors, or invite them over for some socializing, and perhaps even have a party. And it didn't have to be elaborate to be fun. Social gatherings called "Bees," brought neighbors together . . . to help each other with a project; a barn raising, or crop harvesting. Since corn was a staple for many homesteaders, during the fall months, for many it was time to harvest their corn crop, and that was to generate an American tradition, popularly called the "corn-husking bee." A social event where neighbors got together and got needed work done and have a great time while doing it. Some bees were turned into contests, where the young folk would assail a pile of corn, strip off the leaves and toss the ears into another pile. The team that finished their pile first would win. When all the corn was shucked, it was time for a dance!

The fall and winter months also offered another social opportunity for it was time for a quilting bee. Patchwork quilts were used by about everyone to keep beds warm in those pre-central heating days. Neighbors would gather, and the ladies would stitch together a quilt from piles of old blankets, rags, and cotton batting. Meanwhile, the husbands swapped tales and the children played games. Making quilts became an American art-form, with homesteaders creating a variety of designs that literally became a part of the country's cultural fabric; such as the friendship quilts (with the signatures of those who made the quilt sewed in) . . . mourning quilts (with pieces of the clothing of the departed used), and the album quilt (with favorite pattern blocks sewed in). Homesteaders also organized literary societies to discuss anything from the latest books to politics, and also musical societies and recitals.

Because their lives were often hard, there was always a need for a good laugh, and so it was common for neighbors to openly share their most embarrassing moments with their friends. Like that classic tale told by a homesteader as to why he was hosting an impromptu chicken dinner for his neighbors. He explained that the night before, he was awakened by a commotion in the chicken-house. And thinking a coyote had gotten into it, he'd grabbed his shotgun and ran outside . . . dressed only in his union-suit underwear. As he ran out the door, the rear flap snagged on a protruding nail, and got ripped open . . . exposing his bare backside. The homesteader went on to describe to his neighbors, that there he was, standing at the entrance to the chicken-house, intently peeking inside, expecting to see some varmint among his chickens, when his own hound-dog walked up behind him un-noticed and decided to stick his cold/wet nose against the man's exposed bottom to sniff.

And surprised, the homesteader accidentally pulled the trigger on his shotgun . . . and the result was a disaster for the chickens . . . but an opportunity for a good laugh and a chicken dinner with his neighbors.

MULES IN THE MIDDLE OF THE ROAD?

Getting up and over or even down Echo Summit is one of those cardinal mileposts of driving to and from the Basin over Highway 50, especially in the winter. That steep, narrow, winding white-knuckle segment of Sierra roadway, is like a grand entrance staircase into and out of Lake Valley, and has always presented travelers with a challenge. Travelers have long since become used to such roadblocks as fallen rocks, and heavy snowpacks with their treacherous slides.

But one time, there was another kind of roadblock on Echo that created a frustrating delay for a Basin traveler. And not just an ordinary one, for this was April of 1860, and the traveler was attempting to ride his horse as fast as he could from Kingsbury over to Placerville. He was a messenger, a rider for the Pony Express and he was in a HURRY! But he was going to run into an unexpected obstacle high up on the Echo Summit roadway. Late the day before, a muletrain, loaded down with supplies and equipment bound for the Comstock, had started down Echo Summit. It had been snowing heavily and the team had been struggling from Placerville, but had still made their way walking single file through the drifts. But it had taken much longer than the teamsters expected, and the snow on the roadway was getting deeper and harder to walk over. As the last rays of daylight gave way to darkness, they were only halfway down Echo Summit. They couldn't go forward and weren't about to go backwards, so the teamsters took the packs off of the mules and leaving them, hiked back to the top of the summit and set up their camp; with a big bonfire to keep warm. The poor mules were stuck in the snow and couldn't go anywhere and so just stood and waited. Near midnight the Pony Express rider managed to work his way up from the bottom. He too had been struggling in the snowdrifts but he wasn't burdened with the heavy packs the mules had been required to carry, and was able to reach the half way point fairly quickly, when he ran into this unexpected roadblock. With no choice but to proceed, he did the only thing he could; break a path for his horse around each and every one of the two-score stranded mules and their massive packs. This he did, but it took him three and a half hours, and he was late getting into Placerville. That was bad enough, but on top of that, no one at first believed his excuse. He was delayed, he explained, because he had to get around a packtrain of mules in the middle of the night, just standing around in the snow halfway up Echo Summit . . . sure.

NICKNAMES

The saying "A persons good name (their reputation) is more precious than gold," has been around for centuries. A variation of that proverb is even found in the Old Testament. While that certainly seems to make good sense, it's not so clear that a person's nickname has the same degree of reverence. For our history has had its share of people who found themselves dubbed with a nickname that while it wasn't especially complimentary, it was descriptive of the person, and that was probably the whole point anyways. There was "Dirty Mouth Molly (she got her name naturally enough by being an accomplished master of the blue word for it seemed she couldn't put together a complete sentence without adding a colorful invective). "Whiskey Mabel," was also a lady of character. But Mabel wasn't a sipper of that strong elixir; instead she sold it after she made it in a home still! Mabel had quite the business going, with her bootleg brew, and drinkers who put their money down would be served a powerful punch in a glass, compliments of Mabel.

"Slapjack" Liz was to earn her nickname by her generosity. For when a fire over in Virginia City burned out many of the homes, Liz volunteered at one of the emergency soup kitchens that were established to help feed the homeless and the hungry. For weeks, she spent countless hours standing over a hot grill, watching over an endless batch of pancakes. And for that, she found herself dubbed as "Slapjack," but she didn't mind.

There was also "Dead Shot Ike," But his nickname was a bit deceptive, for Ike couldn't hit anything he aimed at . . . including the proverbial side of a barn. He was such a terrible shot that it was a natural for his friends to give him that nickname. He didn't much like it, but once it was given, he was stuck with it. Then too, there was "Donut Bill." His nickname came to him after a single meal. Bill was a gambler that was, more often than not, down on his luck. But he was a man that never hesitated to try his luck. Even if he only had a few coins in his pocket, when he ran into a card game, he'd bet all he had and let fate do her thing. One night he'd done just that. All but broke, Bill bet his last dollar in a game, and came up a winner. He did quite well that night and came away with a small bundle. But Bill was hungry, for before that game he hadn't eaten in two days, but now decided to stuff himself with food. But the only food he could find were donuts, and eat them he did. Instantly gaining the nickname of "Donut Bill!"

And there are many other pioneers with nicknames that we can only guess where those names came from. People like "Gizzy" Graves, "Moldy" Goodwin, "Cornball" Martin, "Chummy" Frost, "Bummer" Adams, and "Bumby" Scott. But then, who said that nicknames needed to make sense?

MONKEYS IN THE SNOWSHEDS

Even their smartest engineers didn't have the vaguest idea of the awesome power of a Sierra winter. Even Theodore Judah, their best and brightest thought that his new railroad near Donner Pass, the Central Pacific, would only need to run a few snowplows back and forth after a snowstorm and the tracks would always be cleared; wrong. His successor, Chief Engineer S.S. Montague proclaimed in an 1865 report that only about a hundred yards of the tracks near the Summit might need some protection from the snows, through a snowshed; wrong again. And that error was to cost the railroad millions of dollars they hadn't expected, but absolutely needed to spend to build miles of sturdy snowsheds over their rail-tracks. For all of the train engines in the world with their massive bucker plows couldn't break through the snowdrifts when they got twenty feet deep. And some drifts were over a hundred feet deep! So this not only spurred the necessity of constructing these protective snowsheds, it also spawned a new way of life for hundreds of railroad men and their families, who also lived under the protection of these snowsheds. For in the old days, there used to be section houses and mountain depots every ten miles for the maintenance crews and the telegraphers that worked the line. And they lived in special freight cars, converted into houses or old sleeper coaches parked on spurs. There were tank cars for water, and railcars just for cooking and eating. The food was brought in to these little stations in commissary cars. The children would catch the day's train to and from school. There were also special fire trains stationed at regular intervals, because of the tendency of these wood snowsheds to catch on fire. And these trains, with their double tank cars full of water, always had a head of steam kept up; 24-hours a day, ready to race after a fire and put it out. And these snowsheds were the scene of so many events; avalanches, sabotage by disgruntled railroad employees and wildfires.

But one incident in particular was a classic. That was when a circus train once derailed in a snowshed and some of the animals got out. A track-checker at the far end of the snowshed, who didn't know about the mishap jumped out of his skin and started screaming when he ran into a full-grown lion coming the track! He went one way, the lion ran the other way. Even though they quickly got the circus train back on track again, it was months before they were able to capture the last escaped monkey. It apparently had found a new home in the rafters of the snowsheds.

THE PRACTICAL
THING TO DO

Back in the early days in this country, and Tahoe was no exception, newspaper editors frequently needed to balance the practicality of making enough money to stay in business against their desire to print what they thought they should. As prudent frontier editors everywhere soon learned the lesson that angry subscribers didn't continue to buy newspapers. The editor of Tahoe's first newspaper, the "Tattler," Robert Wood certainly wanted to stay in business, but he wasn't practical and learned the hard way, with his "tell it like he saw it" editorials. Although they reflected his honest opinion,(like his heckling of some people and places around the lake) they angered and soon cost him subscribers. And primarily because of that his paper only lasted about six months.

Even the usually irreverent Mark Twain, who never shied from writing what he thought, once got a reminder of that practicality principle when he tried to get the newspaper he was writing for at the time in San Francisco, "The Morning

Call," to print his story of outrage after observing some bullies throw stones at a Chinese immigrant. But the papers editor refused to print his story, limply explaining that while that act obviously represented prejudice, it was a prejudice that was common among his papers subscribers, who were mostly recently arrived European immigrants who competed with the Chinese for jobs. Twain confronted the editor, but couldn't get him to change his mind. The editor of course was clearly afraid he'd lose subscribers.

Sometimes, pressure on the frontier editors to "go along to get along" came from their advertisers. One of the most noteworthy examples of this took place in Virginia City when the great Comstock era newspaper, the "Territorial Enterprise" wrote a critical review of a new play being presented at Maguire's Opera House; a big advertiser. So Maguire, not only banished the Enterprises reporters from his Opera House (they had been getting free seats), he removed all of his advertising and gave it to a rival paper. After that, it wasn't but a moment that the editor put out a special edition of the paper, proclaiming that the new play at Maguires Opera House was "absolutely wonderful," and everyone in town should see it as soon as possible. And of course, Maguire responded by giving the Enterprise reporters free seats again and he brought back his advertising. It too, may not have been honest journalism, but it was, in those days, the practical thing to do.

MORRIS AND
THE EMPEROR

Most candidates for a public office need to do a lot of campaigning to get themselves elected. That often includes everything from giving lots of speeches, shaking countless hands, distributing handbills, ads and posters and even kissing a few babies. It would be so much simpler for these office seekers if they could just appoint themselves to that office. Oh, if only they could, that would save "them" a lot of hard work and money. As silly as that sounds, there have been people that actually did just that.

The most famous was a man that declared himself to be the "Emperor of the United States." The year was 1849 when 30-year old Joshua Norton arrived in San Francisco. He didn't come empty handed, for Joshua had with him a tidy sum of money . . . nearly $40,000. He invested it in the booming real estate market that was sweeping the Bay Area . . . all because of the discovery of gold in the Sierra foothills. He managed to push his net worth to a quarter of a million dollars, but ended up losing everything he had when he attempted to corner the rice market. He lost all of his money and it appears he lost his sanity but not his boldness as he then renamed himself "Norton 1st, Emperor of the United States and Protector of Mexico." He even started to walk around town wearing a grand uniform, and people loved his antics and they went along with him. This self-appointed Emperor would spend the rest of his life acting and being treated as if he really was royalty.

Closer to our area was another colorful character that also did a similar thing, although with mixed results. His name was Morris Pinschower; "Colonel" Morris Pinschower. Morris first entered the political arena over in Virginia City in 1868, when he decided he would run for the office of sheriff. For months Morris worked hard, giving as many as a dozen speeches a day while tirelessly campaigning up and down the Comstock country. Morris barely took time to eat or sleep, and people liked Morris all right. But as it turned out, not enough to elect him sheriff, for he only got a few dozen votes. So it was that undaunted, Morris Pinschower decided to appoint himself to a public office. And not just any office, for Morris declared himself to be the "Chief Engineer" of the entire State of Nevada. Now the fact that back in 1868, Nevada didn't even have the position of "State Engineer," let alone a "Chief Engineer," (that wasn't to happen until 1903) that didn't stop Morris, who even journeyed to San Francisco to seek an audience with none other than Joshua Norton to seek his support for new water projects in Virginia City. He managed to get some promises from the Emperor, but of course no money. And in the end Morris resigned his self-appointed position and made yet another run for sheriff. Figuring that even if he lost that election again, he'd just appoint himself (once again) to some other public office.

BREWER'S SURVEY

William H. Brewer in 1863 was a member of the California State Geological Survey. A trusted assistant to geologist Josiah Whitney, he was to travel up and around the state conducting geological surveys of that vast state, recording and mapping the bounty of minerals and also its botanical and zoological treasures.

Brewer's travels would take him throughout the Sierras and into our region. Into the valleys and canyons and onto the mountain peaks Brewer hiked with his constant companions, his canteen, a barometer, a thermometer, rock hammer and collection bag, along with a botanical box for collecting plant specimens. Brewer worked his way northward from Carson Pass, though his journey to the lake wasn't a direct one, as he wandered around Hope Valley and then over towards Pyramid Peak. His route to the top of the Peak required Brewer to cross the Bonanza Road, the grand highway of the day (today's Highway 50) and he was overwhelmed by all the traffic. The continuous line of wagons (each with enormous loads) lumbering down the road, clouds of dust filled the air, the cacophony of sounds coming from a dozen sources, the creaking of wagon wheels, the yelling of the teamsters, the bells hanging from the harness of each horse or oxen team ringing all hours of the day. Brewer left the sounds and chaos of civilization behind and struck out to the top of Pyramid Peak. It took him about 4-hours of steady climbing to reach the summit, but from there he was to record in his journal, that this was "the grandest view" in this part of the Sierra. Lake Tahoe lay below, its waters intensely blue and leaving a lasting impression on the mind. From there Brewer worked his way to the lakeshore. After a short stay on the south shore, he struck out again, to the north end of the big blue lake and was to pass through what his maps had shown as small towns on the slopes overlooking the lake. But instead of a town, he only found a few brush shanties. Centerville only had a single structure with a brush roof and nearby Elizabethtown was little better, a few sagebrush shanties, although it did have a store of sorts that sold whiskey, tobacco, flour and salt. But it too had only a roof made of brush to protect it from the elements.

Brewer was to wander west, to the Truckee River, and there he visited another Tahoe area boomtown called "Knoxville." Two weeks earlier there had only been two miners there, and now (because of a supposed silver strike) there were 600 residents (all miners). Brewer was impressed with all the excitement of the Knoxville miners, for they thought they'd discovered another Comstock Lode, but he himself didn't think much of the place, and continued on his way. William Brewer would soon head back east, to teach at Yale. But he would never forget his travels in the Sierras and of his visit to Lake Tahoe.

BETTINGHIS TEETH?

An 1849 visitor to San Francisco was impressed by all the excitement, the hustle and bustle of the gold rush. A city was being born, as people seemed to be swarming all over the place. Either getting ready to head off into the gold fields of the Sierra foothills, or scurrying around, setting up a new business or simply "hanging out," not really going anywhere. People just savoring the energy of the moment, the charged atmosphere, the intoxicating rumors of wild riches in the mountains and the promise of unheard of wealth, even they added to the overall excitement. But he was most fascinated by the proliferation of new gambling establishments that had grown up all over the region, seemingly overnight. Why, he thought there were more gambling houses just around the Bay Area than there were catfish in the Mississippi River. Everywhere he went he would hear the rattle of dice on a table, the clinking of drinking glasses, the yelling and hooting of drunk or sober customers, the rich sounds of a banjo or a grinding organ or a hurdy gurdy. Street after street was lined with a saloon, a dance hall, a gambling den. Oft-times, the same establishment would be home to all three businesses, something for everyone. The same business location might also be a hotel, a social center and even a post office, but its primary business was to handle the demand for gambling and drinking. And there was quite a demand for both in those days. The score of games that were played would attract many a greenhorn in to test their luck, and fatten the wallets of a shifty card-dealer, a slick swindler, a flimflam artist. Faro was popular, as was draw and stud poker, roulette, Monte, chuck-a-luck and keno and a score of other games would lure the wise and the weak, the hopeful and the needy through the doors to the waiting tables.

Sometimes luck was with those that laid their money down, and sometimes it wasn't, as was shown by the 1888 example of Edward Wolcott, a candidate for the United States Senate at the time. He managed to lose twenty-two thousand dollars at an all-night poker game in a frontier gambling house. His opponent criticized him in a local newspaper for his recreational excess, but Wolcott responded that if he gambled, that was no ones business but his own, and besides he'd won that twenty-two thousand dollars just the day before, betting at a horse race. The voting public must of liked that answer, because they elected Edward Wolcott to the US Senate! But then there was the case of one "Fat Cat Jones." A miner who bet his most important possession while playing a hand of poker, his false teeth. Thanks to his opponent pulling a "full house," Fat Cat Jones ended up gumming his food for the next year!

A VISIT TO
LAKE TAHOE

This Englishman came for a visit in 1870 and didn't want to leave. But while he did head off to Sacramento, he left behind his observations of a world that "was," 130-years ago. A world that has changed in many ways, but not in every way. His name was J.G. Player-Frowd. A man born to privilege, but also a man with a keen eye for detail. He was a copious diarist, recording all that he saw and felt. Fortunately for us, since he was to publish his Sierra and California experiences in a work he was to call my "Six Months in California." Player-Frowd came at a time when the western regions were just becoming civilized. The boom-days of the gold rush and Comstock discovery were in the recent past and this was the heyday of Tahoe logging and mining activities in the foothills.

His journey across the Atlantic to New York was boring, since he'd done that a score of times in recent years. He was to note that on his most recent voyage, the cast of ship-board characters always seemed to be the same, the usual aristocratic set who sat at the Captains table; the men of business, the mysterious passenger who seemed to be pursued by some strange destiny, and the lady who'd make her appearance four days after the ship had sailed, suddenly appearing on deck for the first time, the subject of endless ship-board intrigue. When his ship landed, Player-Frowd immediately booked himself on a train west, into California.

His pen was to capture his experience with a visit to a lake called "Tahoe." He left the transcontinental train at Truckee, and boarded a carriage for the twelve mile trek to the lake, and became thoroughly enthralled at what he saw and felt. Despite the clouds of dust that rose up around the wheels of his carriage, he felt captivated by the majestic Sierra scenery. Here and there, the carriage was stopped, and its passengers given the opportunity to walk around and enjoy the moment. This proper Englishman was hypnotized by the beauty of the wild-flowers loading the air with their perfume, the cascading waters down the Truckee River, the clean and fresh air. Attuned to the sounds of the big cities and the train, he was also struck by the quiet that seemed almost oppressive. Player-Frowd could only hear the winds softly blowing, only the wind. No human voices, no steam whistles, no din of industry, and that was a sound he rarely heard. Arriving at the lake, he once again marveled at the size of the big blue lake and the mighty mountains that surrounded it. He felt a sense of awe. After a few days stay, it was time to leave, to say goodby, and Player-Frowd left with regret. He described Tahoe as the "perfect place of purely natural scenery."

He returned to Truckee, to the train, and was soon on his way to Sacramento. To re-enter the world of 1870's civilization, and there he was to record that at the station he was to observe there was a mass of humanity everywhere, and an unusual number of loafers. Idlers that seemed to have nothing to do but hang around and stare at the passengers getting off the train. Suddenly he longed to return to Lake Tahoe.

A PARADISE OF MEN? BIG DEAL

Weddings are one of those rituals of life that, most people experience. They're something to remember, no matter how many of them you go through. Things were no different years ago. Although for a time in our part of the country, there were fewer weddings. Primarily because there weren't that many women here. And for a time not that many justices of the peace to tie the knot. One of the earlier couples to be married in the Sierra foothills had to formalize their union using a mining claim contract. It was one of the few accepted legal documents recognized, and it clearly "was" a stretch, but it sufficed as a marriage certificate for the two lovebirds. This was an ideal place for a woman looking for a man.

There were stories aplenty of how anyone could find a husband without delay. The few wealthy westerners found it all but impossible to keep an unmarried maid or cook in their employ. One such lady recalled intentionally bringing west with her a new maid from back east that she described as being quite homely. Only to see her run off to get married just a few days after she arrived in Sacramento, with a carpenter who was working on her estate. It was clearly a lady's market. Although at least one pioneer lady, irritated at the boorish behaviors of men was to write in her diary, that though she was in a paradise of men, she was disappointed. It just wasn't as good as she thought it would be.

But for most ladies lucky enough to be out in California during these early gold rush days, it was a treat, for every woman was a princess, and every man (within his limits) was a knight of old; chivalrous and respectful. And many a lady took full advantage of their scarcity to play the field. Engagements were short, and so were the ceremonies: "Do you? 'I do.' I now pronounce you man and wife." Love was where you found it. One couple actually met in jail. They were in for vagrancy, and it was love at first sight, and so they married the next day. And where did they end up spending their honeymoon? Why, in jail of course! Marriages took place on trains, out in the middle of our own Lake Tahoe, on the front porch of a saloon or even in a church. It didn't matter all that much where the ceremony took place, as long as there was love.

FRANK LLOYD WRIGHT

Its natural beauty is known far and wide, recounted in countless travel magazines, in photos and postcards in promotional and personal videos. If Lake Tahoe is known as the "Crowning Jewel of the Sierras," then this is the brightest jewel in that crown. It's the one and only "Emerald Bay." One of its most outstanding features is the lack of any development at the mouth of the Bay with no buildings or high-rise condominiums rising up above the tall pine trees to compete for the attention of the admiring eye. But if he'd had his way, one of the world's most famous architects would have changed all that; of course in a most unusual way.

The year was 1923, and the architect was a young man, just building his awesome reputation for originality, creativity and innovation that was often controversial, radical and yet often ultimately pleasing to the eye. The young man was Frank Lloyd Wright, and he had decided to embark on a mission to incorporate the new culture that was sweeping across the country into a new design. That was the culture of the automobile. And in the early twentieth century it was transforming our society like no other invention before it, for cars weren't just a luxury, they were a necessity. And in the mind of Frank Lloyd Wright there was a crying need to create a new concept of buildings, homes & resorts that would incorporate the new mobility of America, through the automobile, into our structures. Something Utopian, free and unconstrained. So he went to work, creating innovative designs for resorts in places like Beverly Hills, Death Valley and Sugarloaf Mountain in Maryland; using such concepts as spiral driveways, and open terraces extending into the landscape with free form lines that were far different than any of the buildings of the day. And while he was busy trying to sell his new ideas to potential developers, he happened upon a site that instantly stirred his interest as a perfect place for his new designs: the entrance to Emerald Bay. So it was that in 1923 Frank Lloyd Wright laid out plans for what he called the "Lake Tahoe Summer Colony." Based on his expression of "mobility," this 200-acre colony was to have roadways woven into the mountainside, with floating cabins that would change position as the winds blew. And its centerpiece was to be a high-walled inn accessed by a floating bridge.

Unfortunately for Wright though, he couldn't interest the then current landowner Jesse Armstrong to go along with his plans and designs and the project was never built. Guess even Frank Lloyd Wright could be a little too far ahead of the times.

OLD TIME

ADVERTISING

Almost as long as there's been a business, (any business) there's been advertising. The availability of a service or product first becoming known by word of mouth, customers telling friends and neighbors and they doing the same. And over time, the art of advertising took on a life of its own. By the mid-1800's, even in the frontier regions of the country, people were often confronted with signs, billboards, and posters, promoting, sometimes outrageously, the values and virtues of a product, or business establishment. Not surprisingly, some advertisements were blatant lies as products (especially patent medicines, highly popular home remedies in the 19th century) were often being touted as doing far more than they ever could. Curing most anything that ails humankind with just a sip of some magic elixir. Puckish Mark Twain was to observe a century ago "many a small thing has been made large by the right kind of advertising."

One of the earliest elements of early-day advertising was to promote the superiority of one product over another.

How "product A" was so much better than "product B." Bashing a competitor was a part of doing business, and especially in some businesses, where there was a lot of competition, and there was a need to reach out and grab your fair share of customers, and hopefully "more" than a fair share. So, it was that around the Sierras, where there were nearly countless scores of hotels and way stations to serve the Comstock traffic pouring between the mines and Placerville, that advertisements routinely proclaimed that one establishment had the "best food, the best beds, the best whiskey, the best service and the best of everything, all at the best price." Sometimes adding, that the establishment was far better than their neighboring competitor (mentioned by name). Customers of course would easily get jaded over all the claims, and it was always "customer beware." But advertising worked, for the more blatant the claims it seemed, the more numerous the customers.

But one early-day newspaper editor decided that too much competitor bashing was harmful; harmful to the tourists who came to Lake Tahoe for a summer visit, and harmful to the reputation of the lake. Robert Wood was the owner, editor and chief reporter of the "Tahoe Tattler," an 1880's era newspaper printed in Tahoe City's Grand Central Hotel. And in a chiding editorial, he took issue with the advertisements of the various Tahoe hotels that degraded one another in their search for customers. Wood acknowledged that there would always be a jealousy between competing businesses at the lake, but by advertising the "others" shortcomings in their ads that cast a negative air over all the hotels. So he suggested that instead of openly criticizing their competitors, the hotels simply promote how great "they" were, and indicate that those "other" Tahoe hotels, were "almost" as good. So it was that for a short while, that ads in his newspaper anyway, were a bit kinder and gentler.

THE ROWDY FUND

Schools didn't come along right away. But they invariably did arrive, and they were a welcome sight to every parent who wanted a better future for their children. But building a schoolhouse and finding a teacher to face the rambunctious students in the mining camps would sometimes be more difficult than finding gold. As was the case of would-be teacher Prentice Mulford in 1858, when he was told by the interviewing school board members that the town hadn't gotten around to finishing the construction of the school yet. Well, that was ok, but he began to have doubts when he was advised by one of the members that if he got the job, he'd be well advised to shoot two boys that would be in his class, and that particular school-board member declared that "he," wouldn't want the teaching job for $5000 and all the tea in China; the students were that rough! Mulford declined the job, but then he should have been suspicious from the start, when the only criteria for that teaching job, was to be able to spell the words: "cat, hat, rat and mat."

But in fact, many people were poorly educated during the middle of the 19th century, and some of those folks were on school boards. And during the interviews for a teacher position, where one of the primary qualifications of a teacher was to have a knowledge of Latin and Greek, sometimes the applicant would only need to learn a few words of each, and that was enough to get them the teaching job. Largely because the board members had no idea how to speak either language! And while recruiting a qualified teacher was in itself a challenge for some school boards, other towns had all they could do to scrape up the funds for the schoolhouse itself. But that too, was often handled in a creative way. There were lotteries, and community charities and other school fund-raisers.

Two of the most famous involved a pair of outsized shoes that happened to belong to a local politician in Nevada. Now even though no one in town really wanted to own those worn out shoes, a few bid on them in an auction, with the proceeds going towards a new schoolhouse. And that town collected hundreds of dollars, and in the end, the politician even got his shoes back. And the other schoolhouse fund-raiser took place in Carson City, where they were having all kinds of problems raising the money they needed, until two prominent miners decided on the shock treatment! One evening they stormed their way into the town's theater, where a play was going on, waving six-guns, and they then pulled out huge Bowie knives and shredded the curtain while people sat in terror! And when that was done, they started laughing, for it was all a farce! They immediately pulled $1000 from their pockets to pay for the damage and started up a school fund right then and there, and collected thousands more from the audience. It was called the "Rowdy Fund" and showed the lengths people would go to build a school for their children.

SMOKE FROM THE GROUND

We're often reminded how miserable winter weather in the Sierras can become. But at least we have warm homes, apartments or condos to protect us from the cold winds and blowing snow. During the winter of '59 . . . that's 1859, the small number of people that lived in what was about to become a major 19th century boomtown, Virginia City, had to endure an entire winter of constant blizzards often with the barest protection. For silver had just been discovered, and although people were now beginning to flood into the area to stake out their fortune, everyone was so busy searching for that vein no one wanted to waste the time to build a weather-proof shanty, let alone a real house. With winter coming, some of the towns populace of miners had prudently headed down to Carson or Sacramento Valley to wait out the Sierra snows. But a few hundred hardened souls resolved to wait the winter out. And as it turned out, it was one of the worst winters to come along that century. So these fortune seekers holed up anywhere they could find shelter.

And that ranged from a few cozy shanty's, very few, with a good-sized pot belly stove to keep them warm, to pine-board lean-to's, roofed over with ragged canvas tarp's with a half sized do-it-yourself camp-stove as their only heat. These miners swore at the snow and the wind and suffered terribly with the cold temperatures. If the snow drifted in on them, they could only wrap themselves tighter in their blankets and close their eyes to their misery.

There were a number of other miners that found relatively comfortable winter quarters for themselves, below ground in the mines they were digging. Even in the winter, as the miners were discovering, the ground seemed to become warmer the deeper they dug. In fact at the lower levels, the walls of the mine were warm to the touch. And some of these crude dwellings were fairly elaborate. A mineshaft would be widened out to make room for a bedroom, even a parlor and a kitchen with a vent hole that reached to the surface. And so it was fairly common that winter to see smoke pouring out of the ground from an unseen stove pipe a hundred feet below the ground. And what kept all these people huddled against the cold that winter? Why it was that dream of striking it rich as soon as spring came. And that thought alone kept a lot of people warm during the snows of '59.

SOMETHING TO DO
TO PASS THE TIME

Gambling was legalized in Nevada back in 1931. Though, in truth it's always been a part of the historical fabric of the region. Long before Tahoe gaming pioneers Harvey Gross and William Harrah made their mark on the Basin, there were scores of saloons and a few gambling halls. Though places like Truckee and Virginia City seem to have received the most attention, Tahoe had its share of card tables. Oh not as grand or garish as the ones in the bigger cities (the gambling halls in San Francisco were often called "hells" in the gold rush), but they shared the same basic characteristics. A place where a person could go to socialize, to unwind, to be entertained, and of course, a place to risk a few dollars.

One reason they were so popular, was that there weren't many other choices for a place for the workingman to go; whether he be miner, logger or teamster. A person could choose between sitting in his cabin or lodging room, listening to his roommates snore, or he could head out to one of the towns social points, a place where they served drinks and played cards. A place where the lights were bright, the music loud, and perhaps there would even be a chance to catch a dance with a pretty girl; not much difficulty to make that choice. Some of the most popular games of the period no longer have the same lure today, but back when, they were all the rage. Faro, a French card game was a favorite here. Played on a green felt cloth, bettors placed chips on a face or number card laid out on a table. The dealer then dealt two cards from a box on the table, called a "shoe." Bets, based on the number on the first card lost, while those that matched the second card won. Even more popular was the game of Monte. It also required a regular deck of cards, from which the 8's, 9's and 10's had been removed. The dealer exposed two cards from the bottom of the deck, then two more from the top of the deck; face up on the table. Players would bet on either the bottom or top "layout" as they were called, the dealer then turning up another bottom card. A bettor won if the suit of the dealers' last card matched the suit of one of the cards in the layout previously chosen by the bettor. It actually was quite simple to learn and popular, because the advantage to the house was slight, and gamblers felt success was just a matter of skill and daring. Besides it was always better than listening to a snoring roommate.

SPOONER'S

When you drive through the Spooner area today, all you see is a large open area, criss-crossed by Highway 50 and Highway 28. If you wander through the same area, you also see knee high meadow grass waving in the breeze, a small but scenic lake and a modest over-story of aspens, pines and firs. And too, you often also see a lot of people pedaling their way on mountain bikes heading north on the road to Marlette Lake and the Flume Trail, a great bike ride. What you don't see are any remnants of the small vibrant community that used to exist here late in the 19th century, for it's all gone.

The name "Spooner" came from the areas first settler, pioneer French-Canadian rancher and logger Michel Spooner. Who, in the 1850's pre-empted, (filed on) a square-mile of land area that straddled the eastern crest of the Basin. Calling his new estate "The Spooner Ranch," Michel was interested in both the lush mountain meadows for grazing cattle, and he also recognized the value of the timber, if there ever happened to be a market for it. In 1859, a discovery of silver near Virginia City provided that market, and soon others raced to the Basins eastslopes to file on open land, to cut and sell the virgin timbers for the Comstock. Spooner himself negotiated a deal with several of his new neighbors to sell the timbers he owned around the summit, but made it clear they weren't to do anything that would hurt his meadowlands, although a dam was built to provide water for the flume (today's Spooner Lake). It wasn't long before the Spooner Ranch, near today's summit began to grow into a bustling little community, complete with logging mill, livery stables, merchandise stores, hotels and the ever-present saloon. Soon the Spooner area became known as "Summit Camp," and was a regular stopping place for the passengers and freight that rumbled between Placerville and the Comstock. A telegraph line was installed and even Wells Fargo set up an office.

Spooner was more than just a transfer point for the lumber coming out of Glenbrook, for it was also its own community. Smaller settlements sprang up nearby, with such colorful names as "Saints Rest," and "White House." For nearly twenty years this area was alive with people and animals and activity. Until finally the Comstock played-out, and most of the timber gone, little Spooner faded into history. Over time the buildings fell down, and for years, only the iron Wells Fargo safe was left to mark this Tahoe community. And on one day, it too was gone.

TAHOE'S OLD COUNTRY STORES

It wasn't so many years ago that the small and scattered towns that surrounded Lake Tahoe were, in every way, remote mountain communities. There weren't that many people outside of these settlement areas, roads weren't always paved, and there was no such thing as a supermarket, fast food restaurant, convenience or factory store. People here had to depend on small, locally owned and operated general stores for just about everything. There was one in every small community: Stan Meyers store in the south shore, Turnage Grocery, Athertons Market, on north shore, the Bliss Brother's Store in Glenbrook and the Tahoe Mercantile. They were the town's country store. They were also a combination community center, male club, social hall, a place to collect your mail, buy food or anything else you might need. In the windows might be a jumble of spectacles, notions, jewelry, fine and coarse combs. From the ceilings might hang buggy whips, corn poppers, pails, lanterns and kitchenware. Lamp chimneys were hung on wood pegs, with horse collars and harness crowded in between barrels or baskets full of crackers, dried apples, sugar, flour, and sweet potatoes. In the back end of the store were the heavy farming and ranching tools, the shovels, the rakes, and hayforks and sharp-edged axes.

Somewhere around the middle, were the groceries, where the storekeeper kept the Herkimer County cheese under a wire screen cage, the kerosene peanut roaster and the coffee grinder. There too were the latest fabrics, the nine for a quarter "good cigars," the jellybeans and licorice, sharing the shelves with Dr. Price's Baking Powder, J&P Coats Cotton Thread, and perhaps even some Chesapeake Bay oysters. The store smelled with a rich fragrance that stuck in peoples minds long after their visits, the odors of rich leathers, mixing in with coffee, poultry feed, calico and sweet pickles. There was no air conditioning with filters to purify the aroma of the stores varied inventory.

The storeowners themselves were also a vital part of the community. For example, there were the actions of the Atherton's at the turn of the last century near Tahoe City. When winter snows blocked the roads, Mrs. Atherton baked fresh bread for those digging out the streets and would even help with their laundry. They'd deliver groceries in every kind of weather at very reasonable prices, trading fresh vegetables or eggs to help out residents struggling when times were slow. You see, their customers were also their friends. Tahoe country stores are gone now, but here and there, their spirit still lives on.

THEY DEALT WITH PREJUDICE AND IGNORANCE

They prevailed in spite of resentment, discrimination and jealousy. They not only survived, they thrived, but it wasn't easy. They were the immigrants from the east. The Far East; from China. They too, just as were the east coast Euro-Americans, also attracted to the promises of the 1849 gold rush, to "Gum Shan," the Golden Mountains of California. The number of Chinese in California were to jump from less than one hundred in 1848 to twenty-five thousand just a few years later. Within thirty years, that number had reached 115,000 (ten percent of the states 1880s population). The news of the gold discovery had reached the shores of China at an especially opportune time. The recent Taiping Rebellion there had left the countryside in ruins. Poverty and starvation was rampant and people were becoming desperate. Opportunistic ship-owners took full advantage of the news of the Coloma gold strike to stir up a media blitz in southern China, by posting handbills, posters, maps and pamphlets promoting the gold rush and their convenient sailing schedules. And it worked, as thousands booked passage to San Francisco (making the ship-owners wealthy of course).

At first they were welcomed with open arms. There was enough wealth for all, so everyone first believed, and the Chinese were exceptional workers, willing to do most anything, even the laundering, cooking and hard physical labor that the Euro-Americans didn't enjoy doing. Most of the new immigrants were members of the third rank of social classes that then existed in China. They were workers (often called "coolie" after the two Chinese words "koo," meaning "to rent," and "lee," meaning "muscle"), People who made their living by renting out their muscles. This profession was a step above the merchant class, but below the farmers and the scholars. But as the competition for the gold increased, and for jobs, the bitterness of disappointment felt by the 49ers began to grow. And a cry was raised that California's gold "rightfully" belonged to the "Americans." That Chinese, Chilean, Mexican and other so-called foreigners weren't wanted, and state officials initiated a series of taxes and unfair laws against non-Europeans. Some wanted to export the Chinese laborers, and occasionally an anti-Chinese riot broke out. Even Governor Bigler joined in the bashing (the same man who's name was once the official name for Lake Tahoe). But despite the prejudices, due to ignorance and arrogance, the Chinese stayed, and eventually, they received the respect they should always of had.

SENSIBLE
POLITICIANS

As a newspaper reporter and editor in the last half of the 1800's in places like Carson, Sacramento, and Virginia City, Alfred Doten covered every important and unimportant national, state or local election of the times. Not only had he spent countless hours and days at regional political conventions, he'd met and reported on a multitude of governors, senators, as well as on visiting master politicians Ulysses S. Grant and Rutherford B. Hays when they passed through the Tahoe Basin. Doten even ran, though unsuccessfully, for office himself. So Alfred Doten should of understood politicians. Though a contemporary of Mark Twain at the "Territorial Enterprise," Doten at least didn't share Twain's perspective that politicians, especially the ones in Congress, were the only distinctive American criminal class! But Doten did feel they were interesting subjects and spent a great deal of time observing and recording in his journals, what he had come to believe were the various personality types that most politicians could be fitted into.

Doten described what he called the "Positive Man." The member of the legislature that knew what he was going to say, BEFORE he stood up to make a speech. There was also the "Argumentative Man." The politician who was always standing up to object to what everyone else was saying, no matter it seemed what it was they WERE saying. There was also what Doten called the "Oratorical Man." That person who was always ready to deliver a speech on any topic, at a moments notice. There were lots of them, he noticed. And too, he observed the "Cautious Man," who listened to everyone. Rarely speaking up or expressing an opinion unless he had to. On the other side of the coin were the politicians Doten called the "Impudent Man." They got up in front of the legislature whenever they felt like it and spoke their minds even when no one cared to listen. But that never seemed to bother them! Doten's so-called "Reckless Man," was the legislator who seemed to flip/flop back and forth during debates, not really having a position. A person who usually tossed a coin into the air to help themselves decide how to cast their vote. But Doten also admitted, there were also lots of what he called the "Sensible Man." Those politicians that didn't say all that much, but when they spoke, it was usually to say the right thing, the sensible thing. These descriptions were written by Alfred Doten over 115-years ago, but it sounds as if things really haven't changed much at all.

STOVEPIPE GEORGE

He was an original Comstock character, one of those unique individuals that liven up a community and make it a bit more interesting. He was a friend of an old time Comstock editor Wells Drury, and consequently was the subject of several 1870's era news articles. His name was George Cogill, and he made his living as a jack-of-all-trades. Cogill especially loved to act, and he was a fair singer and dancer, and so supplemented his meager earnings by participating in countless little shows . . . theatricals, minstrels, and Shakespearean dramas that were common everywhere between Placerville and the mining towns of the Comstock. He'd appear in Romeo and Juliet, and then wander over to a local saloon and entertain there with a few ballads. It was always good for a few dollars and a few free rounds of beer. Or he just might stand up on a street corner soapbox and solemnly recite some lofty prose and then pass his hat to any onlookers he might of snagged.

Now as talented as old George Cogill was, he was especially sought out whenever there was to be a sporting contest involving large stovepipes. Comstocker's loved to wager, and especially enjoyed the opportunity to bet on an unusual contest. They had plenty of horse races, bare knuckle fights, and bear and bull fights and what-not to keep them entertained. But then someone came up with the idea of betting on a grown man stripped down to his birthday suit, wearing a thick layer of grease, crawling through a series of connected stove-pipes, over a distance of 40-feet or so, as fast as he could. If you could get two different sections of stovepipe and two men, why you'd have the makings of a race! And it so happened that George Cogill was as skinny as a bean-pole, the perfect size for a contestant. And George proved to be a natural. Coated down with thick bear-grease, he'd zip right through those stove-pipes, and come-out first. He was a local champion, and at the height of his popularity. Until that day a big race was scheduled, and he carelessly had been celebrating his presumed victory the night before; wolfing down a huge steak dinner and guzzling far too many beers. The day of the contest, he was so stuffed and still half-crocked, that he lost, and badly. His backers were so angry, they chased him out of town! But after a few months, they did allow poor George to return. After all, he was a town character.

SHE DID A BETTER JOB THAN THE MEN

The role of women has clearly evolved over the last generations. Always seen as the heart of the family, the one who nurtures and protects, a role that has never been questioned nor should of been. But in the outside world, women have often had to prove themselves to be the equals of men. For gender bias, Victorian ideals and social conventions presented a barrier that limited a woman's freedoms outside of the home.

But in the 19th century, there were a few pioneers that challenged the roles of women in rather unusual ways. One such lady, her name is lost to history, so we'll call her "Mary," had a unique job with Wells Fargo that in its own small way, perhaps opened the door a bit for women. At least it revealed that women were as good, even better than men when it came to their courage and powers of observation. The weekly stage between Sonora and Placerville had been held up by roadside bandits, three times in a month. Bandits would waylay the coach and fleece the passengers and that of course was bad for business. The local sheriffs and Wells Fargo's own detectives though, were unable to track down the robbers, for the drivers (all men) were so shook up by the experience they each failed to provide a decent description of the armed thieves. Even the passengers were of little help, providing a mixed and often contradicting description that became frustrating for Wells Fargo managers. The company decided to try a different and admittedly unusual approach: hire a person to ride the stagecoaches to observe and accurately describe the robbers so they might be caught! It was then they hired Mary for the job, believing a woman wouldn't be viewed with suspicion by any bandits. Sure enough, a stage in which she was riding was robbed, and once again descriptions provided by the drivers and other passengers proved to be of little use, but Mary went through the ordeal calmly and gave detectives extremely accurate descriptions of the robbers. Providing details about their facial features, clothing, even scars and hair lengths. Because of Mary's coolness and courage, detectives soon caught up with three men, named Bryan, Benson & Parks, and the stage robberies ended.

Mary went on to other things after that, but she showed that sometimes, a woman could do a better job than a man, as Wells Fargo discovered, and so did three former stagecoach robbers.

THEY HAD BIG FEET

They were ugly and had big feet. They had foul tempers and they also smelled bad. But for a time, these natives of the desert sand were part of a grand government experiment in the west; an experiment that actually worked for a time, though it was never popular. The experiment was to bring camels to the American desert country. It was first suggested in the 1850's, to bring a herd of these exotic animals along with some handlers to the southwest, as part of a military test to see if the exceptional range of these animals, along with their extraordinary ability to carry up to a thousand pounds each, could be used to military advantage here. After all, Army observers had seen them in the Crimea, where camels were often used to carry soldiers and equipment, hundreds of miles with little food or water. A perfect choice, the Army thought, to replace the trusty horse and packmule. Congress appropriated $30,000 to begin the experiment, sending a ship to Tunis and Malta, where they purchased a small herd and brought them back to this country.

The camels seemed to adapt quite well, even when they were taken into a snowpacked Sierra Nevada. The soldiers themselves didn't adapt well, finding the camels an aggravation they didn't need. In addition to their other attributes, they were tough to ride, and difficult to pack right, and besides, they scared just about every horse or mule that came near them. So it wasn't long before camels were "accidentally" getting loose, or shot, and the great military experiment lost momentum and came to an end.

The unwanted camels were sold off, and most put to use by commercial packers as a new enterprise came to life. Using camels, packers began to establish trade routes here and there between central and southern California, from Nevada City to Hope Valley and Virginia City, and from Needles to Fort Yuma, Arizona. They did the job and did it well, but the competition with established freighting companies was strong, and slowly the popularity of the camel train began to fade. They too finally came to a quiet end by the end of the century.

Camels weren't going to be completely forgotten though as what started out as a make-believe story of a supposed camel race by a bored Virginia City news editor in 1959, became a true life contest. Bob Richards had intended it to be a farce. Simply a fun story for a slow news day, but others thought it be a great idea to start up an annual camel race, and so began what's become a major event in Virginia City; an event that honors those animals with the big feet and smelly hides.

THEY HAD
NINE LIVES

Cats are amazing creatures that are blessed with a wondrous sense of vision and hearing. And combined with lightning fast reflexes and an instinct for stealth, it's no wonder they have earned a reputation as a "survivor," and are a subject of an oft-quoted old proverb that's unique in the animal kingdom, the one that says "cats have nine lives." These natural hunters have over thousands of years, managed to adapt to the evolution of humankind and changing civilization without losing their independence and their capacity to put the fear into a lowly house mouse.

But as adaptive and clever as these special creatures are, there was an event in our regional history that was to be a disaster for local kitties, a true cat-tastrophe. An event though that at least brought out a tongue-in-cheek admiration that was felt for these feline residents. It involved a massive fire that suddenly flared up in Virginia City in 1875. The winds fanned the flames until most of the city's largest and most important buildings were in ashes (the church, the school, the opera house and scores of hotels and mercantile stores were gone before the fire was finally put out). Some two thousand people had lost their homes, and also lost was a sizeable number of the city's feline population. The flames ran so fast that even the quickest animals couldn't run fast enough. It was difficult enough to lose a business or to lose a home, but to lose a pet was for many, devastating for it was like losing a member of the family. So it was that soon after the flames had cooled, and the rebuilding had begun, that an article was to appear in the local newspaper, the Territorial Enterprise.

Penned by highly respected writer William Wright, it was intended as a requiem; a tribute, but it lacked a bit in sincerity and compassion. For since the fire, Wright had come to miss the lost kitties, but apparently not all of them. For although Wright was to proclaim that the fire had claimed perhaps ten or twelve thousand poor cats, he personally missed and mourned for no more than several hundred of them. He did have a few favorites however for Wright especially missed those kitty's that used to waltz through his neighborhood late in the evening, entertaining residents with their loud musical selections. How often too, he mused he'd be awakened at midnight by the battle cries of a male feline, challenging the turf of a rival kitty; arched back and erect tail waving like a cedar in a storm. And sometimes there were howls and shrieks when the felines actually did get into a pitched fight. But the battlefield was soon cleared as the mad-cats were pummeled with a rain of soda bottles from the neighborhood and they skittered away. He also missed the pet cats that used to sleep on the newspaper's counter and bite all who stroked them. And the stray cats that used to drop out of the trees to solicit food. All were now gone. Yes indeed, Wright wrote that he missed "these" felines. But even he knew they would return, for after all, they still had eight more lives left!

SAM & JAMES...
TAHOE
DESPERADOES

A century ago, just like today, there were all kinds and all types of people who lived in the Lake Tahoe Basin. And while most people were honest and hardworking, there were a few that were notorious. One of the meanest and nastiest individuals ever to come into the Basin was a longhaired, swaggering bully by the name of "Sam Brown." Before he came to Tahoe in 1861, Texas-born Brown was in Virginia City, where he spent most of his time trying to stir up an army of miners to go south to fight in the Civil War. When he couldn't round up anybody to go with him, he drifted into the Tahoe area and hung out at the Sierra House & Saloon on the south shore. But here, "Long Haired Sam Brown" started to spend all his time picking fights. And preferably a fight that involved a gun or a knife, and he didn't mind if his opponent was looking the other way when he pulled out his gun; in fact he preferred it. And in a short time Brown had carved out 20 notches on the butt of his pistol. And there's no doubt that he was planning on adding a few more notches, but fate had other plans, as Sam Browns bullying and back-shooting came to an end at the hands of another area resident, Henry Van Sickle, who effectively defended himself against Browns pistol, with a shotgun. And for a long time Tahoe residents breathed a sigh of relief, peace had returned to the lake.

A few uneventful years went by when yet another gun-totting bully drifted into the Basin. It was now the 1870's, and the man, a burly logger by the name of James Stewart, had moved into Tahoe City, where he quickly established a solid reputation as one of the best lumberjacks in the Basin. He could cut down more trees in less time than anyone else around the lake, but he also was a hard drinker, and like Sam Brown, liked nothing better than swaggering around with his six-guns, shooting at just about anything and anyone. It got to the point, whenever he went into town all the residents would take off for their homes and wait until Stewart had passed though. But strangely enough, he too ran into some buckshot. Courtesy of a frightened barkeeper by the name of Fred Scott, who had James Stewart coming at him just because he was in a mean mood and there was no one else around to pick a fight with. Stewart was buried above the golf course in Tahoe City and there was a big celebration that day. So while these tales of notorious Sam Brown and James Stewart aren't widely known, they do show us that the Tahoe Basin back in the 1860's and 70's truly was a part of the wild west.

THEY WOULDN'T
HAVE SAID A WORD

The Sierras and our Tahoe Basin were never going to be the same after that fateful Monday in January 1848. It was the day that a man by the name of James Wilson Marshall, a 35-year old carpenter picked up a few small gold nuggets out of the stream that fed the sawmill he had built and operated for the rancher-farmer John Augustus Sutter. The mill was located on the South Fork of the American River, and of course it wasn't long before word leaked out about Marshall's find, and the country stampeded into California, and our Sierras. Within just the first few years, about $350 million had been taken from the ground.

But what ever became of the men who started this bonanza, Marshall and Sutter? James Marshall, who started the whole thing, didn't even get to keep the first nugget he had found, for he had given it to the lady who did the cooking for the sawmill crew for safekeeping, but she ended up spending it for supplies. The sawmill where Marshall worked went broke and closed down, and although he tried to do some mining on his own, it seemed like all his luck had left him. He finally moved up towards Placerville, where he worked as a blacksmith, and then later he even wandered around trying to make a living as a lecturer, retelling the story about how he had discovered the gold at Sutter's Mill. But that didn't work out, for by 1872 Marshall had to petition the California legislature for a $200 a month pension "in recognition of his considerable service to the state." At first he got that pension, but the next year, they cut it in half, and in 1878 the state cut him off completely when he showed up drunk one day at the state capital; on a day they were holding a hearing to decide whether he should be getting more money for his pension. During James Marshall's last years, he was completely broke. He died in 1885, but a short time later, a historical group did build a ten-foot high monument to Marshall so he wouldn't be completely forgotten.

John Sutter, the man who owned the sawmill, also faced hard-times after the discovery. With everyone running around looking for gold, his pride and joy, Fort Sutter was falling apart; squatters were moving in on him from all directions and eventually he even lost the title to his land and had to leave the Sacramento Valley. Sutter eventually moved back east, and similar to Marshall's efforts, petitioned Congress to give him a grant to repay him for his services to the country. But Sutter passed away of old age before Congress made their decision. So while the great California gold rush had stirred up a nation, it had left the two men that started it all wishing that if they had only known what that discovery was going to do to them, they probably wouldn't have said a word.

ONE BOOK
TOO MANY

During the early days of the region, even though this was a relatively isolated area, residents still had a strong interest in keeping up with current events, with the cultural arts, with the latest novels and the oldest classics. Newspapers served the needs of most, but they weren't enough for those seeking Shakespeare, Longfellow or Whitman, or a greater understanding of history and the sciences. Magazines like "Harpers," & "Atlantic Monthly," which began life in the late 1850's were instantly popular, and were eagerly sought but hard to find in the Carson and Washoe Valleys. People wanted something more. Individuals stepped in and opened up private libraries; offering their own collections . . . sometimes just a single book. But it was a start until public libraries could be created. For a time there was a thriving industry in mail-order book-sales, especially reference books.

But for one man at least, that turned out to involve a lot more books than he bargained for or even wanted. A butcher in Carson City was approached by a book salesman, hawking a new and comprehensive series of history books, still being written by then famous historian Hubert Howe Bancroft. The butcher was excited, for he had an interest in learning more about the regions history, and so signed a contract to purchase each volume as it was completed. He didn't believe that Bancroft could possibly complete more than one or two of his big and expensive, volumes a year, tops. But Bancroft was both prolific and he had a team of researchers helping him, and so in no time, there were ten volumes delivered to the butchers shop. And more volumes would soon be on their way. This was starting to become an expensive proposition! And the books were beginning to take up a lot of shelf space. But, the butcher was going to honor his contract. But after the 38th volume arrived, he was clearly upset. When the book salesman arrived with the 39th, the butcher was livid . . . enough-was-enough! When he was given the book, the butcher flipped, for he took the book over to his chopping block, and hacked it up with his meat cleaver. Then, gathering the splintered pages, he mixed them in with some chopped liver and handed the mess over to the salesman; the contract was cancelled. Clearly, this was a case of getting too much of a good thing.

OLD NUMBER "2"

It's 125-years old and sits on a small section of track down in Carson City. A relic of days long gone. There's some obvious wear showing on its brass fittings, but for the most part, it's still sound and ready to be fired up again and put back to work if the need arose. She was once only known as "Number 2," but her admirers felt that wasn't grand enough, so they called her "The Glenbrook." She was a locomotive on a proud little railroad, operated by the Bliss family of Glenbrook in the late 1800's. A logging railroad that was part of the Carson & Tahoe Lumber and Fluming Company. The Glenbrook was forged by the Baldwin Locomotive works of Philadelphia. One of two such steam powered engines that were initially ordered for delivery at Lake Tahoe.

Even before the railroad tracks from the lumber mills of Glenbrook were laid, the Baldwin Company was hard at work, building a powerful engine with six driving wheels forty and one-half inches in diameter, and a wood fired boiler with an operating pressure of 130-pounds per square inch. Weighing in at 46,000-pounds, the locomotive could easily pull eight loaded flat cars, loaded with Tahoe wood, up the steep grade to Spooner Junction with seventy tons of lumber.

With its polished brass, flared funnel smokestack, shiny paint and gold leaf lettering, the little engine was an impressive sight. Bringing it here from back east was surprisingly easy. Partially disassembled it was shipped across country on a Union Pacific flat car. It arrived in Carson City in May of 1875. There to be prepared in the machine shops of the Virginia & Truckee Railroad for transport to the lake, which was accomplished by loading the engine on a large wagon, and pulled over the mountain by a double team of oxen and mules. Here it was to dependably serve the Bliss family for many years, spending some of those years hauling passengers & freight between Truckee and Tahoe City.

But in the 1930's the lakes railroad hit upon hard times and the locomotive was sold for spare parts to a line near Grass Valley. There it might of ended its days, as scrap iron. But the Bliss family came to its rescue in 1943, buying it back and then donating it to the Nevada State Museum. There, with public donations, it was lovingly restored to most of its original glory, and is now on display. A part of Tahoe history.

THE OLD TAHOE GENERAL

He was an old Indian fighter. A firebrand that often depended on his Colt .45's or a blast from his rifle to save his neck or to stand for his principles. He was also a Tahoe pioneer and sometime protector of the forest. His name was William Phipps: "General" William Phipps. Originally a plainsman from Kentucky, Phipps as a young man had been swept up in the Indian Wars taking place in the east and south. Earning the respect of his fellow soldiers for his bravery, and quickly earning the title of "General." A few years after those wars had ended, Phipps decided he wanted to see the west, and gathered up his bedroll and his weaponry and headed off to California; landing in Georgetown. After a few years of panning for gold, he had enough to buy himself a homestead, but wasn't quite sure where he wanted that homestead to be, until the day he wandered into the Tahoe Basin. "This" was the place, he decided and quickly filed on a 160-acre plot on the west shore. It was here, that one of his legendary gun battles was to take place.

Phipps had been hard-at-work hacking out logs for his new cabin, when a musket ball suddenly slammed into a tree near his head. He ran for his pistols, hanging on a peg nearby, grabbed them and jumped behind a deck of logs, safe for the moment. His old Indian fighter instincts came alive again, as he cautiously slipped around the logs into the underbrush and waited. A minute became an hour, and still he sat motionless, until a branch across the way softly moved. Instantly Phipps blasted away at that branch; he emptied his pistol! A cry rang out and a bronze figure fell to the ground. Phipps's intended assailant was an old Paiute warrior from the Truckee Meadows. A renegade named "One-Eyed-John," who'd been raiding Tahoe settlers. That was the warriors last battle, but it wasn't Phipps, as over the next few years he had to fire scores of shots at trespassers intent on cutting and stealing some of the majestic old growth sugar pines that graced his 160 acres of Tahoe shoreline.

Phipps also had to do battle with state fish & game wardens, when they set out to stop the General from collecting spawning trout eggs in a pond he'd dug out by the lakeshore. They were out to protect the native trout, but Phipps resented government interference. After saving the country during the Indian Wars, the old General declared "no-blue-noses," were going to stop him and fired a volley of rounds through the roof of his cabin; they left. Phipps too, finally left Tahoe to return to Georgetown, but his name is honored around the lake even today. For on the lake's west shore, you can find "Phipps Peak," & "Phipps Pass," and a tributary that is known today as "General Creek." The old Indian fighter would have been proud.

THEY WANTED
TO BE A CHIEF

There was clearly a pecking order in the world of the "Chief's," the gunfighters that lived, some say infested the west. There were the loud mouthed, "wanna-be's," the "barely were's," and here and there, the without a doubt major league, get out of their way if you value your life bona fide "Chiefs." All kinds lived around our region. Around Tahoe was an especially notorious bully named Sam Brown. Also known as "Fighting" Sam Brown, or because of his flowing locks: "Long-Haired" Sam Brown. He only had to walk into a saloon and people would scatter. He sat on top of the pecking order and knew it. His local reputation was every bit as formidable as "Billy the Kid" or gunman "Rattlesnake Dick," until he ran into Henry Van Sickle, Brown was the most feared gunslinger in the region.

Somewhere around the middle of the pecking order was a man named Langford Peel, locally known as "Farmer Peel." He first came to the Carson Valley in the late 1850's, already sporting six notches on his handgun. But at least his victims, were "wanna-be" gunfighters, who had heard that Peel had a lightning-fast draw, and so challenged him to prove their own prowess; unsuccessfully it seemed. Which brings us to the low end of the pecking order. A brash and ultimately foolish man named "Johnny." "Eldorado" Johnny, he called himself, and he arrived in Washoe country in 1861, looking to establish a reputation for himself as a fearless gunfighter; a Chief. He wasn't in the area very long before he began hearing stories about a local farmer named Peel & his six notches. This was exactly what Eldorado Johnny was looking for, a chance to face-down Farmer Peel, and gain fame as the fastest draw in the valley. Eldorado did have a sense of style about himself. A Chief, he felt, should also look the part, and since he soon expected to become one; after doing-in Peel, he decided to spiffy himself up before the gunfight. First visiting the barbershop, getting his whiskers trimmed, his hair washed and his boots polished to a bright shine. That done, he stopped by the local tailors shop, donning a stylish suit of clothes with a dapper new hat. Then he was ready for the shootout, which he fully expected to win. But, it didn't work out that way, as Farmer Peel easily beat him to the draw, and Eldorado Johnny discovered that just looking like a gunfighter, didn't mean much if you weren't faster on the draw.

THE DIRTY
WOMAN'S INN?

From practically none in the 1850's, by the 1860's there were nearly a hundred way stations and hotels between Placerville and Virginia City. The light patter of travelers that had been going east or west through the Highway 50 corridor turned into a stampede, attracting scores of entrepreneurs who recognized a good business opportunity when it walked by. Some of the new hotel operators were families, some individuals and others, partnerships. All clamoring to attract their share of the throngs of people needing a good meal, warm bed, perhaps a stiff drink for themselves and a corral for their trusty horse or herd of cattle.

Competition could be stiff and that fostered some creative advertising as one operator had a sign placed that claimed that at "his" establishment, he would provide comfort to the weary, he would "feed the hungry," and "would cheer the gloomy." All of that for a reasonable price. Another operator of a modest, no-frills, remotely located way station, was understandably anxious to attract customers, and recognizing that selling "service," was just as important as providing comfortable accommodations, created some effective though perhaps unrealistic advertisements, claiming that every room was lavishly furnished with scenic views, impeccably cleaned, every meal would be perfect, piping hot, and always served with a smile by spit and polish waiters, every guest a king or queen. It may not have been true, but it did attract needed business, and these "were" the days before the Better Business Bureau.

Early day way station operators also learned the importance of giving your business an attractive name. Around the south shore were places like "Lakehouse" & "Bijou House" & "Heritage House." There was also "Frosts Homestead," and "Old Mother Velty's" and the "Cornelian Springs Sanatoria." There was even a business near Spooner called the "White House." But not every way station fared so well, picking up such non-appetizing names as "Dirty Mikes," and one pioneer way station was ingloriously dubbed as the "Dirty Woman's Inn." Named, it was said, after an especially untidy innkeeper. Somehow though, they still managed to attract customers, for these were the golden days for area hotel owners. Days when the demand for rooms far exceeded the available supply.

THEY LEFT THEIR UNDERWEAR AT HOME

During the mid-years of the 19th century, there weren't that many women around the Sierras. While census counts weren't complete, it was determined for example, that in 1850, there were all of seventy-two women over the age of eighteen in Butte County (Chico area), and 194 women in Calaveras County. And around here, other than the Native American Washoe ladies; there were none, not a single one. All of which made courting, which hasn't always been easy, a lot tougher when a man set his cap for a lady. And scarcity wasn't the only obstacle. One 1800's disgruntled father described to his daughter his opinion of the young men that were swarming around, trying to win her hand. He said they could all be compared to a coal oil lamp: "They smoke a lot . . . they're not especially bright . . . they are often turned down . . . and they go out a lot at night." And despite this particular father's concerns, one young miner finally did win her hand, but he had to work for it.

As did all of the men that became interested in a woman in those days, for many of the miners and loggers were men with little or no education and generally few social skills, but once they became interested in a lady there was no end to the lengths they'd go for self-improvement. One of the most popular catalog mail order items of the time was a toupee. All they had to do was to draw the size of their bald spot on a piece of paper and send it in, stating whether their hair was either straight or curly, and enclose a lock of it along with a few dollars and they'd receive their toupee in the mail along with a tube of glue to make it stick. And so, feeling more sure of themselves, off they'd go a'courting.

And there was potentially some risk that went along with the search for a wife especially during cold weather. That was due to the tradition of the Saturday night social. For when the few ladies that were around would come into town to dance, the eligible ones would often be quickly surrounded by a bevy of lonely miners. And since every man just had to put his best foot forward, all the serious suitors would do something drastic. Something they otherwise seldom did; they took off their extremely itchy & often needing to be washed woolen longjohns before the dance, so they could impress the ladies with their courtly manners. Avoiding the ungentlemanly distractions of scratching while in the middle of a hoe-down! But on cold evenings this was a bit risky, and more than a few miners shivered their way back home after the dance, risking pneumonia. But certainly the Chinese laundries appreciated the boom in the Saturday night long-john business, and hopefully the ladies at the dances appreciated the sacrifices of the men who'd do most anything for love. For sometimes, back in the 1850's anyway, that's what it took!

UNDERWATER HISTORY

An awful lot of Lake Tahoe's history is under the surface of the lake, sunk many years ago. The first sizeable vessel to go under was called the "Meteor." An iron-hulled steamship, the Meteor was an eighty-foot-long workhorse that began life as a powerful towboat. Pulling massive floating logs across the lake, to waiting sawmills. Later on, she carried passengers, and the mail. Ending her days in 1939, when she was sunk by her owners. Another sunken nautical treasure is the eighty-five foot long steamer, the "Nevada," who also plied the waves of the lake through the early days of the century. There is also the proclaimed "Queen of the Lake," lying in the darkness on the sandy bottom; the steamer "Tahoe." This 166-foot long beauty was originally launched in Glenbrook in 1896 and was to carry passengers, freight and the mail all around the Basin until a windy August morning in 1940, when she too, was sent off by her owners to retire beneath the waves.

But there are other sunken historical treasures down

there. Not as grand as a white-hulled steamship, nor as large, but still historic, and interesting in their own way. They're over in Emerald Bay, under the water. They've been there for most of the last century, and have likely been observed by divers some years earlier, but in 1988 a marine biologist and marine archeologist brought attention to a number of sunken barges, dories and launches that had been hidden under the Bays waters. Here, was an interpretive opportunity! One barge, down about thirty-five feet below the lake surface, is eighty-five feet long and twenty-five feet wide, and was once used to haul cordwood across the lake. It was probably towed by the Meteor or Nevada. Another one is even larger, 106-feet in length! They were both sketched and photographed using sophisticated underwater cameras. And what's more exciting, was the decision by the California State Park System to designate the area as a "State Underwater Park." Also visible are a multitude of old relics; refuse from the old Emerald Bay Resort, old piers, and tires, and telephone batteries and parts of old automobiles. A unique bit of Tahoe history just waiting to be visited, for all you need are air tanks.

THE LADY WAS
SOME DRIVER!

She was an unlikely pioneer of a new age. It was the dawn of the automobile age and the sunset of the horse and buggy era. She was a twenty-two year old housewife and mother from Hackensack, New Jersey. But Alice Ramsey was about to make history as the first woman ever, to drive a car from coast-to-coast. It was a journey of 3800-miles across the backroads of this country; when in 1909, few of those roads were even paved. It was that summer that the Maxwell-Briscoe Motor Car Company decided it wanted to stir the imagination of the country and sell some of its automobiles, by sponsoring a cross-country road-trip that would grab some headlines. And what better way than to ask a local lady, Alice Ramsey, to drive their Maxwell from New York to San Francisco. Alice (her only qualification was her flair for adventure) accepted, and accompanied by three lady companions (Nettie Powell, Hermine Jahns and Margaret Atwood . . . none of whom ever drove during the trip), she set off, headed west.

They ran into all sorts of problems along the way . . . the lack of road signs, the lack of paved roads, the weather. In Nebraska, they were stopped by a posse of lawmen who were looking for a pair of escaped killers. The posse was suspicious of the four ladies and searched their Maxwell thoroughly, thinking they might be hiding guns for the escapee's. In Wyoming, they were nearly washed away when a flash flood caught them while crossing a river. In Utah, they hit a prairie dog hole so hard they broke a tie bolt! The two front tires caved inward, busting a spring and breaking the front end. Eventually, after two months on the road, the end was in sight as she pulled into Reno. After a nights sleep, Alice headed for the last challenging leg of her cross-country trip: the roadway between Carson City and Lake Tahoe. A roadway that she described as a "poor excuse for a road." Her Maxwell sputtered and coughed in the thin air, but she limped into South Shore, where she spent the night. Next morning, she was off again, over Echo Summit, and after another day, into San Francisco. There she was greeted and escorted by a whole fleet of Maxwell's. Alice Ramsey, the unlikely pioneer, had done it!

SLEEPING WITH STRANGERS

The very first lakeshore hotel here at Lake Tahoe sure wasn't much to brag about. It was variously called the "Lake Bigler House," or more often, simply the "Lake House." And while it did fulfill the basic needs of the 1860's traveler through the Basin, its owners, like so many of these early day way stations, weren't prepared nor able to provide more than minimum accommodations for their customers. In the case of the Lake House, part of the problem was the unexpected large crowds that descended on the hotel. The discovery of the Comstock generated a flood of traffic and Tahoe was abuzz with people; and there was standing room only at the Lake House. The proprietors did their best, but there weren't enough beds (even with two to a mattress), and not enough food (though they sliced the meat thin), and not near enough good drinking whiskey. The Lake House had to substitute their homemade "rattlesnake juice," to meet the demands of their customers. Visitor John Ross Browne blasted the hotel for its noise and its dirt. Also for its congestion; its lack of good food, and of course, the shortage of decent sipping whiskey. Though the hotel later improved its services and amenities, it at first was typical of what the early day traveler had to endure when they took a trip out west.

Also common was the practice of sleeping several men to a bed. Sometimes three to a single bed if the bed-frame was wide enough! Lady travelers would also, of necessity, end up sharing a bed with a stranger; another lady of course, but also with the lady's children. And as every mom knows, babies and very young children can make for a sleepless night. There was no such thing as privacy for couples or individuals. Men slept in one room and women in another.

Also common, too common, was the presence of bedbugs, fleas and small vermin. And few travelers ever had much good to say about the food they were served at the various way stations, whether it be in our area or on the open frontier. Many times travelers would need to guess what kind of meat it was they had been served, for you couldn't tell by the taste; was it buffalo, beef or prairie dog? There was so much grease and seasoning! Travelers learned to put up with these little challenges but demanded improvements. And so, over the years, things did become better. Nowadays, we get clean, private rooms and perhaps even a vibrating bed that practically gives you a massage if you have enough quarters; and that's progress!

THE BATTLE OF THE STATE BOUNDARY

As we all well know, a boundary line between two states (California and Nevada) runs down the length of Lake Tahoe; a line with a substantial bend in it that had been disputed for many years. The subject of multiple surveys, lawsuits and countless debates, its only been since 1980, after a ruling by the United States Supreme Court, after California filed a lawsuit against the State of Nevada, that the permanent boundary line would be as we've marked it on today's maps. The confusion started back in 1850 when California was admitted to the Union. Congress then set the eastern boundary of the new state along a meridian that was believed to approximate the summit of the Sierra Nevada mountain range . . . but it wasn't exact. And things became more complicated when, in 1861, the Nevada Territory was formed, its western boundary was also approximated, so that portions of Nevada overlapped into what people had accepted to be inside California, and conversely, part of

California overlapped into Nevada. And that was to spark a war of sorts from both sides of the disputed boundary.

Residents of Honey Lake Valley had believed they were Nevada residents, but unexpectedly found themselves approached by tax-collectors from California, intending to collect taxes for "that" state . . . they refused, and the debates began, as California maintained this area was in truth, a part of "Plumas County." Things soon heated up, as Nevada judges issued injunctions restraining California judges from exercising their perceived authority. This was met with California-side judges passing their own orders against Nevada-side judges and sheriffs. Up in Susanville, on February 15, 1863 issues boiled over . . . for this town too had found itself fought over by the two states . . . both declaring the town lay within its particular boundary. Nevada supporters barricaded themselves in a log house (they called Fort Defiance), and a gun battle broke out with a California posse. They fought for hours, and a number of men were hurt. Eventually an armistice was called and a new survey was promised to once and for all determine the state line. This was done, but while the Susanville battle was over, the debates over the dividing line between the two states would continue for years. One surveyor, Von Schmidt actually placing all of Lake Tahoe entirely inside California. But it was all finally resolved, just a few years ago.

TRAINS ALONG
THE TRUCKEE

During the golden years of the Comstock, it spent its days hauling ruff-cut lumber from the mills at Glenbrook to Spooner Summit where the wood was offloaded and then placed in a V-flume for the ride to the bottom of the grade. But when the mines closed down, the sturdy trains weren't simply scrapped along with all the other now useless logging and mining equipment that seemed to lay everywhere between Tahoe to Virginia City. For another bonanza was about to begin around the Tahoe area. A bonanza of tourists, and the owners of the great Glenbrook railroad, the Bliss family, weren't going to miss out. So they closed down most of the operations of the Carson & Tahoe Lumber & Fluming Company and formed a new corporation, the Lake Tahoe Railway and Transportation Company. In 1899 they began construction of a railroad down the Truckee River Canyon while at the same time moving all of the necessary rolling stock to Tahoe City, including the locomotive and tracks. After a years work, the sixteen mile long narrow-gauge railroad was opened. It was also about this time the Bliss enterprises constructed the classic steamship "Tahoe" and built the luxurious Tahoe City hotel known as the "Tahoe Tavern." And to serve the railroad, and its steamer, the company also constructed machine shops, docks and a marina on the north shore.

The little locomotives were perfect for the tourist business, with polished boilers, high drive wheels, and shining brass; they were impressive to look at. They usually pulled a baggage car, two or three miniature passenger coaches and an open-air observation car, and it was a lot of fun to ride. During the height of the tourist season, there would be three trains running back and forth between Tahoe City and Truckee. The highpoint of the route was always that last mile, just before the train reached Tahoe City. There was a steep grade to get past, and sometimes the little trains couldn't quite make it the first time, so they'd have to back up and make one or more runs at the hill, always at full throttle. And sometimes too, the tourists would get a treat by catching a glimpse of one of the big logs that were still being shot down the Truckee River. Pushed on by way of the check dams that still dotted the river corridor. And when they got to the lake, there was one more thrill waiting. After the train reached the pier near Tahoe Tavern, it was switched around a few times, and it then pulled up right next to the steamer Tahoe. The train passengers would then board the steamer and from there sail off over the lake. If only Tahoe had something like this today!

THE LADY NEEDED
A SHAVE

Gamblers during the heyday of the Comstock and Gold Rush eras weren't only men. Ladies too, joined the ranks of professional gamblers, though they were (at first) a novelty and a rarity. And when they first appeared, they were enormously popular. The first lady cardsharp in California was one Madame Simone Jules. A dark-haired beauty in her early twenties, she also graced the roulette wheel at a San Francisco gaming hall called the "Bella Union." Her beguiling smile attracted throngs of patrons, who it seemed, found it refreshing, even enjoyable to lose their bets to a lady instead of to a male dealer.

In 1854, another lady was to join the ranks of California gamblers. She arrived by stage in Nevada City, and immediately created a small sensation among the all-male miners. Well dressed, resplendent in her traveling suit and jewelry, she had a noted French accent and a manner about her that conveyed her self-confidence and her independence. She introduced herself as Madame Eleanore

Dumont. She booked herself into a hotel, and for the next week quietly sized up the town. Deciding there were opportunities there, a good place to practice her chosen profession: gambling. She rented a room in a store on Broad Street and opened up a game of chance. Predictably, the rowdy miners flocked to her table, but Madame Dumont insisted they act as gentlemen, requiring them, to play at her table, to take off their hats, wear jackets, not engage in fighting or brawling, and to keep their swearing down to a minimal level. The miners of course, tried their best to comply with any request from the attractive dealer, and her business was a thriving success. So much so, that within a short period, Madame Dumont was able to expand her business, and moved to a larger location, and added more dealers and tables.

When Nevada City's fortunes began to ebb in the mid 1850's, Madame Dumont decided it was time to move on, and so adopted a life of a wanderer. Migrating over the next two decades from mining camp to boomtowns, to wildcat towns, to wherever the money was flowing and the prospects were brightest, she wandered into and around Nevada and California. Sometimes showing up in far away places like South Dakota, Oregon and Montana. But she also lived a wild and a hard life, and her beauty began to fade.

By the time Madame Dumont reached her 30's, she had put on weight and her features began to turn coarse. Most notably, soft downy hairs above her lip had darkened giving her the appearance of having a mustache, and she became known as "Madame Mustache." She must of enjoyed the notoriety of her new nickname, for she causally ignored her appearance. Madame Dumont was to end her days in Bodie, passing away there in 1897. Madame Dumont was to be honored by the town citizens for being a good-hearted person, a pioneer in her field, and a legend in her time.

ROLLING HOMES GATHER NO MOSS

During the boomdays of the 1800's, when someone struck it rich, it wasn't long before "boomers" (as they were called), flocked to the site of the discovery. If it was big enough, merchants and miners would throw-up buildings, and a town would be born. If the discovery played out, or flat busted, the so-called boomers would abandon the town and head off for greener pastures. And more often than not, they'd leave behind everything they couldn't carry since freighting costs were sky-high and if it didn't fit in your wagon, you simply left it. So it was that everything from furniture to unsold merchandise was left behind, for people had little choice. This was to spawn a most unusual industry: house moving. For the abandoned homes also presented an opportunity, and they were a perfect answer for those places where there was a shortage in building materials. This was especially the case in remote parts of Nevada (where there were few trees). With a strong team of mules and a specially built wagon, entrepreneurs would jack up an abandoned house, or a saloon or even a multi-story hotel and haul it to another area. And many a house was to be moved this way . . . time and time again. As a new strike was discovered, and a new town sprung up, these mobile houses were moved in and occupied. One hotel was moved six different times over ten years, finally ending up right back where it started after an old claim was found to contain previously undiscovered riches.

Around our own Lake Tahoe, before a road system was constructed, it was a common sight to see floating barges, transporting just about everything you can imagine. Every spring, dairy cows were floated over the lake to the various resorts and private estates. For without roads, they couldn't be herded. Sometimes you'd see a pile of lumber and stones, and you knew that someone was building a home, for these were their building materials. But one of the stranger items to be floated across our lake were the remnants of the Bliss family's railroad at Glenbrook. The locomotives, the rails and the cars were towed over to Tahoe City, where they would begin a second life, carrying freight and passengers from Truckee to the lake. And too, even though we had lots of trees here from which to build a house, it was still cheaper to move a constructed building than to make it from scratch. So it was that laker's were treated to the unusual sight of a score of one and two-story buildings floating across Tahoe, to join the railroad stock, providing housing for the employees. They were literally, Tahoe's very first mobile homes.

THEY'D BET
ON ANYTHING

Perhaps it was all the excitement of the times. The abundance of so much money, or at least the promise of it, and the carefree atmosphere that accompanied the gold rush, and the discovery of the Comstock Lode. And perhaps, it was a simple case of human greed and sense of adventure. For certain, it reflected a recklessness and departure from common sense. It was the tendency of the times for men to wager, to bet, on almost anything. While standing at a bar sharing a drink with a co-worker, while working a mine, or sawing a tree, idle conversations might well evolve into a friendly disagreement that led to a bet. It was fun, and it provided some entertainment, and sometimes it was also risky, as there were some interesting wagers. Common were those bets on athletic contests: boxing matches, foot races, horse-races. And also those staged events, like the bear and bull contests, and badger and cockfights. But there were also those odd bets. For example, there was once a spittoon spitting contest. After filling up on some chewing tobacco, the contestants would back off ten feet away from a brass spittoon and let fly! The most accurate marksman would win the bet.

Another early day resident of Eldorado County, was visiting his local saloon, and got to bragging about how good he thought he was with his throwing arm. He bragged that he could hit most anything he wanted to within fifty feet. Others challenged his prowess, one person suggesting the miner couldn't even hit the bar mirror with a beer mug from twenty feet. And so a bet was set, and the miner grabbed an empty beer mug. He stepped off twenty feet, then flung the mug at the bar mirror, and smashed it! For that he won a paltry two dollars, but had to cough up $175 for a new mirror! Another high stakes contest involved a pie-eating contest. The bets flew, and a man from Folsom won the culinary contest by downing an impressive seven pies with only twenty-three bites. This was before the days of Guinness, but that must be a world record! There was also that bet between two men to see which 150-pound block of ice would melt first. It was July, and idle conversation stimulated a question about how fast ice would melt in the blistering sunlight. So a contest was arranged as two blocks of ice were set out in the sun, and the men waited. And while it took all day, one block of ice did melt faster than the other, and a bet was won and another was lost. Other, less complex bets include the one between the men that, following a rainstorm, wagered which hour and minute the last raindrop would fall from the town's courthouse roof. Others mentioned such Mark Twainish wagers as which bullfrog would leap the farthest, or which ant would run the fastest, or which rabbit would hop the highest.

But even the more traditional betters had to take their chances, as was shown during that classic boxing contest where two men squared off against each other. The bell rang, and each man charged to the middle and let loose a roundhouse punch. And both men went down! They'd knocked each other out in the first round!

SAD ERA AND
A BRAVE LADY

When news of the discovery of gold in the California foothills reached China, like everywhere else, it stimulated a sudden migration of adventurers; mostly men. Twenty thousand by 1852 sailed into San Francisco Bay to look for their fortunes. Women from China came to America in small numbers at first. That trickle however would soon increase as hundreds of women would soon find themselves shipped to the land of the free as slaves. Every bit in bondage as any slave in the American South, they were sent here in large padded cages like animals. Put into crowded ships, victims of a system that often treated women like property. Where poor families would sell their young daughters into prostitution, into slavery. When they arrived they might be herded into an examination room where agents would select individuals for wealthy customers. The others would be forced to hawk themselves in small rooms, some no more than four by six feet in size, to poor laborers, teenage boys, sailors and drunkards for as little as twenty-five to fifty cents.

These women were intentionally taught little or no English. Just enough to entice customers into their tiny buildings and trade money for sex. Treated more like a wild animal than a human being, exposed to physical abuse, including beatings, drug addiction, and disease; some tried to escape, but only a few made it.

But one woman decided she was going to try to stop this slave trade. Donaldina Cameron was a wealthy woman. A reformist at heart who found herself devastated at the plight of the young Chinese girls. Girls as young as nine and eleven were being forced to endure the existence of the cribs. Donaldina launched a crusade to rescue any and all that she could. Leading raids through opium dens and into back alley bordellos, chopping down doors if necessary, or ripping out trap doors, she would grab every young girl she could and whisk them away to a secure place where they would be cared for. Donaldina founded a charity and a home shelter to provide for the Chinese women and girls. Given their freedom, taught English and Christianity, the girls also received something they'd rarely experienced in their lives: love. Over three thousand were rescued. Saved from a lifetime of misery, thanks to a brave woman, Donaldina Cameron.

TAHOE MYTHS AND MYSTERIES

During the 19th century there were a fair number of scientists that studied Lake Tahoe, trying to figure out how big it was and how deep, and too, how it was formed. Trying to unravel some of the mysteries of the big blue lake. One of the most persistent early myths was that there was no bottom to the lake! That it was lying over the top of a volcanic caldera that disappeared into the bowels of the earth, and so the depth could never be measured. Eventually that theory was discarded. But even in the same year of 1883, some scientists, like Professor John Le Conte from Berkeley, claimed the bottom of the lake was exactly 1645 feet, and that's the depth we use today. But others insisted that the "real" depth was precisely 2,800 feet with no apparent reason for the difference.

Another mystery was the belief that since Tahoe didn't freeze over during the winter, then there "must" be some hotsprings in the lake. And this belief was reinforced by the fact that there were some hotsprings on the north shore.

This supposedly was confirmed one day in 1866, when 250-yards off the northshore, a number of people spotted a column of water, 5 or 6-feet high, rise up out of the lake, then dropping back and forming a whirlpool. And this happened several times! So someone rowed out to see what was happening, and stuck their hand in the water at that point and discovered it was "quite warm." But other than that, all they could see was a hole in the lakebed; about forty feet deep. They never did figure out what had caused the water-column and waterpool. The real reason the lake doesn't freeze over has more to do with its great depth and the strong winter winds that stir up the surface than any possible influences coming from a subterranean hotspring.

To add to the natural mysteries of such a big and deep lake, are some myths and tales that were also common during the mid-1800's, told by early day Tahoe pioneers. These pioneers may well have chuckled at one supposed local legend that claimed superstitious Indians were afraid to even try to cross the lake in a canoe or raft for fear that an evil spirit might grab them and pull them down to the bottom. But they took seriously their own beliefs that it would be dangerous for "them" to try to swim in the lake as the lake's altitude was so high and the air so thin, that it was deemed to be impossible to float, and they'd sink like a rock. Nowadays, we know that's baloney of course, and these myths are forgotten. Only one natural mystery remains today: that's where in the lake does Tahoe Tesse live? Perhaps someday, we'll find out!

THE GENERAL

Summertime in the Sierras was once a time for hunting bears. Although bear meat was nourishing, though a bit on the tough and dry side, bears weren't hunted so much as a source of food, as they were tracked down because they were feared and were considered nuisances. These aggressive animals, in particular the once prominent California grizzly, often pillaged food stocks, killed livestock and scared off ranchers horses & mules. To many, they represented a hazard and a pest, and it wasn't long before bounty's were placed on bearskins. Certainly, in the case of the California grizzly, this was to mark the beginning of their end. And if annihilation wasn't bad enough, these majestic, though occasionally aggravating bruins also found themselves used as a source of entertainment before they met their end.

The practice of matching a captured bear, usually a grizzly with another large animal, sometimes another bear, most often a bull with long & sharp horns, actually originated before the gold rush, during the days of the "Californios;" the days of the great ranches that occupied vast stretches of California. Bears were viewed as sport, but this was oft-times

412

a cruel sport and a dangerous sport. Few of the grizzly's lived long enough to develop any measure of notoriety.

But there was "one," that was to become a legend in his time. Weighing around 1200 pounds, he was soon to be known as a formidable opponent, a terror to face, if you were a bull. He was dubbed "General Scott," or more familiarly known as the "General." Every bull that was thrown in a ring with him was to end up as a steak dinner. So it was that the General was hauled around the Sierra foothills while promoters would stir up a match and a paying audience. When word came that the General was to appear, the crowds would clamor to lay their money down, as side-bets were soon made and expectations of a spectacle grew. One eyewitness to an 1851 General Scott contest near Placerville described the event as packed with the curious, the bored, and the gamblers. A wooden amphitheater had been constructed to contain the combatants. An internal arena, about 40-feet in diameter was enclosed by a strong five-barred fence; a tier of seats encircled the dirt-floored arena. The General was at first confined in a cage; a heavy wood box lined with iron, with open-iron bars on one side. A chain, anchored in the center of the arena led to the cage, and to a collar on the bears neck. At first the promoters let in first one, then a second large bull to battle the grizzly. Fairness was never a concern for the promoters, OR the crowd, who never seemed to mind a one-sided contest.

The General was to engage and endure hundreds of these fights before his days were done. He always fought a magnificent fight, but probably if given a chance, he'd rather have foregone the experience and preferred that instead of being a grizzly, that he'd been born a rabbit.

THE LADY HAD A TEMPER!

The way west in the 1850's was a long, and difficult journey that put a strain on even the best marriage and tended to widen any fractures in a troubled one. The ordeal of months on the trail, the hardships, the strain was wearing and some families grew stronger, learning to pull together to make the journey to California. But then there were a few cases where tempers flared and a marital skirmish would begin. Usually the anger would boil over and soon enough be forgotten, but not always.

One of the more volatile episodes took place on an 1848 wagon train to California. It was apparent that this wife never did like the idea of coming out west and was being compelled against her wishes to leave their farm and make the long trip. She reluctantly had gone along for the first few months, but somewhere on the backsides of Nevada she'd had enough and refused to go any further. And, she wasn't going to let her children go anywhere either. So, on the side of a trail, she and her husband had a terrific argument. For three hours they stood there and yelled and debated and she held her ground. Finally, several men, from neighboring wagons, came to the husbands assistance; grabbing the children and placing them in the family's wagon. The husband then drove away, leaving his still angry wife standing by the wayside. But their fight wasn't over just yet, as she followed the wagon train; walking behind it, thinking and planning her next move. When the wagons finally pulled up to camp for the night, she made that move. First quietly making sure her children were safely out of the way, she grabbed a still-burning ember from a campfire and with it, she set the family's wagon on fire. She may not have won the argument, but certainly had made her point.

Sometimes, these angry outbursts had less to do with the strain of travel, but had more to do with a bad disposition. As was shown by the experiences of a group headed west in 1853. Jake Fouts, his young wife and his parents were bound for California on a wagon train. It seems that Mrs. Fouts had a nasty temper, and she loved to argue about anything, with anyone, anytime. When she couldn't stir up a quarrel with her husband, she would try to strike up an argument with someone else on the wagon train, and soon everyone tried to avoid her. The poor lady it seemed couldn't be happy unless she was causing a commotion . . . and would start screaming if someone crossed her. At several points during the trip she even tried to shoot her father-in-law, and in general was a pain in the neck to everyone. Enjoying every moment of the clamor she was causing. She kept things quite lively for much of the long trip west. But eventually, her husband Jake had enough, and when the wagon train reached California, he sold his wife (for $300) to a trapper that his wife had taken a fancy to, and happily continued on. The trapper took his new wife to Placerville. But once there, he traded her to a gambler, and quickly departed to parts unknown; obviously having discovered his lady love had a nasty temper. There's no telling what happened to her after that. But likely, we should pity the poor gambler.

IT WAS TIME TO CHANGE JOBS

Merchants during the old days weren't beyond a little larceny or price manipulation, especially if that made the difference between making a profit and going out of business. As was the case of that storekeeper who had heard of a potential gold strike just up in the hills a ways, and so he decided to acquire a sizeable quantity of gold pans to sell. After all, it was prudent to strike when the iron was hot. He invested every spare cent he had, filling up his store, his storage-room, and even his front porch with new gold pans. And then, he sat back with high hopes and great anticipation. But they didn't sell. That gold strike fizzled, and no one was interested in buying a now useless gold pan. It was then a now desperate storekeeper came up with a new idea. Quietly and craftily he spread some gold dust he had, on the dirt street in front of his store, and stomped it in a bit, then sat back and waited. The trap was baited and soon came the first prey. A man walking down that street caught glimpse of the gold and dropped down to take a closer look. Soon he was joined by a second man, and in no time, a cry of "gold" rang out. A crowd gathered and in minutes, that storekeeper had sold most of his pans to gold-hungry customers. It was sneaky, but it worked.

Another merchant though, wasn't quite so lucky. His name was William Coleman and in the 1850's he ran a grocery store in Placerville. Winter was setting in and the roads would quickly become impassible, but Coleman managed to get a large wagon, full of flour, into town just before an exceptionally big storm hit. The roads would probably be closed for several months Coleman thought, and this would be an opportunity for him to make a bundle on his flour. All's he had to do was to wait until the town supplies ran short and the scarcity would drive up prices. So he waited. And for a while the winds did blow and the snow piled up on the roads and eventually everyone in town was running out of their last precious sacks of flour. But Coleman still sat back and waited, until the going price was sky-high, and people were beginning to go hungry. But just as he decided it was finally "time to sell," unfortunately for Coleman, the weather suddenly warmed up, and the snow melted just enough for some mule-trains loaded down with shipments of flour to punch their way through into town; sent by Sacramento merchants who also wanted to capitalize on the Placerville flour shortage. Coleman had waited too long. He sold his supply of flour at a now much lower price and then quietly left town; deciding that he wasn't cut out to be a merchant.

TAHOE WAS ONCE FULL OF FISH

Back when Lake Tahoe was often called a "piscatorial bonanza," this clearly was a fabulous place for anyone with a fishing pole, or for that matter, anyone who just had a knack for telling fishing tales. The size and abundance of the Tahoe trout were constantly making the regions newspapers. As early as 1863, people were passing stories about the twenty and thirty pound trout being caught here. Up until 1872 the largest trout caught here weighed in at twenty-nine and one-half pounds. In 1911, a thirty-one and one-half pound monster cut-throat was pulled in off the south shore! During the "Great Fishing Sweepstakes of 1881," ten young ladies and their escorts managed to hook 112 fish in a three-hour period, one at a time. That at least was sporting, as others weren't so patient with baiting and waiting.

Tahoe's fisheries were once thought to be limitless, as our lake began supplying local markets as early as 1858, and markets (after the transcontinental railroad was completed), in places like San Francisco and Chicago by the 1870s. And too, by the 1870's, twenty-five commercial operators were using long seines, a half a mile long, and large trawlers to harvest tons of Tahoe's trout. In 1880 alone, seventy thousand pounds of fresh lake trout were shipped by railroad from Truckee. Wagons loads, one thousand to two thousand pounds each were also working their way to Virginia City. By 1904, the numbers of commercial fishing boats on Tahoe's waters reached sixty vessels. And their methods of catching the fish were oft-times, wasteful. In their hurry to catch as many fish in as short a time as possible, many lake operators were using nets and grab hooks and traps. But also in use were tributary check dams, poison and even dynamite. These methods were so aggressive, so destructive, that it was only a matter of time that there would be a decline in fish populations. A series of laws were passed, even in the 1860's, in an attempt to provide at least some protection to the fish here, as the methods of fishing were supposedly regulated . . . though that didn't work without enforcement. After 1911, the limit was reduced from a hundred pounds per day per fisherman to fifty pounds. But that wasn't enough as the occasional illegal net was still being used.

Wide-scale commercial fishing was finally prohibited in Lake Tahoe by the California legislature after 1917. Happily, individuals can still fish the lake, even though it's not quite the piscatorial bonanza it once was, it's a lot of fun to try to catch that "big one." And there are still a few down there.

TIME FOR A PICNIC!

They've been proud traditions in this country ever since the days of the pilgrims. Warm days, filled with bright sunshine lure people outside and before you know it, people are having a picnic! Washington Irving would note that in spite of the interruption of the flying or crawling insect, or the threat of rain, the opportunity for camaraderie, for savoring the fresh air, the sunshine, the wondrous beauty of nature, made the fare of cold sandwiches, hard-boiled eggs, wine and fruit a veritable feast. In the early years of the 19th century, summer picnic parties were all the rage. They weren't the casual affairs we have today. People then, dressed in their Sunday best; suit and tie or a flowing dress. Long tables laid out, wicker baskets brimming with food, perhaps containing a true feast of roasted chicken, ham, cheese, biscuits, champagne and a delicious home-baked apple pie.

Even around our neck of the woods, a weekend community picnic was a regular event. A chance to socialize, a day of fun and a day for laughter. Glenbrooker's would hop on the freshly cleaned wood-train and journey to Spooner Meadow. There, they were entertained by their own brass band, play games and eat a banquet. These community picnics took place all over the region at the turn of the century. For communities then were small, and people weren't just neighbors, they were friends. A major annual event was called the "Grand Picnic," and everyone in the area was invited. There was no admittance charge, but there was a small fee for some special food treats: lemonade, fresh ice cream, baked pies were available for a dime. But there was more than eating on the minds of the attendees, for after the meals, it was a time for the contests, the games. A tug of war, between the married men and single men, which the married men usually won (they must of had more determination); high-jump contests among the ladies, sack races with your sweetie or wife, or running backwards foot races. For the athletically challenged, there were the potato rolling races, throwing a ball at a pie plate, or even a story-telling contest.

The community picnic also provided a great opportunity for young and not so young couples to walk hand-in-hand around the meadows or near the picnic-grounds. Savoring the opportunity to be alone as well as enjoying the summer afternoon. And certainly, more than one proposal of marriage must have been stimulated by the sweetness of the moment; there's something about fresh air and apple pie. When the Grand Picnic was over, the community would pack up and head back home, plans already being made for the next year's event. They couldn't wait for the next picnic.

THE BIGGEST
LITTLE CITY

It's the largest city close to the Tahoe Basin, with about 165,000 residents. A concentration of high-rise hotels, office buildings, and casinos surrounded by a sprawling carpet of shopping centers, subdivisions, and shrinking open space carved out of a sagebrush valley called the "Truckee Meadows." It's widely known as the "Biggest Little City in the World," but most locals simply call it "Reno." This growing metropolis, which is slowly expanding into a megalopolis with Carson, like most large urban areas, had a simple beginning. What would one-day become a modern city, was to rise from the sagebrush because it happened to be in the right place at the right time.

There wasn't much to see in the early years of the 1800's, not even a settlers cabin. But the California Gold Rush was to stimulate a new era in the west and sew the seeds of a future city. For a few years after the initial 1849 rush for gold, three temporary trading posts (way stations) were established in the Truckee Meadows to serve the flood of overland emigrants that were heading west into California. For this was part of the California Trail, a major artery through the Sierras, a good place to re-supply before heading over the Sierras. The 1859 discovery of the Comstock Lode affirmed the importance of this location as this site became a transportation hub for commerce to and from the mines of the Comstock. A hotel and a log toll bridge were constructed over the Truckee River by Charles William Fuller that year, and the place became known as "Fullers Crossing." But he soon sold it to Myron Charles Lake; a man who not only expanded the hotel, but also would give the site a new name: "Lakes Crossing." But it was the coming of the railroad that assured the permanency of this settlement. Following its slow completion through the Sierras, Charles Crocker, one of the owners of the Central Pacific Railroad, was determined to make up for lost time as his tracks were laid to the east . . . through the middle of Lakes Crossing, heading toward a rendezvous with the Union Pacific. So Crocker approached Lake with a deal. If Lake would deed him land on which to build a railway station, in exchange he'd give Lake additional lands . . . lands which were about to jump in value with the arrival of the Central Pacific. Lake of course agreed and the tracks and station were constructed, but yet another name was chosen by Crocker for his new station. The site was to be named after Jesse Lee Reno, a Union Army general who'd fallen in battle.

Over the years, until an upstart Las Vegas began to challenge Reno as the neon and glitter heart of the state, it was to be the state's brightest star. But even in the 1920's Reno boosters felt it needed something unique to give it a distinctive identity. A slogan was needed, and so there was a contest. A man from Sacramento was to submit an entry with his suggestion for a new city slogan . . . based upon a flyer he'd once seen for a Reno prizefight. That flyer heralded that the prizefight was being held in the "Biggest Little City on the Map." So, with a little paraphrasing, he submitted the suggestion that Reno be known as the "Biggest Little City in the World." He won the contest, and in 1927, the first of four Reno Arches were constructed to promote its new identity, and a city became a legend.

NO LONGER
A QUACK

Getting sick or hurt in the old days was bad enough, but sometimes the so-called doctor that people went to for a cure made the problem worse. For there were all kinds of charlatans practicing medicine without either a license or without training. Sometimes these quacks dispensed patent medicines full of alcohol and herbal tonics. But there were also those miracle cure machines that became wildly popular during the 1800's, pushed by an unprincipled practitioner. The most notable of which ran off portable batteries. Through a rejuvenating jolt of electrical current, these shocking treatments promised to cure just about every ailment of mankind. Chairs were fitted with what were called "Galvanic Faradic Batteries," so patients could sit in comfort while electrical currents titillated their bodies and their pocket books.

Other pseudo-doctors of the day were also known to direct malaria patients to take ice-cold water baths for treatments, and people with snake-bites were told to drink a concoction of tobacco juice and whiskey. Most patients got sicker, but a few actually did get better. But not all of the people who pretended to be a doctor were so inept. One of the most capable was a young man by the name of W.C. Jones. Now, he was a very bright young man who longed to study medicine, but his family just didn't have the money to send him to school, so he learned the practice of medicine from his father, who was the local barber. For in those days, the barber also set bones, and dug out bullets and bandaged the wounds of the men around the mountain communities. And so young Jones learned the basics of a barber/doctor, and he got his chance to begin a real medical practice when in 1867, he heard that the Central Pacific Railroad, which was building tracks through the Sierras at the time, was looking for a doctor to tend to the wounds of the Chinese laborers who worked for the Central Pacific. It turned out that the superintendent of the railway didn't really care if Jones was actually a trained doctor or not, for he just wanted someone to mend their broken bones, sew up their wounds, and pass out the caster oil and the laudanum when the Chinese needed doctoring; and he was hired! And for the next two years, young Jones learned more about emergency trauma treatment than any country doctor would have. For building a railroad was dangerous business and Jones saw countless crushed bones, bruises and banged heads, and in fact when the railroad was completed he actually did go to medical school, and with all that he had learned, young Jones became "Dr. Jones," after only two years. Always a fair doctor, but now, no longer a quack!

TAHOE'S THUNDERBOATS

Many called them "thunderboats." Their powerful engines would blast these half-planes, half-boats across the lake at speeds that often reached 165-miles an hour. The throaty roar of their exhaust pipes sounded like thunder as their drivers raced across the lake's waters. At full throttle, water plumes a hundred feet high churned up towering behind them! These hydroplanes, these greyhounds of the waterways, were built for shear speed. The most powerful ones could touch 200 miles an hour! And until 1964, they used to come to our lake for a regular high stakes regatta. Powerful racing boats have long been using Tahoe's waters. Even in the 1920's racing boats (like the 26 foot Liberty-powered "Lucky Strike II") were zipping across the lake at 85-miles an hour; a new marine record at the time. By the late 1940's, racers were regularly topping 140-miles an hour.

A Reno Hotel, the venerable Mapes, in 1953 encouraged local boat racing with a new challenge cup, they called the "Mapes Cup." For it helped to stimulate Tahoe trophy races.

And in conjunction with the Lake Tahoe Yacht Club, racing became a regular summer Tahoe event. Races would alternate, moving between various Nevada lakes. The races shifted back and forth for years. In the early 50's they raced from the lake's north end, then the races shifted to Pyramid Lake, near Reno, returning to Tahoe in the early 1960's. In those years, races were also conducted on Lake Mead. Thousands of spectators would pour onto the shores to watch the spectacle; people came from all over the country, for this was quite a spectator event! Wealthy and sporting enthusiasts brought their meticulously maintained and carefully tuned hydroplanes. People like Bill Harrah, Stanley Dollar and William Kaiser being among the most well known. There was also inventor/rancher Bill Stead, who was both boat owner and driver. In 1948 he purchased Stanley Dollar's racer, the "Miss Golden Gate," and re-named it the "Fury," and learned how to drive these powerful machines. In 1953 Stead purchased the "Hurricane IV" and learned to become a champion. Bill Harrah was to establish his own trophy for the lake: the coveted "Tahoe Trophy." And he did well with his "Tahoe Miss" and "Miss Budweiser" unlimited class hydroplanes.

But eventually the difficulties of racing at the lake's high elevations, the great expense of racing, and possibly changing times at the lake, combined to put an end to the summer hydroplane races here, and Tahoe's thunderboats were gone.

THE EXPLORER

He was always a risk taker. At times he was even reckless and foolish. But then, these were the qualities that were to make him a great explorer. That, and an intrepid nature, and more than his share of good luck. John Charles Fremont was born out of wedlock in 1813. His mother having endured a miserable marriage before running off with a dancer named "Charles Femon," who died soon after John was born. He spent his young years enduring the stigma of his birth, and learned to be independent of others. Everyone but a beautiful, strong willed young lady named Jessie, who John instantly fell in love with. Her father, though, was a powerful US Senator; Thomas Hart Benton, and their efforts to get married were barred by the Senator. And so it was that John and Jessie were secretly wed. The Senator, when told, was furious and he threw his daughter out of the house. As she was leaving she told her father, if he didn't accept her marriage to the man she loved, he would never see her again. The powerful Senator, the man who counseled presidents, who controlled the votes of others in Congress, had met his match, and he gave in. Over time, the Senator was to become John Fremont's benefactor and patron.

One of the Senator's dreams was to survey the west, to discover what was there, and perhaps to open it up to new settlements. Through his son-in-law, and a former mountain man (Christopher "Kit" Carson) he was to achieve much of that dream. Fremont joined the Corps of Topographical Engineers, and was to participate or lead explorations into Oregon, Nevada and California. His 1844 expedition was especially noteworthy for its difficulties, and for its discoveries. His experiences were recorded in his later report to the Chief of Engineers. He had started out with sixty-seven horses and mules, but half of them didn't survive the whole journey. Fortunately none of his men were lost, but they went through some miserable conditions that left several traumatized and most malnourished and all exhausted. It was the middle of the winter, and most people would of thought twice before trying a winter crossing of the Sierras, but John Fremont had that indomitable spirit and moved from the desert country of the Carson towards the American River.

By early February, the winter cold and the snowfall had made the journey both hazardous and nearly impossible, but Fremont continued on. On February 5th, his horses were giving out, it was too cold to sleep, and his local guide had deserted him. But he continued on. They set trees on fire for warmth and wrapped silk scarves around their faces: protection from the winds and the blinding glare off the snow. His men took to pounding the snow with mauls and shovels, beating the snow down so they could get their animals through the drifts. On February 14th, Fremont made an entry into his log that he had observed a beautiful mountain lake in the distance; the first recorded sighting of Lake Tahoe! But he was in a hurry to press on, and kept going. And he had harder days ahead. He eventually escaped the Sierra's finally arriving in the Sacramento Valley, and then it was time to return home to Jessie.

THEY SET THE FOREST ON FIRE!

He was one of the most famous people to ever visit the Lake Tahoe Basin during the last century. He wrote about it some years later in a book, called "Roughing It," even though he didn't have a particularly good time here. In fact he might of lost his life; but fortunately he didn't. His experiences are well worth the retelling because few will read the book, but it's worthwhile for anyone that has an interest in Tahoe history. The story began with two men; the author and his friend "Johnny," deciding they were going to take a look at a big lake they kept hearing about in Carson City. Grabbing a couple of blankets, a few supplies and an axe, they headed up into the mountains, plodding on what seemed to be forever, when suddenly, there it was; Lake Tahoe! A massive blue sheet of water surrounded by a lush green forest. There was no wind blowing that day, and the lake's surface was like a perfect reflecting mirror. They stood for a time to try to take in all the lakes beauty, before heading down to the waters edge. Finally settling down to camp for the night along the eastshore, they looked around the lakeshore and concluded they were almost alone, thinking that there were perhaps, only a dozen people at Tahoe.

After a refreshing nights sleep they began to explore around the lake, marveling at its clarity, the pure air, the scenic splendors. But they also had a mission: to make their fortune from the dense forest. Trees a hundred feet high and five feet thick were everywhere, and they only needed to stake out some land and build a house to become wealthy men. Neither man was cut out for hard physical work, and they were barely capable of constructing a primitive cabin made of brush, but they were satisfied with it; it would do. They were all set to begin their new logging business, but wanted to spend a few more days relaxing and fishing. It was then that their dreams went up in smoke. A gusty wind blew their poorly watched campfire out of control; the sparks jumped high into the air, branches caught fire, and trees exploded in flame. The winds roared, the heat was intense, and the two men raced for their lives! They jumped into the lake, clamored aboard their small boat, and they watched as the wildfire ravaged the lakeshore. Their visit to Lake Tahoe was over, and Johnny's friend, was one-day to write about it. His friend was fellow arsonist, Mark Twain.

TROUBLEMAKER

It was inevitable, that given the multitude of unruly and rambunctious people that drifted into the Sierras during the 1870's, that odd incidents would happen. And so several did in Truckee. According to an article in an 1875 edition of the "Truckee Republican," an especially seedy individual by the name of James Ray had drifted into town, looking for some excitement and a chance to stir up some trouble. Ray wasn't going to be disappointed as he soon managed to pick a fight in one of the town saloons. It wasn't long before fists started flying, Ray and his opponent swinging and kicking, they slammed against packed gaming tables, and bounced off other patrons who crowded around to watch the spectacle. And it wasn't long before these bystanders started pushing and shoving each other and suddenly another fight broke out, and then another, and soon people everywhere it seemed were spilling out into, and down the street, swinging and fighting! James Ray had somehow managed to spark a town brawl!

That was bad enough, but two men, who had been in a neighboring saloon when the street fight broke out, happened to have a real grudge match going, involving a wayward wife, and as this was as good a time as any to settle their quarrel, they joined the melee. But for them, fists weren't near enough, and soon lead was flying as the angry husband and his wife's paramour were blasting away at each other with their six-guns. Shots began ricocheting off the walls, and people dove for cover behind the bar as the two went at each other. Their shots were wild, but those bouncing bullets did somehow find their marks, and both men were wounded. But then it seemed like all the anger disappeared! Perhaps it was their pain or perhaps they'd vented it all out, or perhaps they'd decided the cavorting wife wasn't worth all the trouble, but the fight was over, as the two men, grabbed on to each other and struggled over to the doctor's office to seek treatment. But as for the man who started the town brawl, James Ray, he was to hang around town for another day, still stirring things up, as he started yet another fistfight! But perhaps because he sensed it was time to leave, since Truckee's residents were getting weary of his constant brawling, or because he'd temporarily satisfied his need for excitement, Ray suddenly left town. For a short while anyway, for at heart, he was still a boisterous soul, and sometimes, a troublemaker. At least he never came to Lake Tahoe; for James Ray, it was just too quiet here.

SELECTED
BIBLIOGRAPHY

Angel, Myron ed. *History of Nevada 1881.* Reprint, Thompson & West. Howell-North, 1958.

Bancroft, Hubert Howe. *History of Nevada: 1540-1888.* Reno: University of Nevada Press 1981.

Boessenecker, John. *Badge and Buckshot: Lawlessness in Old California.* Norman: University of Oklahoma Press, 1988.

Brands, H.W. The Age of Gold: *The California Gold Rush and the New American Dream.* New York: Doubleday, 2002.

Brewer, William H. *Up and Down California in 1860-1864.* New Haven: Yale University Press, 1930.

Browne, John Ross. *A Peep At Washoe.* 1860. Reprint, Balboa Island, Calif., Paisano Press, 1959.

Canfield, Chauncey L. *The Diary of a Forty-Niner.* New York: Turtle Point Press, 1992.

DeGroot, Henry. *The Comstock Papers.* Reno: Grace Dangberg Foundation, 1985.

Doten, Alfred. *The Journals of Alfred Doten: 1849-1903.* Edited by Walter Van Tilburg Clark. Reno: University of Nevada Press, 1973.

Downs, James F. *The Two Worlds of the Washo.* New York: Holt, Rinehart and Winston, 1966.

Drury, Wells. *An Editor on the Comstock.* Palo Alto: Pacific Books, 1948.

Earl, Phillip I. *This Was Nevada.* Reno: Nevada Historical Society, 1986.

Farquhar, Francis. *History of the Sierra Nevada.* Berkeley. University of California Press, 1965.

Glasscock, C.B. *The Big Bonanza.* Bobbs-Merrill Company, 1931.

Hinkle, George and Bliss. *Sierra-Nevada Lakes.* Bobbs-Merrill Company, Inc. 1949

Hungerford, Edward. *Wells Fargo: Advancing the American Frontier.* Bonanza Books, 1959.

Jackson, W. Turrentine. *Treasure Hill: Portrait of a Silver Mining Camp.* Tucson: University of Arizona Press, 1963.

James, Ronald M. *The Roar and the Silence.* Reno: University of Nevada Press. 1998

James Ronald M and C. Elizabeth Raymond editors. *Comstock Women: The Making of a Mining Community.* Reno: University of Nevada Press, 1998.

James, George Wharton. *The Lake of the Sky: Lake Tahoe.* 1915 Reprint, Stanley Paher, Nevada Productions, 1992.

Kowalewski, Michael. *Gold Rush: A Literary Exploration.* San Francisco: Heyday Books (cooperation with California Council for the Humanities), 1997.

Lekisch, Barbara. *Tahoe Place Names.* Lafayette: Great West Books, 1988.

Levy, JoAnn. *They Saw the Elephant: Women in the California Gold Rush.* Norman: University of Oklahoma Press, 1990

Lord, Elliot. *Comstock Mining and Miners.* 1883. Reprint, San Diego: Howell-North, 1959.

Lyman. George D. *The Saga of the Comstock Lode.* New York, Charles Scribner's Sons, 1951.

Muir, John. *My First Summer in the Sierra.* Reprint. San Francisco: Sierra Club Books, 1988.

Scott, Edward B. *The Saga of Lake Tahoe.* Sierra-Tahoe Publishing Company, 1957.

_____*The Saga of Lake Tahoe Volume II.* Sierra-Tahoe Publishing Company, 1973.

Stewart, George R. *Ordeal By Hunger: The Story of the Donner Party.* Houghton Mifflin Company, 1960.

Stone, Irving. *Men to Match My Mountains: The Opening of the Far West.* 1956 Reprint, Edison, New Jersey, Castle Books, 2001

Strong, Douglas H. Tahoe: *An Environmental History.* Lincoln: Univ. of Nebraska Press, 1984.

Strong. Douglas H. Tahoe: *From Timber Barons to Ecologists.* Lincoln: University of Nebraska Press, 1999.

Thompson, David. *Nevada: A History of Changes.* Reno, Grace Dangberg Foundation, 1986.

Twain, Mark (Samuel Clemens). *Roughing It.* 1892 Reprint, New York: Harper and Row Publishers, Inc. 1980.

_____Ed. Ken Chowder. *Gold Miners and Guttersnipes: Tales of California.* San Francisco, Chronicle Books, 1991.

Wright William (pseudo Dan DeQuille). *The Big Bonanza.* 1876 Reprint, New York:Alfred A. Knopf, 1953.

Wright, William._*A History of the Comstock Silver Lode and Mines.* 1889 Reprint, New York: Promotory Press, 1974.

MANUSCRIPTS AND REPORTS

History of the Tahoe National Forest 1840-1940. Jackson Research Projects. Special Report 15, May1982.

Kehlet, Pearl. *George Edward Kehlet:* Personal Narrative. Forest Service history files. 1970.

Richardson, Cora. (Camp Richardson) Personal Narrative. Oral History. Forest Service history files. 1990.

A Contextual History of the Lake Valley Railroad, Pioneer Timber Sale. Heritage Resources Report No. TB-96-5 Forest Service history files, 1997.

Emerald Bay Route Studies. State of California-Department of Public Works Report, 1960.

Contextual History, Evaluation Methodology and Management Plan for Prehistoric and Historic Roads and Trails Within the Lake Tahoe Basin Management Unit. HRR Report, July 1998.

Supernowicz, Dana E. *An Historical Overview of the Eldorado National Forest,* MA thesis, California State University, Sacramento, 1983.

_____. *Highway 50 Historical Overview: 1850-1895.* Report for Eldorado National Forest. Placerville, 1985

South Lake Tahoe Estates: An Historical Study. Forest Service Report 39-4696. San Francisco, 1974.

Lake Tahoe Watershed Assessment. Forest Service General Technical Report PSW-GTR-175. 2000

Tahoe Tattler Files. Penny Rucks File. Reno, Nevada 1995.

ADDITIONAL RECOMMENDED READING

Jill Beede. *Tahoe's Magical West Shore.* Tahoe Country. 2001

Landauer, Lyndall Baker. *The Mountain Sea: A History of Lake Tahoe.* Flying Cloud Press. 1996

Mark McLaughlin. *Sierra Stories: True Tales of Tahoe.* Mic Mac Publishing, 1997.

_____.Sierra Stories: Volume 2 Mic Mac Publishing 1998
David J, Stollery Jr. *Tales of Tahoe.* Western Printing & Publishing Company, 1969.

_____. *More Tales of Tahoe.*1988.

Carol Van Etten. *Tahoe City Yesterdays.* Sierra Maritime Publications, 1987.